MEDIA EDUCATION AND THE LIBERAL ARTS
A Blueprint for the New Professionalism

COMMUNICATION

A series of volumes edited by
Dolf Zillmann and Jennings Bryant

Barton • Ties That Blind in Canadian/American Relations: Politics of News Discourse

Becker/Schoenbach • Audience Responses to Media Diversification: Coping With Plenty

Beville • Audince Ratings: Radio, Television, Cable, Revised Edition

Biocca • Television and Political Advertising, Volume 1: Psychological Processes

Biocca • Television and Political Advertising, Volume 2: Signs, Codes, and Images

Blanchard/Christ • Media Education and the Liberal Arts: A Blueprint for the New Professionalism

Botan/Hazleton • Public Relations Theory

Brown • Television "Critical Viewing Skills" Education: Major Media Literacy Projects in the United States and Selected Countries

Bryant • Television and the American Family

Bryant/Zillmann • Perspectives on Media Effects

Bryant/Zillmann • Responding to the Screen: Reception and Reaction Processes

Cahn • Intimates in Conflict: A Communication Perspective

Dobrow • Social and Cultural Aspects of VCR Use

Donohew/Sypher/Bukoski • Persuasive Communication and Drug Abuse Prevention

Donohew/Sypher/Higgins • Communication, Social Cognition, and Affect

Edgar/Fitzpatrick/Freimuth • AIDS: A Communication Perspective

Ellis/Donohue • Contemporary Issues in Language and Discourse Processes

Flagg • Formative Evaluation for Educational Technologies

Gunter • Poor Reception: Misunderstanding and Forgetting Broadcast News

Hanson/Narula • New Communication Technologies in Developing Countries

Huesmann/Eron • Television and the Aggressive Child: A Cross-National Comparison

Johnson-Cartee/Copeland • Negative Political Advertising: Coming of Age

Kalbfleish • Interpersonal Communication: Evolving Interpersonal Relationships

Kaufer/Carley • Communication at a Distance: The Influence of Print on Sociocultural Organization and Change

Kelly • Fund Raising and Public Relatins: A Critical Analysis

Kelly • Mass Communication and Political Information Processing

Kraus • Televised Presidential Debates and Public Policy

Kubey/Csikszentmihalyi • Television and the Quality of Life: How Viewing Shapes Everday Experience

Masel Walters/Wilkins/Walters • Bad Tidings: Communication and Catastrophe

McLaughlin/Cody/Read • Explaining One's Self to Others: Reason-Giving in a Social Context

Narula/Pearce • Cultures, Politics, and Research Programs: An International Assessment of Practical Problems in Field Research

Olasky • Central Ideas in the Development of American Journalism: A Narrative History

Olasky • Corporate Public Relations: A New Historical Perspective

Richards • Deceptive Advertising: Behavioral Study of a Legal Concept

Richmond/McCroskey • Power in the Classroom: Communication, Control, and Concern

Salvaggio • The Information Society: Economic, Social, and Structural Issues

Salvaggio/Bryant • Media Use in the Information Age: Emerging Patterns of Adoption and Consumer Use

Semetko/Blumler/Gurevitch/Weaver • The Formation of Campaign Agendas: A Comparative Analysis of Party and Media Roles in Recent American and British Elections

Sprafkin/Gadow/Abelman • Television and the Exceptional Child: A Forgotten Audience

van Dijk • News Analysis: Case Studies of International and National News in the Press

van Dijk • News as Discourse

Welch • The Contemporary Reception of Classical Rhetoric: Appropriations of Ancient Discourse

Winett • Information and Behavior: Systems of Influence

Wober • The Use and Abuse of Television: A Social Psychological Analysis of the Changing Screen

Zillmann/Bryant • Pornography: Research Advances and Policy Considerations

Zillmann/Bryant • Selective Exposure to Communication

MEDIA EDUCATION AND THE LIBERAL ARTS
A Blueprint for the New Professionalism

Robert O. Blanchard
William G. Christ
Trinity University

LAWRENCE ERLBAUM ASSOCIATES, PUBLISHERS
1993   Hillsdale, New Jersey   Hove and London

Copyright © 1993, by Lawrence Erlbaum Associates, Inc.
All rights reserved. No part of the book may be reproduced in
any form, by photostat, microform, retrieval system, or any other
means, without the prior written permission of the publisher.

Lawrence Erlbaum Associates, Inc., Publishers
365 Broadway
Hillsdale, New Jersey 07642

Library of Congress Cataloging-in-Publication Data

Blanchard, Robert O. (Robert Okie), 1934–
    Media education and the liberal arts : a blueprint for the new professionalism / by
Robert O. Blanchard and William G. Christ.
      p. cm. — (Communication)
    Inspired by a symposium held at Trinity University in Feb.
1987.
    Includes bibliographical references and index.
    ISBN 0-8058-0488-9
    1. Mass media—Study and teaching (Higher)   I. Christ, William G.
II. Title.   III. Series: Communication (Hillsdale, N.J.)
P91.3.B55   1992
302.23′071′1—dc20   91-22047
                                                                                                          CIP

Printed in the United State of America
10 9 8 7 6 5 4 3 2 1

Contents

Preface   ix

PART I: THE FOUNDATION FOR REFORM

1   The New Liberal Arts   3

2   Media Education and Technology   22

3   The New Professionalism and the University:
        A Blueprint for Renewal   34

4   The New Professionalism and Media Practioners:
        A Blueprint for Reconstruction   60

PART II: BUILDING FOR REFORM

5   Frameworks for the Enriched Major   81

6   Building Toward the New Professionalism   103

7	Teachers and Students on the Front Line of Reform	**122**
8	Accountability and Accreditation	**142**
	References	**162**
	Author Index	**175**
	Subject Index	**181**

Preface

We hope reading this book will be as liberating for fellow media educators nationwide as writing it has been liberating for us at Trinity. It is a by-product of a decade-long philosophical and practical search for solutions to problems facing our field. We believe confronting, debating, and acting on the issues, information, and ideas surrounding our problems will lead to more effective and honest responses to them. We educators in "media," journalism, mass communication, telecommunications, speech communication, communication, and so forth, are facing conflicting realities of individual campus resources and missions, intellectual and philosophical ferment in the field, changes in undergraduate education and the liberal arts canon, and the dynamic "information age" in which students will be living and working for the next 40 or more years. We believe that, because of these changes and ferment and because the future is impossible to predict, media educators for some time to come will have to rely on experimentation and enterprise, rather than established methods, to find ways to meet the new challenges.

Experimentation and enterprise can be unnerving and painful. At Trinity, we realized we could not even consider new approaches unless we faced and challenged outdated orthodoxies, structures, and relationships that acted as built-in censors to new ideas. Only after having dealt with those obstacles could we begin to consider new forms.

The purpose of this book is to help academic reformers overcome daunting and potentially immobilizing conditions and thoughts that preserve and protect the status quo; to provide them with concepts and information with which to attack the myths, illusions, and dogmas of the academy and the occupational constituents upon which so many of the nation's media education programs have been built; and to help them begin experimenting with new approaches toward a New Professionalism.

Most of the concepts and content of the New Professionalism are not new, having emerged from the academic ferment and reformist impulses of the 1980s. They can be found in James Carey's advocacy of the university tradition and his intellectual assaults on the excesses of professionalism; in the pioneering works of Paul Dressel, Everette Dennis, Jean Ward and others, including those involved in the discourse leading to and following the Oregon Report; in the reformist literature of Ernest Boyer and others in the higher education establishment; and in studies of professional and liberal education at Syracuse and Michigan. There is no shortage of ideas and we have attempted to compile and synthesize the most promising and germane of them. But they cannot take root, or even find a plot in our field, until some of the academic and philosophical groves, and our minds, are cleared of undergrowth and debris. Some of the interrelated and overlapping concerns addressed in this book are:

1. the notion that the liberal arts canon, fortunately under siege in these postindustrial times, still adequately reflects knowledge, perspectives, technology and multicultural and institutional changes that have taken place since it was presented in the 19th century as an industrial-age alternative to classical education;

2. the dogma that "liberal arts" are content driven, residing exclusively with the "traditional" disciplines—even though they have become fragmented and professionalized during the past 40 years and do not offer, even at the best schools, the unity of knowledge, integration, and coherence of an undergraduate liberal education;

3. the myth that undergraduate preprofessional programs, including media programs that encompass newer technologies and institutional systems, have nothing of substance to offer to the liberal arts or liberal learning for the 21st century;

4. the illusion that there are substantial distinctions—justifying separate colleges, schools, departments, divisions, sequences and faculty specialties—between oral and written communication, interpersonal and mass communication, electronic and print communication, public relations and advertising and other field-fragmenting, faculty-featherbedding fairy tales;

5. the seldom-questioned assumption that communication and media education undergraduate programs exist primarily to serve the narrowly defined, short-term needs of media industries by producing unquestioning, industry-socialized, job-specific, entry-level, plentiful, cheap labor;

6. the fantasy that industry- or occupational-specific "professional" mass communication programs and courses are "neutral" or "objective" and

ideologically or value free; that they contain only "skills" training that have no auxiliary or latent content or values that can have either liberal or illiberal outcomes or consequences; and

7. the tragedy of media education programs, especially journalism and mass communication programs, that are sacrificing potential intellectual leadership in media studies for roles as "placement directors" for the media industries.

This book outlines the challenges and changes facing media education and provides a guide for negotiating change through the development of a New Professionalism and participation in the New Liberal Arts.

The book is broken into two parts. Part I presents two challenges facing media education and the curricular implications of those challenges. The first challenge, reform of undergraduate education in America and the emergence of a New Liberal Arts, is described in chapter 1, and the second challenge, the communications revolution, in chapter 2. These challenges call for reform in media education; rethinking of traditional orthodoxy and the development of a New Professionalism. This New Professionalism repositions media education within the university, chapter 3, and in relationship to practitioners, chapter 4.

Part II develops, with specific examples, the idea of the New Professionalism and media education reform. The New Professionalism challenges the status quo by questioning programs' missions and curricular structures, chapter 5, their university and practitioner alliances, chapter 6, teaching strategies, chapter 7, and outcomes assessment and accreditation, chapter 8.

Three major outcomes for the undergraduate curriculum in higher education generally and in media education specifically should result from the reform called for in this book. The first is more diversity, because each program will reflect the general university tradition and its community values, and the specific mission, distinctiveness, resources, and geographical mandate of its college or university. The second is a commitment by units to the institution's general or common curriculum. The third is the promise of interesting, innovative, integrative ways of delivering media education. There are many challenges ahead for media education. The hope is that this book provides a blueprint from which media educations will be able to, at the very least, ask the relevant questions.

Throughout this book we use interchangeably several terms such as *media education, media and communication studies, communication, mass communication, journalism and mass communication* (see Arcenas, 1991). There is not yet one term, such as "communication" or "communication science," that would be both widely accepted and used by those in the field to designate their programs and recognized and understood by those outside the field. We use *media education* and *media educators* in our title and preface, and in the chapters, to encompass 1,164 college and university programs and faculty in communication, speech, media studies, journalism, radio, television, film, advertising, public relations, and new technologies as listed in *The Communication Disciplines in Higher Education: A Guide to Academic Programs in the United States and Canada,* published jointly by the Association for Communication Education and the Association of Schools of Journalism and Mass Communication, compiled and edited by Garland C. Elmore (1990), Indiana University and Purdue University at Indianapolis.

ACKNOWLEDGMENTS

In February 1987, a small group of academics held a symposium at Trinity University to discuss professional and liberal arts education. It was from that meeting and subsequent discussions that this book was inspired. Among those original members, a special thanks to James Fletcher (University of Georgia) who suggested we write this book. Also in that group, thanks to Thomas Bohn (Ithaca College), Stewart Hudson (Pepperdine University), and Drake Mabry and Jeffrey McCall (DePauw University).

We would like to acknowledge those who corresponded with us about their philosophies and curricula. You will see many of them quoted in this book. Their insights and examples were invaluable. They include: R. C. Adams (California State University—Fresno), Jo-Ann Albers (Western Kentucky University), Douglas Anderson (Arizona State University), Samuel Becker (University of Iowa), William Biglow (University of Wisconsin, Oshkosh), Donald Brod (Northern Illinois University), Trevor Brown (Indiana University), Walter Bunge (Ohio State University), David Clark (Colorado State University), Richard Cole (University of North Carolina–Chapel Hill), William Elliott (Southern Illinois University), Robert Finney (California State University–Long Beach), Jon Franklin (Oregon State University), F. Dennis Hale (Bowling Green University), Robert Kolker (University of Maryland), Val Limburg (Washington State University), Barry Litman (Michigan State University), Michael McGregor (Indiana University), Nikos Metallinos (Concordia University), Robert Moore (Elizabethtown College), John David Reed (Eastern Illinois University), Hampden Smith III (Washington and Lee University), Charles Warner (University of Missouri), James Webster (Northwestern University), and Brain Winston (Penn State University).

In addition to those pioneers most visible and frequently mentioned in the text, we thank our colleagues at Trinity—James Bynum, Richard Gentry, Harry Haines, Sammye Johnson, Bob Luk, Marion Pfrommer, Gladys Schuchard, Scott Sowards, Carolyn Warmbold, Suzanne Williams, and

Wayne Woodward who, as partners in reform, helped us formulate, articulate, defend, rationalize, implement, adjust, and sometimes abandon our intuition, ideas, rhetoric, proposals, and experiments. And we are grateful for the enriching and nurturing resources and leadership of Trinity University, an exciting place to be, where a New Liberal Arts and New Professionalism are emerging. We are grateful to our fellow reformers everywhere, who have been charting and implementing, without fanfare and rhetoric, curricular approaches to a New Professionalism.

We would like to thank the editors at Lawrence Erlbaum Associates, especially Hollis Heimbouch and Robin Marks Weisberg, for their thorough, careful, and useful comments.

On a more personal note, the second author would like to acknowledge those teachers and mentors who have challenged, befuddled, excited, and supported him. They include: Helen Kovacs, Frank Diamond, John Nash, Rick Hutto, Dick Lawson, Bob Bohlken, Bob and Marie Christ, Nathan and Jonathan Christ, and especially, my true friend, Judy Christ. Thanks.

I THE FOUNDATION FOR REFORM

1 The New Liberal Arts

*The disciplines have fragmented themselves
into smaller and smaller pieces, and undergraduates
find it difficult to see patterns in their courses
and to relate what they learn to life . . .*
— Boyer (1987, pp. 5, 6)

*Liberal education seems to be making another comeback
these days, although there seems to be less agreement than
ever on just what it is.*
— Ahlgren and Boyer (1981, p. 173)

*Today's weak conception of the liberal arts is useful only
as an advertising gimmick for beleaguered universities.*
— Botstein (1979a)

Beginning in the 1980s, harsh criticism of U.S. colleges and universities exploded both within and outside the higher education establishment. The result has been campus ferment and change in undergraduate education that is likely to continue through the 1990s and from which we believe a New Liberal Arts will emerge. Because of the transformation of the liberal arts, as well as the technological and economic convergences of media technologies and institutions, media education is now faced with its own conceptual and curriculum turmoil, reexamination, and restructuring. From this ferment, we believe a New Professionalism will emerge.

In this chapter, we highlight some of the public concern expressed about undergraduate education over the past decade, followed by review of the influential critiques conducted by the higher education establishment. We discuss how these decade-long efforts herald new meanings for liberal arts, new principles for curriculum design and new roles for professional education. We argue throughout this book that these and other changes present both challenges and opportunities to communication and media educators. We believe that for the survival of the field, the revitalization of the liberal arts and the benefit of society, these challenges should be met with a restructuring of undergraduate curriculums in media education toward a New Professionalism that replaces the uniformity and expediency of the occupational ethos of today's media programs with the diversity of a liberal ethos more reflective of the university tradition and community values.

REFORM AND THE NEW LIBERAL ARTS

In reviewing the 1980s critiques of undergraduate education, we found there to be three interrelated, broad criticisms. The first is that undergraduate education lacks integrity and purpose. The second is that its content, especially the liberal arts "canon," needs revitalization. The third is that it is too vocational, narrow and fragmented, and needs integration and unity of knowledge. Interconnected with each of these criticisms is an intense debate over the relationship between liberal and professional education.

Widespread concern in the 1980s over insufficient coherence and rigor in bachelor's degree programs turned the national spotlight on what usually had been a matter of concern solely in academic circles. It was the higher education version of the "Why-Can't-Johnny-Read" syndrome that occupied the popular press of the 1950s. Business, government, and professional leaders, including media people, were repeatedly confronting educators with embarrassing questions: "Why can't college graduates read with critical understanding, think clearly, and express themselves cogently? Why can't educators develop adequate programs of collegiate studies to provide the nation with literate, thinking, responsible citizens?" (AAC, n.d. p. 8).

The National Institute of Education issued a report in 1981 on the "decline of U.S. undergraduate learning." Other reports of national commissions found specific deficiencies that were "serious, if not shocking," in such fields as foreign languages, international and foreign cultures, and science and technology (pp. 8–9).

In 1983, Secretary of Education Terrel H. Bell said, perhaps prematurely, that the nation was "in a renaissance of American education . . . the greatest, the most far-reaching, and the most promising reform and renewal of education we have seen since the turn of the century" (Scully, 1983, p. 1). He warned that pressures for "job-related education" could lead to a crisis in American higher education. "Pragmatic vocationalism and careerism" in colleges and universities is turning many of them into "glorified work-preparation institutes." He added: "We must beware of the crowding out of student time for the liberal arts because of the professional school's propensity to demand more and more time of students" (pp. 1, 21).

Following Bell, Secretary of Education William J. Bennett wasted little time expressing a major theme throughout his tenure: "the extraordinary gap between the rhetoric and reality of American higher education is so wide that we face the real possibility . . . of an erosion of public support for the enterprise" (Text of secretary Bennett's address, 1986, p. 27). He charged that American colleges, in fact, are "ripping off" their students with ill-conceived curriculums (Fiske, 1987, p. 36).

By 1987, the American Council on Education reported that at least 86% of the colleges in the United States "had revised, or were revising, their general education programs" (p. 1). By that time, the Association of American Colleges had issued a report, based on the assumptions that "the meaning of baccalaureate degree has become obscure and that undergraduate education no longer has an accepted purpose," and "that the most used plans for organizing undergraduate education are open to serious question" (Jaschik, 1985, p. 1; Palmer, 1986, p. 13).

There is Little Liberal Arts "There"

Higher education and especially the traditional or classical liberal arts caretakers have lost their way, according to critiques that attacked undergraduate education's lack of integrity and purpose and its content and ethos.

Public concern with undergraduate education seemed to have reached its peak when Allan Bloom's (1987) *The Closing of the American Mind: How Higher Education Has Failed Democracy and Impoverished the Souls of Today's Students* hit the best-seller list. Bloom wrote that a "crisis of knowledge" had developed in undergraduate education (p. 262) in which the social sciences and humanities had ceased performing their function of providing a liberal education for undergraduates. He argued that especially since the 1960s these "traditional" disciplines had lost the unity of knowledge that had been their special responsibility. They had "decomposed," becoming fragmented hosts of specialisms. In a similar vein, the "tribalization" of the disciplines was described nearly a decade earlier in *The Academic Tribes* by Hazard Adams (1976).

It is important to note that Bloom was writing about the curricula in only the top 20 or 30 highly selective, prestige colleges and universities in the nation, which should be expected to be the caretakers of liberal education. What he described, however, generally coincides with other critiques of higher education:

> Thus, when a student arrives at the university, he finds a bewildering variety of courses. And there is no official guidance, no university-wide agreement, about what he should study. . . . Each department or great division of the university makes a pitch for itself, and each offers a course of study that will make the student an initiate. . . . Most professors are specialists, concerned only with their own fields, interested in the advancement of those fields in their own terms, or in their own personal advancement in a world where all

the rewards are on the side of professional distinction. They have been entirely emancipated from the old structure of the university, which at least helped to indicate that they were incomplete, only parts of an unexamined and undiscovered whole. (pp. 338–339)

An AAC-sponsored review of more than 25,000 student transcripts from 30 colleges and universities seemed to support Bloom's critique. It "revealed unstructured liberal-arts curricula that lack depth and all but ignore mathematics and natural sciences. (DeLoughry, 1989, p. 1)" According to the *Chronicle of Higher Education* (DeLoughry, 1989), Robert M. Zemsky of the University of Pennsylvania, director of the study, added that "the relative lack of temporal focus and depth of study across the humanities is consistent with [Bloom's] observations (p. 1)" He continued:

Too often . . . humanities courses are open to beginning and advanced students alike, without any sense that some things must be learned first or that experience within the humanities itself makes one a more advanced learner. . . . Our explanation . . . is that in market-driven undergraduate curricula, the humanities have attracted sufficient numbers of students by essentially practicing a kind of internal open admissions. (DeLoughry, 1989, p. 1)

In other words, because there is little study in depth or little unity of knowledge, there is little liberal arts "there." As educators in undergraduate professional programs who have endured the self-serving "back to the liberal arts" rhetoric on our campuses, we find it ironic that the titled caretakers of the liberal arts—especially the humanities and the social sciences—have become narrow and fragmented, scattering the knowledge among their fields into tiny research or preprofessional-PhD modules.

"It is no secret," Hudson (1988) wrote, "that generally inaccessible specializations based on theoretical and historical minutiae have proliferated even in the humanities. . . . [reflecting] an arcane specialization and, thus, vocationalism, that classical liberal arts, and communication theory, would find unacceptable" (p. 13).

In analyzing the historic and very complex set of circumstances that led to "the unhappy disarray, the loss of integrity in the bachelor's degree," the AAC task force on redefining the undergraduate degree, placed blame on the following:

The dispersal of authority over the curriculum . . . the grip of departmental authority and a misguided marketplace philosophy on the curriculum . . . the transformation of the professors from teachers concerned with the characters and minds of their students to professional, scholars with Ph.D. degrees with an allegiance to academic disciplines stronger than their commitment to teaching or to the life of institutions where they are employed . . . doctoral programs that have certified successive generations of college teachers . . . the bias [for research that] has entered the ethos of institutions by virtue of the way that professors have trained and therefore evaluated. (1985, pp. 4-7)

Bashing Professional Education

What is the significance of these negative critiques of the traditional liberal arts disciplines? For communication and media educators and other professional education educators, it is important that they introduce and articulate these arguments in campus discussion and debates with their traditional-discipline colleagues who attack professional education for its specialization. It makes little sense to single out the popular professional programs as the sole or even the major sources of narrowness and vocationalism in the undergraduate curriculum, as many spokespeople of the traditional disciplines have done.

After all, as we see in our review of the reform literature, specialization or study in depth, in the context of broader historical, social, economic, and ethical issues, is an important component of liberal education (Boyer, 1987). The primary role of professional programs is to offer specialization. The traditional and primary responsibility of the humanities, arts, and sciences, on the other hand, is to provide another important component of a liberal education—coherence and unity of knowledge or the liberal arts "canon." Unfortunately for undergraduate students, the traditional disciplines have generally failed to perform that primary responsibility and they should be reminded repeatedly of their failure to do so.

Yet, instead of addressing their own failures as stewards of humanities, arts, and liberal arts, representatives of the traditional disciplines have bashed professional education, mostly in the form of self-serving proposals for "a return to the liberal arts." Blaming professional education had become so widespread by 1986 that Shirley Strum Kenny, president of CUNY's Queens College, told the annual convention of the Association of American Colleges that "liberal-arts advocates" had been so upset by the recent dominance of professional programs in undergraduate education, that they had been defensive and "morally superior." Their attitude, she said, was, "If we can't have the dollars, at least we can wrap ourselves in our own virtues" (Jacobson, 1986, p. 24).

Leon Botstein (1979a), president of Bard College, 7 years earlier questioned the motives of those faculty who were advocating more emphases on traditional subjects such as literature, philosophy, and history, that he found happened to be entirely "consistent with their [faculty] vocational aspirations." Most proposals for "more liberal arts" were "being used as a facile, acceptable front to shield us from addressing more serious social and cultural issues" (p. 17; See also Botstein, 1979b).

To repeat, it is important for communication and media educators, and other professional program educators, to clearly establish in their campus curriculum discussions the culpability of the traditional disciplines in the overall excessive fragmentation and narrowness of undergraduate education in the United States. It is even more important that representatives of the traditional disciplines on their campuses are told that, because they are the titled caretakers of the liberal arts, their fragmentation and narrowness is far more damaging to liberal education than the specialities of the professional programs. After these points are clarified and put on the table of curriculum reform, professional program representatives can then address their campus colleagues with the important issue of what professional programs can contribute to the revitalization of the liberal arts with the new skills, perspectives, and knowledge that their programs can contribute. This issue probably will not be welcomed, nor even understood, until the liberal-versus-professional education myth is dispelled.

The Professional Versus Liberal Education Myth

Bloom, Bennett, spokespeople for "more liberal arts," and others have popularized and exploited the undergraduate curriculum crisis. But, except for some vague and dated "return to the great books" solutions and self-serving proposals similar to those mentioned above, they have provided no substantial or constructive alternatives to the conditions they so forcefully describe. For this reason, except for perhaps contributing to public and political pressure for reform, they have had very little constructive impact inside the academy where real reform must originate.

The most influential agendas for change have been provided by the reform efforts of the Association of American Colleges (AAC), the National Institute of Education/U.S. Department of Education (NIE), and the Carnegie Foundation for the Advancement of Teaching (Carnegie Foundation). Their reports offer specific recommendations and they have been widely circulated and summarized by the academic press and debated among academic associations.

Directly linked to AAC, NIE, and Carnegie Foundation reports are two major examinations of the relationship between liberal arts and professional studies—the Professional Preparation Project ("Strengthening the ties," 1988) at the University of Michigan, supported in part by the Fund for the Improvement of Postsecondary Education, and The Syracuse Experiment (Marsh, 1988) at Syracuse University, supported by the Andrew W. Mellon Foundation. We would add to these reform efforts the Sloan Foundation's New Liberal Arts program (see later).

The ACC's Project on Redefining the Meaning and Purpose of Baccalaureate Degrees culminated in its 1985 report (Association of American

Colleges, 1985), which *The Chronicle of Higher Education* characterized as "a blistering attack on the quality of undergraduate education" (Jacobson, 1986, p. 1). The NIE's Study Group on the Conditions of Excellence in American Higher Education resulted in its 1984 study (National Institute of Education, 1984). The Carnegie Foundation capstone was *College: The Undergraduate Experience in America,* by its president, Ernest L. Boyer (Boyer, 1987). The Professional Preparation Project at the University of Michigan formed a nationwide voluntary coalition of faculty members, administrators, and accrediting officials—a "Professional Preparation Network"—representing both liberal arts and professional programs that resulted in a report, *Strengthening the Ties That Bind: Integrating Undergraduate Liberal and Professional Study* (1988). The Syracuse Experiment brought together Syracuse University faculty from the arts and sciences and the professional colleges to explore the interrelatedness of their fields and to implement their findings in the curriculum, the goal being a reordering of the relationship between professional and liberal studies. The 2-year project resulted in *Contesting the Boundaries of Liberal and Professional Education: The Syracuse Experiment,* by Peter T. Marsh (1988).

The concept of a New Liberal Arts appears to have originated with the Sloan Foundation's program of that name, launched in the early 1980s, to encourage the integration of quantitative reasoning and technology into the curricula of liberal arts colleges. This resulted in grants for pilot projects to more than 50 institutions and to the establishment of the Council for the Understanding of Technology in Human Affairs, to promote the development of technological literacy. Discussion of the meaning of the New Liberal Arts and reports on some of the Sloan Foundation projects resulted in a variety of publications (cf. Kanigel, 1986; Koerner, 1984; Lisensky, Pfnister, & Sweet, 1985; Morison, 1986; Truxal, 1986; White, 1981). Our use of the term *New Liberal Arts* is derived from this effort to integrate technology and liberal education. Although much of the emphasis in pilot projects so far has been on integration of engineering and liberal arts, we extend the concept to new communication technologies, media and information systems, and the field of communication and media studies. We do not address them in this book, but we would, of course, include in the New Liberal Arts "movement" issues that have received perhaps the widest public attention so far—attempts to revise the liberal arts "canon" with new diversity perspectives, including race, multiculturalism, ethnicity, and gender.

Not all of the critiques listed above set out to redefine liberal arts, but most of them, from various perspectives, challenged assumptions about distinctions between liberal and professional studies. Specifically, the AAC, Carnegie Foundation, the Michigan Professional Preparation Project, and Syracuse Experiment challenged two interrelated myths. One was that professional programs are the antithesis of and have no role in liberal education. The other was that professional studies, even though they may have to be recognized and tolerated because of their student popularity, should remain separate from the so-called traditional liberal arts.

Persistence of these myths, sad to report, still can be found in the NIE study that states that "it is clear that [4-year professional programs] offer few opportunities to develop the capacities and knowledge that most institutions would expect of baccalaureate graduates" (NIE, 1984, p. 43). As we see here, the other studies contradicted—and both the Michigan Professional Preparation Project and Syracuse Experiment reports forcefully challenged—the NIE on this and similar positions (Marsh, 1988, p. 4; "Strengthening the ties," 1988, p. 17).

The AAC, however, believed that professional or vocational programs may "provide a strong, enriching form of study in depth . . . if based on the skills and attitudes of our minimum curriculum and presented in a liberal spirit." Study in depth, if it is to be disciplined and complex, "cannot be restricted to the offerings of one academic department" (AAC, 1985, p. 30). Thus, the ACC held the traditional disciplines up to the same standard, because many "have an abstraction and a narrowness that do not recommend them to students . . . who do not contemplate academic careers." This is a nice way of saying many traditional disciplines have become PhD-prep programs to perpetuate their own narrow vocationalism (pp. 30-31). This is not a recent development. In his classic study of liberal arts and journalism, Paul L. Dressel (1960) found that "deans of arts and sciences colleges. . . . commonly pointed to the specialization in their liberal arts departments as equalling or exceeding that in journalism [departments]" (p. 79).

Secretary of Education Bell's criticism of excessive "careerism" was documented and shared by these studies and by other critics and students of undergraduate education. The Carnegie Foundation found many cases of "rootless vocationalism" in 4-year universities and colleges (Boyer, 1987, pp. 102-115) and reforms were clearly needed. Vocational excesses in communication and mass media education are addressed in chapters 3 and 4. In the meantime, it is important to reemphasize that all of the traditional, older academic disciplines have become vocationalized and, in this way, they share the excesses of professionalism, even if they are less apparent because of the mystique of the liberal arts label associated with the older disciplines.

Peter Marsh (1988) best summed up this issue in the report of the 2-year Syracuse Experiment:

> It became clear that the conventional distinction between liberal and professional education has disintegrated. Their assimilation has been going on as

long as the two forms of education have existed. The explosive expansion of specialized knowledge over the past century has not only professionalized the disciplines of the arts and sciences, but also reduced the historic rationale for purely liberal education to a faint memory. While the arts and sciences now stand to a large extent on professional foundations, there are liberal components at the base of professional education. (p. 12)

Career Preparation: The Historic Purpose

The futility of debating dogmatic distinctions between professional and liberal studies becomes apparent when the suggestion is made that the primary purpose of a liberal arts education is not career preparation — or, at least, it was not in the "good ol' days."

"The point is that all students, regardless of their major, are preparing for productive work," Carnegie Foundation President Ernest Boyer (1987) argued in the Foundation's capstone study. "As with engineering and business and computer science," he added, "a student who majors in English or biology or history will, it is assumed, someday become employed and use what he or she has learned for some useful end. Even the most traditional colleges expect their graduates to move on to careers. And a great embarrassment for a department occurs when its graduates 'cannot get placed' " (p. 109).

The Carnegie Foundation report challenged those in higher education who have opposed new career-related majors because they are "too novel" or "too new."

> Overlooked in such debates was the fact that most disciplines that now have status within the academy — modern languages, laboratory sciences, for example — were themselves once considered too novel for the academy to embrace. . . . We propose that the "newness" of a proposed field of study is not sufficient reason for its rejection, nor should tradition alone be used to justify holding to an existing major. (p. 107)

Boyer also criticized the resistance to new majors because they were in less prestigious fields, such as nursing and social work.

> We heard it argued, for example, that it is all right to prepare students to be doctors, but not nurses. To educate future college teachers is applauded, but to prepare students to teach in elementary school is not considered a respectable career objective. To dig ruins of the past as an archaeologist is considered a respectable career objective, but to work with ruined lives in an urban jungle as a social worker is a less well-regarded field of study. Lost in these debates was the recognition that college graduates, instead of being

demeaned by all but the prestigious professions, can, in fact, lift up a job and give it meaning. (p. 108)

He also disputed the argument posed by Secretary of Education Bell that some programs are "too job related." Boyer responded: "What we found missing in these discussions was the recognition that a university education has always been considered 'useful' " (p. 108).

Indeed, Sheldon Rothblatt (1976), in his classic analysis of the development of liberal education, found that resistance to career preparation in liberal education historically "has caused more difficulty for the theory of liberal education than perhaps any other aspect. The idea that a liberal education must be a broad or general education and that under no circumstances must it ever be subservient to a specific career . . . has only been possible for a leisured class and at a stage in the evolution of society when expert knowledge was not necessary for the exercise of political and economic leadership" (p. 200). Higher education historian Frederick Rudolph (1984) found that "liberal studies were from the beginning eminently useful even if they were not specific in their vocational focus" (p. 15; see also Rudolph, 1979).

Stewart Hudson (1988) noted that classical Greek and Victorian English education "prepared the upper classes for the exercise of authority in the Greek and English civil services and armed forces by the study of heroic models and by ascetic physical training," whereas "scholastic education in effect prepared the clerics, lawyers, and doctors of the middle classes" (p. 12).

William F. May (1986) argued that in addition to "cultivating the well-rounded person . . . and training the skilled person," the university "must pursue what the ancient Greeks saw as a fundamental purpose of education . . . the cultivation of the civic self or the political self—the self as it readies itself for public affairs." Universities must do this especially in professional programs "because modern professionals function as members of the ruling class; they wield power in society." He concluded that "it is . . . strange to have a ruling class without nurturing and cultivating a sense of civic responsibility in that class" (p. 27).

There is no question that today's view of higher education is pragmatic. In economic terms, it is viewed as an investment and its product is human capital for the economy and productive careers for the graduate. We return to this economic perspective in chapter 3, for it is crucial to a debate similar to the liberal versus professional issue—the specific versus general debate within professional education.

We would emphasize at this point that although we would defend the role of professional education and expose the hypocrisy of many of its tradition-bound critics, we believe reform of undergraduate professional education generally, and of communication and mass media education specifically, is long overdue. In media education, reform must include a shift from media- and occupational-specific curricula to those that are more general or generic—toward a New Professionalism. As we see here, there are both sound philosophical and economic reasons for seeking these reforms. Overemphasizing specific job-related and entry-level job skills in professional education not only leads to what Boyer termed "rootless vocationalism" but it leads to problems of oversupply and obsolescence (Boyer, 1987, pp. 102-115; Gomery, 1986).

BASIC PRINCIPLES FOR REFORM

Challenging the myth that the liberal and the professional studies are separate is a key element of the current transformation in undergraduate liberal education. But questions remain: What is a liberal education and what is the meaning of liberal arts?

There has always been disagreement and even confusion within the academy about what is meant by undergraduate liberal education. Most colleges or universities purport to offer their students a liberal education, but when pressed for particulars educators provide conflicting definitions (Ahlgren & Boyer, 1981; Kimball, 1986; Rothblatt, 1976). Andrew Ahlgren and Carol M. Boyer (1981) have concluded that endless faculty debates (and, we would argue, public debates) over what a liberal arts education is are not resolved because educators and others entertain fundamentally differing conceptions of liberal education. And they always will.

Ahlgren and Boyer (p. 180) found that some educators argue that particular courses, certain distributions of courses, or certain processes or methods taught in courses are most important for a liberal education. Others believe faculty intentions, whatever faculty "value and think the students should learn" is the measure. Others emphasize outcomes—"skills and character of the liberally educated person" as a reflection in graduates of liberal arts curricula—is what counts. If it turned out that college graduates "were in no way distinguishable from those who did not attend college" we would expect content-oriented faculty to "change the measures," the outcomes faculty to "change the curriculum," and the faculty-intent proponents "perhaps not even to care."

Of the three approaches, we believe that the outcomes method is the most tangible and rational measure. And we believe it is the only measure society will ultimately accept. Outcomes are at least implied by most everyone—ranging from students and parents, admissions recruiters, and to those who decide how much private contributions or taxpayers' money go to higher education, to probably most faculty and administrators and scholars on the subject. Even content-oriented and faculty-intent-oriented proponents would be hard pressed to demonstrate that their philosophies do not imply outcomes.

In any case, faculty cannot afford the luxury of not caring. Although faculty, empowered as "officers of instruction," traditionally have final say on curriculum matters, only the most reckless and monkish would make such decisions without taking note of market or political conditions of support for their institutions. This reality today is behind public outcries for "accountability" or "assessment" of academic programs (see chapter 8). And it is reflected in all of the major critiques of undergraduate education. The NIE study concluded that "adequate measures of educational excellence must be couched in terms of student outcomes—principally such academic outcomes as knowledge, intellectual capacities, and skills" (NIE, 1984, p. 16). Similarly, the Carnegie Foundation report recommended assessment programs because "a quality undergraduate college is concerned about outcomes" (Boyer, 1987, p. 295). The AAC study recommended guidelines for assessment after noting that "one of the most remarkable and scandalous aspects of American higher education is the absence of traditions, practices, and methods of institutional and social accountability" (AAC, 1985, p. 33).

In the context of our current political and cultural expectations, we believe that the meaning of liberal arts or liberal education will be—and perhaps always has been—defined by outcomes. And we believe the New Liberal Arts will continue to be defined by outcomes, which are, in turn, determined by curricula. If current outcomes are not deemed satisfactory and changes in them are desired, then the curricula will be changed to produce the desired outcomes. That is what undergraduate education reform in America is all about. So what outcomes are desired in a liberal education and how are they achieved?

Convergence of Outcomes: Liberal-Useful Integration

Drawing on a broad base of experience and knowledge, both the Carnegie Foundation and the AAC reports outlined desired outcomes. Labeled, in one case, "essential undergraduate experiences" and, in the other, important "capacities," they are authoritative guidelines for establishing the outcomes for undergraduate liberal education graduates.

The Carnegie report includes such goals as language skills; "understanding the unique ability of the arts to affirm and dignify our lives"; awareness of tradition, heritage, and meaning beyond the present; acquaintance with the major institutions that "make up our world"; knowledge of "the ordered yet symbiotic nature of the universe"; understanding "the universal experiences of producing and consuming, and [placing] . . . work in larger context"; "the understanding of oneself and a capacity for sound judgment" (Boyer, 1987, pp. 92-99).

ACC goals include skills in "inquiry, abstract logical thinking, critical analysis"; ability in "literacy, writing, reading, speaking, listening"; "understanding numerical data"; "historical consciousness"; understanding of science; ethical values; appreciation for art; "international and multicultural experiences"; and "study in depth" (AAC, 1985, pp. 15-24).

After comparing the AAC and Carnegie outcomes with a synthesized list of professional education outcomes, the Michigan Professional Preparation Network Report ("Strengthening the ties," 1987) concluded that, although there are important differences, "one cannot fail to notice that the goals of professional program educators overlap with those traditionally espoused by liberal arts educators" (p. 26). Derived from literature in various professional education fields, the professional education list "bears a striking similarity to" the Carnegie and ACC outcomes. The Michigan report concludes that "it is erroneous to view the enduring attributes of education as the sole domain of any single group of academic programs" (p. 26).

The overlap of each of the Michigan-compiled 10 potential professional outcomes with liberal education outcomes is apparent. A student pursuing a professional degree that exemplifies the 10 outcomes would be achieving most of the outcomes of a liberal education, as the following brief overview of the 10 professional outcomes, compared with liberal outcomes, demonstrates ("Strengthening the ties," 1987 pp. 23-25):

1. *Communication competence* is the ability to read, write, speak, and listen and to use these processes effectively to acquire, develop, and convey ideas and information. These skills, which are highly valued by most professional curriculums—especially communication—are also fundamental to "desired liberal outcomes of informed citizenship and continued personal growth."

2. *Critical thinking* is the ability to examine issues rationally, logically, and coherently—a universally recognized and desired liberal outcome. Professional graduates seek to possess "a repertoire of thinking strategies that will enable them to acquire, evaluate, and synthesize information and knowledge." Professionals also are taught "to develop analytical skills to make decisions in both familiar and unfamiliar circumstances."

3. *Contextual competence* is an understanding of the societal context or environment in which one is living and working. The liberally educated person needs "to comprehend the complex interdependence" between one's

profession or work and society. Likewise, the "ability to make judgments in light of historical, social, economic, scientific, and political realities is demanded of the professional as well as the citizen."

4. *Aesthetic sensibility* is an enhanced aesthetic awareness of arts and human behavior for both personal enrichment and application in the enhancement of work.

5. *Professional identity* is a concern for improving the knowledge, skills, and values of the profession. This "both parallels and supplements the liberal education goal of developing a sense of personal identity."

6. *Professional ethics* is an understanding of the ethics of a profession as standards that guide professional behavior. "Liberally educated individuals are expected to have developed value systems and ethical standards . . . [T]he study of ethics provides a context for development of professional ethics."

7. *Adaptive competence* is anticipating, adapting to, and promoting changes important to a profession's societal purpose and professional's role. "A liberally educated person has an enhanced capacity to adapt to and anticipate changes. . . ."

8. *Leadership capacity* is exhibiting the capacity to contribute as a productive member of the profession and assuming appropriate leadership roles. "Not only does leadership imply both functional and status obligations, it requires the intelligent, humane application of knowledge and skills."

9. *Scholarly concern for improvement* is recognizing the need to increase knowledge and to advance the profession through both theoretical and applied research. "The heart of the intellectual process is attention to a spirit of inquiry, critical analysis or logical thinking."

10. *Motivation of continued learning* is exploring and expanding personal, civic, and professional knowledge and skills through a lifetime, both appropriately liberal and professional outcomes. "All knowledge . . . is liberal (i.e., it enlarges and liberates the mind) when it is committed to continuing inquiry" (Bell, 1968, p. 8).

How these 10 outcomes compare with the outcomes of communication and mass media studies programs, and how these programs have their own distinctive outcomes in a New Professionalism, are discussed in chapter 8.

Does Subject Matter Matter?

If outcomes define a liberal education, does it really matter what programs of study a student pursues? Asserting a general equality among academic subjects is as American as apple pie. Nearly 130 years ago, educational pioneers Ezra Cornell and Charles William Eliot called for an end to the mandatory classical curriculum. The debate then was between those defending the classical curriculum against the new, emerging technical and trendy disciplines of natural science and modern languages. Eliot, in his landmark inaugural speech as president of Harvard in 1869, called for an end of "the endless controversies" about which field of study was more superior or liberal than another. "We shall have them all and at their best," he said (Boyer, 1987, p. 63). Boyer, in his account of this change in American higher education, added:

> In Eliot's day the philosophical linchpin of the liberal arts college was to affirm that the *formation* of the "whole student" was immensely more important than particular *information*. Thomas Babington Macaulay, the great nineteenth-century English historian, went so far as to suggest that no academic subject is intrinsically superior to another . . . By the end of the nineteenth century, business leaders had joined academic reformers in opposing classical education. They argued that if a thorough mastery of any body of knowledge — and it didn't matter which — is really the formative element of a liberal education, why not study those bodies of knowledge that are commercially valuable? (pp. 63–64)

If subject matter does not matter, what does? Even boosters of the superiority of liberal arts education over professional education reject the simplistic notion that traditional-discipline content alone determines liberal outcomes. In an exploration of just why "liberal arts" (i.e., nonprofessional program) graduates apparently do better in careers than graduates of professional programs, the authors (Woditsch, Schlesinger, & Giardina, 1987), quoting Daniel Bell (1968, p. 8), argued that the *method* in which knowledge is presented is more important than the knowledge. The authors, reviewing literature on cognition and pedagogy, emphasized formation over information. Although they concluded that the traditional liberal arts and sciences should be "the disciplines of choice," they doubted whether the learning processes they prescribed actually took place in many liberal arts and sciences programs. They pointedly rejected "back to a liberal arts curriculum at any price" arguments. A liberal arts curriculum that does not meet their criteria of liberal education was "not worth the price." Because they valued liberal pedagogical processes over content, they looked for them wherever they could find them, including in professional programs.

> We . . . would readily pick a liberal Accounting 101 over a dogmatized French Renaissance 212. Evidence of liberal educators' wielding their distinctive capability well beyond the boundaries of what we call the arts and science is not uncommon. A careful look at liberalizing [professional education] programs doing good work outside liberal arts institutions reveals that they

employ much of that very tradition, often more sensitively than do many of its titled caretakers. (Woditsch et al., 1987, p. 57)

Frederick Rudolph (1984, p. 41), other critics, and reformers including the Carnegie, AAC, and NIE decade-long studies and reports, have reasserted the century-old concept of the general equality of subject matter. But most agree that this concept from its inception created a vacuum. What is missing today is what still has not been fully achieved in American undergraduate education since classical education was dropped: coherence and unity of knowledge. The solution to this problem is some form of an integrated, common, or "general education" core where subject matter and a liberating pedagogical spirit are fused together by a clear vision of anticipated outcomes.

THE BACCALAUREATE

Ernest Boyer and Arthur Levine (1981) concluded that liberal education should include a balance, approximately one third each among three components of a baccalaureate degree—the general or common core (integration of knowledge), the major (study in depth), and the electives. We examine each.

The Core Solution: Part One

Throughout the reform literature, and in this chapter, one major theme is that less fragmentation and more coherence is needed in the American baccalaureate. What is needed is a unity of knowledge, an understanding that "if the college experience is to be worthwhile, there must be intellectual and social values that its members hold in common" (Boyer, 1987, p. 66).

At the most fundamental level, as Boyer of the Carnegie Foundation expressed it, the issue is striking a balance between two powerful, but contradictory, American traditions—individuality and community. Individuality encompasses "the personal benefits and the utility of education" where students pursue their own goals, "follow their own aptitudes" to become "empowered" human beings. By community, Boyer meant "an undergraduate experience that helps students go beyond their own private interests . . . develop a sense of civic and social responsibility, and discover how they, as individuals, can contribute to the larger society of which they are a part" (pp. 67–68).

The integrated core would ensure not only that community values and goals are included in the undergraduate experience, but that there is a pool of knowledge and perspectives or outcomes shared by all students, a commonality. Reformers call for the equivalent of what Boyer called an integrated core—"a program of general education that introduces students not only to essential knowledge, but also to the connections across the disciplines and, in the end, to the application of knowledge to life beyond the campus" (p. 91).

This core would include areas of inquiry "that can relate the curriculum to experiences common to all people," for the community. Boyer's seven areas—language, art, heritage, institutions, nature, work, identity—are representative of a variety of reformers' nominations for common core areas (pp. 91, 92). The development of a truly integrated and comprehensive core is the top priority of undergraduate reformers. This is where coherence and unity of knowledge are expected to begin. Toward this goal the traditional academic disciplines should be taking the lead. This is their historic role. Their active participation in successfully developing integrated cores in undergraduate curriculums in the United States would be some compensation for their abandonment of their traditional stewardship of coherence and unity of traditional knowledge.

But the educational reformers are abundantly clear on another point: The core curriculum is not the sole "turf" of the traditional academic disciplines. The integrated core must include contemporary, as well as traditional, knowledge that reflects new, emerging understandings—a New Liberal Arts. The professional fields encompass the newer technologies and powerful institutional systems, which tradition-bound and preservation-bound disciplines historically are slow to assimilate. Because many of these systems and technologies are ubiquitous and central to our culture, they provide a basis for the cross-disciplinary exploration of commonalities vital to the maintenance of our otherwise fragmented society: integrating traditional knowledge and newer professional knowledge and perspectives for a New Liberal Arts (Kanigel, 1986; Koerner, 1984; Lisensky, Pfnister, & Sweet, 1985; Morison, 1986; Truxal, 1986; White, 1981).

As the Michigan study ("Strengthening the ties," 1988) argued, professional programs bring to the academy a number of educational outcomes that are, by any measure, liberal. And it is through their contributions that true integration of the useful and liberal arts—for the development of a New Liberal Arts—can begin. In chapter 3, we discuss the role of communication and mass media education in this enterprise of enriching the university's integrated core.

The Depth Problem: Part Two

Although the integrated core is for the community, the major or specialization in an academic discipline or professional field is for the individual. The ACC calls this "study in depth." In the spirit of integrating professional and liberal studies, Boyer (1987) went further that the specialization implied in "study of depth." He recommended the "enriched major" concept.

> By *enriched major* we mean encouraging students not only to explore a field in depth, but also to help put their field of special study in perspective. The major, as it is enriched, will respond to three essential questions: What is the history and tradition of the field to be examined? What are the social and economic implications to be understood? What are the ethical and moral issues to be confronted? (p. 110)

The heart of the Carnegie curriculum proposal is that "the liberal and useful arts [professional subjects]" should be "brought together in the curriculum just as they inevitably must be brought together during life" (p. 112). The liberal and useful arts should be integrated, rather than kept in their unhealthy separate domains. Instead of worrying about the newness, status, or utility of a discipline or program, the "basic test" of any study-in-depth major should be: Does it have "a legitimate intellectual content of its own and does it have the capacity to enlarge, rather than narrow, the vision of the student?" (p. 109)

As we noted previously, the AAC study finds that the "study in depth" component in an undergraduate liberal education can be met by any academic discipline or professional program if they are "based on the skills and attitudes of our minimum curriculum and presented in a liberal spirit" (AAC, 1985, p. 30).

The concept of integration within the enriched major is crucial. As reform progresses, it is not enough that the role of professional education is recognized or tolerated in the undergraduate curriculum, but kept apart from the liberal arts. Frank H. T. Rhodes, president of Cornell University, argued instead that:

> In an effort to counteract a perceived narrowness in their students, too many institutions have simply added more liberal arts courses to already burdensome programs of professional education. Rarely have they attempted to integrate liberal and professional education in ways that have meanings for all students; rarely have they been able to link high standards of scholarship and professional practice to critical thinking on the fundamental issues of life. ("Strengthening the ties," 1988, p. v)

The Professional Preparation Project also noted that the response to reform critiques has been merely to increase the separation of professional and liberal education (p. 1).

Electives: Completing the Three-Part Baccalaureate

As important as the core and study in depth are, there is another equally important element needed to fulfill the liberal education requirements for the baccalaureate—the electives. Although electives have been subject to misuse, reformers have not overlooked their abundant, often serendipitous advantages and relevance to liberal education. They provide opportunities to "kick tires"—to sample widely the intellectual offerings, broad learning experiences, and challenging teachers they would not otherwise be required to do; acquire learning skills, sometimes in a nonthreatening pass/fail environment, that they might not attempt under other circumstances; develop interests and talents in drama, music, painting, film, video, athletics, and the other performance fields; and satisfy curiosity about unfamiliar subjects (Carnegie Foundation, 1977).

Although the major belongs to the discipline, the common core belongs to the university, and the electives belong to the student. A liberal education does not reside exclusively in any one of the three components. The absence of one short changes liberal education.

Joining the Mainstream of Undergraduate Education

The professional programs should be both flattered and challenged by the conclusions and recommendations of the undergraduate curriculum reformers and the New Liberal Arts. Their historic role of providing specialized education in undergraduate education has been reaffirmed and new meaning and legitimacy have been given to the concept of study in depth or the enriched major. A new and important role for professional programs has been suggested in the essential experiences or capacities to be included in the integrated core for the 21st century. The importance of electives is reemphasized.

But, more realistically, the professional programs are being challenged by the New Liberal Arts. They are not in the mainstream of the general education or common core curricula on most of their campuses. Many professional programs are too narrow to be considered enriching to a student's undergraduate experience. Many do not offer any or enough opportunities for nonmajors to explore their fields. Developing the New Liberal Arts will be at least as challenging to the professional programs as it will be to the traditional arts and sciences. The solution for communication and media education, at least, is nothing less than a New Professionalism.

2 Media Education and Technology

Convergence, of course, is a coming together of the ways and means of communication, from message formation and processing to dissemination and storage. In today's world there isn't much difference at either the abstract or operational level between a newspaper, a television station, a database and a telephone system. What is different is human intention and purpose of communication.

—Dennis (1989, pp. 3, 4)

How we conceptualize, produce, and deliver information is shown to be rapidly changing (cf. Bell, 1973; Brody, 1990; Dennis, 1986b; Dizard, 1989; Porat, 1977; Rice, 1985; Rogers, 1986). Whether it is called a communication, information, or technological revolution, rapid changes within the U.S. media system coupled with new ways of thinking about communication processes and content challenge media educators to rethink curricular structures and what and how they teach. This challenge calls for flexible, integrated, and innovative media courses and curricula; it means a movement away from narrowly conceived media-specific sequences based on industrial configurations toward broad-based, cross-media, integrative models; the teaching of ideas and skills that transcend the narrow occupational focus of specific, entry-level, job-related protocols; "de-massifying" the concept of communication to incorporate the study of intrapersonal and interpersonal communication and their relationship to "mass" forms of communication distribution; and, finally, rethinking how people teach and how learning environments can be enhanced with the use of technologies. There are many ways of implementing curricular changes that take into account technology's impact. This chapter suggests general curricular approaches while leaving the specifics to Part II of this book.

TECHNOLOGY AND DEFINING THE SCOPE OF MEDIA STUDIES

The following example could have been repeated in any number of communities. A local parents' group, trying to get its bus service reinstated

TECHNOLOGY AND DEFINING THE SCOPE OF MEDIA STUDIES 23

after the school district took it away, uses the telephone for networking, strategically placed road signs for communicating displeasure, and a local television station's reports to apply pressure on the district. For scholars to describe the impact of technology on this persuasive process would require them to expand the scope of typical "mass" media studies to include telephones, signs, and interpersonal communication. Of these three, signs are closest to a "mass" communication form, whereas telephones, along with the ubiquitous answering machine, might come closer to the new, emerging interactive technologies being developed.

New interactive technologies (cf. Dominick, 1987; Kipper, 1989) are changing the way scholars think about media communication. When Rogers (1986) asked rhetorically: "What is different about human communication as a result of the new technologies?" he came up with three main points including the new technologies interactive quality:

> Interactivity is a desired quality of communication systems because such communication behavior is expected to be more accurate, more effective, and more satisfying to the participants in a communication process. These advantages usually come at the cost of more communication message exchanges and the greater time and effort required for the communication process (Rafaeli, 1984). (Rogers, 1986, p. 5)

Second, he argued the de-massification capabilities of the new technologies: "The high degree of de-massification of the new communication technologies means that they are, in this respect at least, the opposite of mass media. De-massification means that the control of mass communication systems usually moves from the message producer to the media consumer" (p. 5).

Finally, he discussed the asynchronous aspect of the new technologies. "In the new communication systems, the participants don't have to be in communication at the same time" (p. 5). This "attack" on the time-boundedness of the communication process gives more flexibility to how media are used.

The use of "fax" by students during the spring 1989 Tiananmen Square rallies and subsequent suppression helps illustrate the challenges of defining mass communication and the interactive characteristics of "new" technologies (cf. Schell, Nixon, & Gardels, 1989). In the spring of 1989, Chinese students and workers staged massive rallies in Beijing's Tiananmen Square asking for reforms in the Chinese government. These protesters kept each other informed through a distribution network that included loud speakers, small printing presses/mimeographs, posters, couriers on bicycles, motorcycles and cars, and word of mouth (Cherrington, 1991; Lull, 1991; Shen, 1990).

During the initial stages of the protest, Western journalists were able to move freely and to report on the various marches and demands. As the events leading to the military resolution of the protest reached its climax and the Western media were literally shut off and shut out, protesters who wanted to hear reports from outside China had to depend on their people network, short-wave radios, smuggled papers, and a fourth, unexpected medium: the fax machine. Chinese students in the United States and elsewhere used fax to communicate the facts, as they knew them, to people in China.

As a point-to-point distribution technique, the fax resembles interpersonal communication. Usually, people use it to communicate to other specific individuals. However, in the case of the Chinese protest, the fax "network" resembled a mass communication network. Messages were sent to many locations without the assurance that they would be received or fall on sympathetic eyes. That is, messages were "broadcast" to a variety of people some of whom would not like or appreciate or read the messages.

Perhaps only those who remember the use of copy machines in the 1960s and 1970s as an inexpensive method for reproducing posters to communicate events to people on the streets (stapled to telephone and light poles, bulletin boards, and construction barriers) in and around college campuses could have foreseen the Chinese students innovative method for using fax as another media tool in people's political arsenal. Again, to understand the protest requires an understanding of how people use different kinds of communication technologies to communicate their ideological perspectives; challenges us to re-define what we consider "important" or mainline media.

Besides moving into the area of interactive technologies, media scholars are exploring how mass media tend to impinge on face-to-face communication and how face-to-face communication impacts media use (cf. Kubey & Csikszentmihalyi, 1990; Lull, 1988). Scholars are using variables that are normally associated with interpersonal communication research to describe and explain media use (cf. Rubin & Rubin, 1985).

Of course, academic turf and epistemological concerns have often created a tension among interpersonal and mass communication scholars and between interpersonal (i.e., speech) and mass (i.e., broadcasting or journalism) communication departments (see chapters 3 and 6). However, a comprehensive study of communication processes would require acknowledging both interpersonal and mass communication perspectives; how media impacts and intertwines with people's lives requires a realization that previously useful categories like "interpersonal" and "mass" may impede media studies research in the future.

So questions are raised: How mass is mass communication? What does it mean to be a mass medium as the process of communication begins to turn back on itself allowing for immediate feedback where before there was limited two-way communication? Rogers argued that it requires a new way of modeling the communication process, a modeling that challenges the very foundations of mass communication research and education.

TECHNOLOGY AND THE NEW MEDIA INDUSTRIES

Two points should be made about technology's impact on media industries. First, print and broadcast companies can no longer afford to think of themselves simply as print and broadcast companies. Second, the low cost and proliferation of technologies is changing who has access to and control over media content.

Media companies, by affirming that they are in the information business, rather than the business of a single delivery system, are breaking down old distinctions between print and electronic communication. Take, for example, the production of the information delivered in a newspaper. From the writing of the story to layout to printing, much of what is done is accomplished electronically (cf. Hanson, 1988; Junod, 1989; "New York, New York," 1990; Truitt, 1988). Electronic "newspapers" are now available. News, as written word, is now available on a "television" screen. News, as graphics, is now available in the "newspaper." Erasable laser disk storage devices will allow "a personal computer . . . [to] control the press . . ." (Consoli, 1989, p. 13). As de Sola Pool (1983) wrote, the lines between the technologies of print and the electronic media have blurred: "In the coming era, the industries of print and the industries of telecommunication will no longer be kept apart by a fundamental difference in their technologies" (p. 42). The Office of Technological Assessment (OTA) argued that the very conception of the "press" will be redefined through technology:

> Satellites, high-speed computers, electronic bulletin boards, global communications networks, "intelligent" machines and low-cost storage media "of astonishing capacity"—these are the kinds of technologies that will affect the structure of communications and, consequently, OTA says, the manner in which the press gathers and publishes information. "In changing the way in which information is produced and disseminated," OTA adds, "technology may change who and what is considered 'the press.' " ("Technology redefines," 1988, p. 133)

Newspapers that realize they are in the information business and not just the paper and ink news business are developing a variety of delivery systems including direct mail and audiotex (cf. Fitzgerald, 1992). In fact, those newspapers that do not face the challenges of new delivery systems may find themselves in financial trouble. As was reported in *Presstime:*

> Mailboxes get fuller every year with catalogs, fliers and shared-mail packages as the boom in direct mail advertising continues. . . . All this means that direct mailer's share of total ad spending has been going up, while that of newspapers has been slowly dwindling. Most newspapers have responded with

total-market-coverage strategies, some with their own shared-mailed programs. (Rambo, 1989, p. 5)

Audiotex involves phone services by companies, including newspapers. These services include the time and weather, stock prices, baseball scores, and horoscopes. For example, "At 28 cents a call, *Newsday's* New York weather line generated 35 million calls in 1988. . . . The paper kept only 15 percent of the resulting $9.8 million in revenue." Other newspapers offer the service for free but play advertisements as part of their message. Still other uses of automated voice information services include "voice response mailboxes for classified advertisers (no need to stay home on Sunday afternoon to wait for a call . . .)" (Lessersohn, 1989, pp. 12-14).

Certainly direct mail and the telephone services are not new. However, by seeing themselves in the information business, media companies are breaking down old distinctions based on media-specific delivery systems:

> Despite all of this "electronic publishing" activity, no one (not even Ted Turner) is currently predicting the disappearance of the printed newspaper. But at a time when fewer and fewer people under the age of 35 are reading newspapers and more and more are growing up taking computers and sophisticated telecommunications for granted, newspapers cannot afford to ignore new means of distributing the information they gather and edit. (Lessersohn, 1989, p. 14)

The trend to move away from a single delivery to a broader information approach has implications for other media as well. Like some newspapers, radio stations are turning to the telephone to enhance profits. *Radiotrends* ("New telephone," 1989, p. 1), for example, reported that, "First of all, *stations could carry advertising for 900 lines. Second, radio could tie in with record companies or retailers to offer listeners who call in coupons for discounts on records or other merchandise.*" They cited the fact that DJ Jazzy Jeff and the Fresh Prince 900 line has brought in *"an estimated $4 million in revenues so far"* (p. 1). Furthermore, the circular sees interactive telephone capability giving radio stations the ability to develop a listener database: "All of the systems have the ability to collect information from callers thus allowing stations to develop a data base of listeners for future direct mail efforts" (p. 2). (See also, Courson, 1989; Hume, 1991.)

A television station that realizes it is in the information business might use excerpts from the evening newscasts to develop educational videotapes or laser disks. Telephone companies that realize they are in the information business have challenged cable companies for the right to distribute programming.

Since the early days of the mass media industry there has been cross-ownership of media properties. Newspaper companies have owned radio stations; television and radio stations have been owned by the same company; companies have owned both television stations and newspapers. However, today, as perhaps never before, it is clear that those companies that see themselves in the "information" business, will feel free to produce, distribute, and sell a wide variety of information using a wide variety of media vehicles.

The curriculum implications are clear. Training people to think of themselves as simply print or electronic communicators is counterproductive. What is needed is a broadbased, fundamentals approach to media education.

Second, print and electronic technologies are becoming less expensive. Three examples illustrate this point: the computer, the recorder, and the telephone. Hand-held computers can now be purchased for under $20; personal computers for word processing and graphics for under $1,000. These kinds of prices have major impacts on the media industry. In terms of production, it makes it possible for even the smallest newsroom to become an electronic newsroom. Newspeople, using portable computers, can write their stories on the road and download them over the nearest phone to their editor. Small suburban newspapers can be more quickly and easily produced. Students in schools can have their articles more easily accessed and corrected using newly setup electronic class rooms (cf. Adams, 1987; Behnke & King, 1986). Computers, through desktop publishing programs, now give graphic capabilities to people who had to rely on "professionals" before. For example, small public radio stations now have the ability to produce more graphically sophisticated program magazines with less effort and cost. Both internal and external publications can be more easily produced (cf. Morgan, 1988).

In terms of sales and management, the low cost and proliferation of computers makes it possible for even the smallest radio and television station to subscribe to software programs that allow them to analyze their audience or sales or programming. Many of these programs allow salespeople to individualize and "configure" their sale package based on different subsets of the latest ratings. Hours of analysis can now be done quickly and impressively with the touch of an "F1" key. Computers, including in some cases the use of computers for automation, are used to keep track of operations, traffic, personnel, budgets, programming, stories, and billings.

"Recorders" is a generic word under which the proliferation in visual and audio recorders can be grouped. Perhaps no recording technology has challenged the television and film industries as has the home videocassette recorder (VCR). Zipping, zapping, and time-shifting are concepts made possible through the VCR and remote control technology. People can zip through commercials of programs they have recorded. They can zap commercials by using their remotes. They can watch programs when it is convenient to them. Through local video rental stores and cable companies, the supremacy of network prime-time programming has been eroding. Like desktop publishing, low cost video recording allows many companies and schools to get involved in the production and distribution of programming.

The telephone, including mobile paging and wireless telephony, allows for the instantaneous bridging of space. Its ubiquity makes it somewhat invisible in terms of appreciating its importance. Although we have discussed its new found importance at newspapers and radio stations, one more example is appropriate.

In his book, *The Next Hurrah: The Communications Revolution in American Politics,* Richard Armstrong (1988) wrote:

> By 1906, use of the telephone in politics had become widespread enough for a writer in the trade journal *Telephony* to lament that no one had yet made a serious study of the subject: "It is time for someone to write a book, or at least an article, on 'The Telephone in Politics.' The telephone has made it possible for one man to wage a campaign over an entire city. It has curtailed the functions and responsibilities of a district manager as the cable has those of the ambassador. It enables a canvass to be made, or a list of distinguished signatures secured for some 'call' or manifesto, without the expenditure of several days' time or the employment of a large corps of workers." (p. 140)

Armstrong argued, "It doesn't take a genius to realize that this is probably the most powerful political tool ever invented" (p. 142).

For media educators the challenge is clear. What do we study and how do we study it? Do we study all communication technologies? What is it about communication technologies that should be taught and learned? We address this in our last section.

TECHNOLOGY AND MEDIA CHANNELS AND CONTENT

As computers have allowed the combination and easy analysis of enormous quantities of data, the ability to describe and segment people along a variety of demographic, psychological, and behavioral dimensions has increased. The need of advertisers and "producers/publishers" to reach specialized audiences has encouraged the growth of specialized channels in such media as cable television, radio, film, magazines, and books. This in turn has increased the quantity and type of information available to people. A brief

TECHNOLOGY AND MEDIA CHANNELS AND CONTENT   29

review of four media (cable, radio, magazines, and books) shows the enormous quantity of content now being produced and distributed.

Cable.   In the electronic distribution of information, perhaps the variety and quantity of information is most evident in the cable industry (cf. "Filling the upcoming," 1991). For example, in San Antonio, a media market in the high 30s/low 40s (depending on how the market is defined), the cable company delivers 46 television channels and 30 music channels. Besides the three local television network affiliates, local independent stations, and two of the superstations (WTBS and WGN), specialized information channels are available that feature news, sports, weather, Spanish language programming, children's programming, old movies, new movies, music, religion, business, and shopping. Hundred-channel cable systems are becoming more commonplace.

Radio.   Radio's content has also changed since its "commercialization" in the 1920s. What were once all-purpose stations, stations that played live music, delivered news, and performed drama, are now stations that specialize in a variety of formats. The Standard Rating and Data Service (*"SRDS's spot radio rates and data,"* 1991) lists nine standard format classifications (Music, Sports, Talk, Air Personalities, News, Farm, Religious, Entertainment, and Commercial Policy), and over 200 syndicated format titles. These titles, which differ based on the syndicator, include: *Roots of Rock N'Roll* (targeted to men 40+ and women 36+), *AC Christian* (targets the 25-49 AC [Adult Christian] audience with alternative music), and *Kaleidophonics* (full or part-time new age format services . . . targets upscale/professional demos . . .). The impact of technology is not only about quantity but also about variety and specialization of content.

Magazines.   There has been a proliferation of magazine titles and book publications since the late 1970s. Older magazine titles like *Life* died and came back in a different form. Mass national publications like *Newsweek* have space set aside for regional advertising that allows for more focused targeting. *Ulrich's* (1991) lists 118,500 serial titles. Although not all of these serials are magazines, in the United States, there are over 85 consumer magazines with paid circulations of over 750,000 (Johnson, 1991). The titles of these magazines do not include the numerous consumer magazine subtitles or the variety of business publications. Under the "TV & Radio/Communications Electronics" heading, for example, the *SRDS's Consumer Magazine & Agri-Media Rates and Data* (1991) section lists 28 titles including such specialized magazines as *Audio/Video Interiors, Popular Communications, and Satellite Orbit*. In the *SRDS's Business Publication*

Rates and Data, (1991) there are 50 periodical titles under the heading, "Telecommunications Technology" including *Cellular Business, Fiberoptics Product News, Mobile Radio Technology, Satellite Communications, Telemarketing,* and *Telephony.*

Books. Book titles also continue to exemplify the quantity, variety, and specialization evident in the information revolution. The recent *Books in Print Index* (1991) for example, states that there are presently "some 1 million titles produced by over 40,000 publishing houses" (p.v.). There are over 42 pages of books beginning with "How-To. . . ."

New Forms. Besides the quantity and variety of information content increasing, the communication revolution has seen the creation of new forms or the new packaging of old forms. Music videos are an example of a "new form." The marriage of music and film has always been a popular one even before *Don Juan*'s (1926) first synchronized musical score. However, by linking one song with one video, music videos became analogous to records. Music Television (MTV) became a visual jukebox. With their use of visual techniques such as slow motion, superimposition, colorization, and unexpected editing, music videos forged new ground in the media content.

Another development in the creation of new forms is the marriage of different types of content. These marriages tend to be controversial. For example, the marriage of advertising and editorial content, which is called *advertorial,* does not always make clear that the articles were paid for by the advertiser (see "Cover story," 1988). The marriage of historical or news events and drama, which has become known as *docudrama,* usually takes enough liberties with the historical record to cause consternation among scholars.

The repackaging of old forms is another attribute of the information revolution. Perhaps the best example of this is *USA Today,* which began publication in late 1982. It combines "*Splashy graphics and liberal use of color. *Short, easily digested stories—the longest average about 100 words. *Extensive use of graphics, charts, and tables. The sports section in particular is crammed with statistics. *A full page devoted to weather. *The use of factoids" (Dominick, 1987, p. 106). *USA Today* is not without its critics. It has been called the Disneyland of newspapers, bubblegum or fast food journalism. Yet, at the very least, it has had an impact on how people expect a newspaper to look (see Badgett, 1989; Terrell, 1989).

How do media educators address the changes in content and delivery systems? Some decide to keep up with the changes by developing courses or sequences of courses that reflect new subspecialties in the industry. This, we think, is ultimately shortsighted. The development of new media forms suggests the need of media educators to experiment and to be enterprising in working to create new communication forms with new content. This experimentation is at the heart of the media laboratory discussed in chapter 6.

TECHNOLOGY AND THE WORKPLACE OF THE FUTURE

Janis (1991) suggested that "the media workplace of the future will be an information-technologies theme park, where technical distinctions among the attractions will blur and everyone will speak the same language— digitial" (p. 18). Her predictions include the use of voice-controlled workstations that could eliminate keyboarding; computer screens with full-motion video capabilities that would allow for the monitoring of multiple sources; infrared networks that could surround a building and eliminate expensive wiring; artificial intelligence that could be used to "customize news products to individuals"; hand-held computers for tracking distribution of newspapers; eye-activated electronic systems that could accommodate physically challenged individuals; advanced database technology to assist in customizing consumer products; and high-definition television.

The impact of digital reinforces two points. The first is that the "worker" of the future will need to be as comfortable with technology as today's children are with video games. Second, due to the increasing accessibility of new technologies to "untrained" practitioners, there is the possibility of more "voices" being "seen" and heard on local and national issues. This "democratization" of the media can be seen in the proliferation of newsletters on many campuses that attempt to supplement the campus paper. With desk-top publishing, almost anyone can become an editor and publisher. This can lead to more personal stories being told in the media (see chapter 6 discussion of "laboratories").

TECHNOLOGY AND CURRICULAR CHANGES

Can We Talk?

Technologies now in place are leading media scholars to the clear linkage between interpersonal and "mass" communication. What this means on college campuses is the need for scholars and teachers from a variety of traditional speech and mass communication programs to sit down and talk (see chapters 3 and 6). Political and epistemological differences need to be faced face to face for the students' sake. The New Professionalism looks for the interrelatedness among the subspecialties and calls for presenting a communication perspective that transcends the traditional compartmentalization of subdisciplines and moves toward an integration of the field of communication.

Cross-Training: Ahead to Fundamentals

Cross-training refers to exercises that help an athlete compete in a variety of sports. The analogy with media education is preparing students to prosper in a variety of media settings. Overly drawn distinctions being made between print and electronic media systems are, if not obsolete, then counterproductive. As media companies move to define themselves less within the confines of discrete delivery systems and more as information companies, media educators need to re-think what they are doing. Schools that see themselves as graduating print or electronic people are doing a disservice to their students (see chapter 4). The new media environment calls for a New Professionalism, a flexible, fundamental, integrated approach to media education, one that looks for linkages and common concepts and skills that will allow students to understand and move easily among different information forms and companies (see Webster, 1989). The move by some media units to change their names from departments of broadcasting to departments of telecommunications or communication or communications, or from departments of journalism to the more inclusive journalism and mass communication reflects a positive move (cf. Carroll, 1985; Eastman, 1985, 1987; Head, 1985; Kittross, 1989; Sterling, 1985; Welke, 1985). Of course, it is not enough. What is needed is a hard look at fundamentals.

On one level, this discussion about curricular structure turns into a question of breadth and depth. There may be those who may see the specialization and fragmentation of the industry and decide to develop curricula that mirror those specializations. This approach is often justified under the rhetoric of providing depth to students. These programs might develop sequences for many types of communication: television or video or corporate production, audio or radio production, print or broadcast journalism, or advertising and public relations. Or, they may promote sequences that reflect each new technological development. These programs might develop writing courses for a variety of specialties or subspecialties: writing for broadcasting, writing for television, writing for radio, writing for newspapers, writing for magazines, writing for newsletters. These programs may develop courses in each new technology like videotex or teletext. Unfortunately, as it already has, this approach can drain limited resources and lead to a narrowness of scope that keeps students from understanding the broad communication picture (see chapter 3).

The New Professionalism seeks an approach that looks for underlying principles. Students need a curriculum that will encourage them to think of themselves as communicators and not simply as radio, television, or newspaper people. Courses, like media writing, that cut across a variety of media formats, channels, and content are the kinds of courses that help foster the New Professionalism.

Technology or Not?

The new technologies affect what and how media educators teach. For example, new graphic developments challenge the way we understand and present images, challenge us with new ways of seeing, require educators to think and study media images in new ways (cf. Zettl, 1990). Technology also has the potential, through its ability to distribute enormous amounts of information, for having a negative impact on people including, according to Salvaggio (1987, p. 147) "information overload (see Branscomb, 1979; Gabor, 1973; Pelton, 1983), invasion of privacy (see Diebold, 1973; Donner, 1981), information inequity (see Evans, 1979; Oettinger, 1980), psychological isolation (see Silberman, 1977), centralization of information (see Schiller, 1981; Salvaggio, 1983a,b,c), information monopoly (see Wicklein, 1981) and information misuse (see Parker, 1983)." Also see Leiss (1989), Teeple-Hewes (1983-1984), and Slack and Fejes (1987).

Media educators should be in the forefront of the discussions and debates about the ongoing transformation of the media industry and our symbolic environment; of making sense of the media's political, economic, legal, social and cultural impact. At the very least, and perhaps most importantly, media programs should study technology's impact.

How deeply a program addresses technology depends on school and departmental philosophies, financial resources, and administrative and faculty interests, among others. For those programs with the facilities and the will, internships, workshops, laboratories, and apprenticeships, which create opportunities for students to directly confront the communication technologies, are important possibilities (see chapter 6). Through the use of audio, video, laserdiscs, and computers, media educators can be on the forefront of developing innovative ways of using technology not only to communicate but to enhance the understanding of students (see chapter 7).

Understanding and using technology is a direct challenge to media education. By impacting on media processes, industries, and content, technology requires educators to rethink their discipline, what and how they teach. In the next chapter we discuss the revolution taking place in media studies.

3 The New Professionalism and the University: A Blueprint for Renewal

When a subject is presented as received doctrine or fact, it becomes an aspect of specialization and technique. When it is introduced with an awareness of its contingency and of the conceptual frame that guides its organization, the student can then proceed with the necessary self-consciousness that keeps his [sic] mind open to possibility and to reorientation.
— Bell (1968, p. 8)

[M]ass communication study may be essential if liberal education is to empower the student to act independently in a social fabric spun from contemporary message systems.
— Fletcher (1988, p. 30)

We are a century and more away from the time when going to college meant instruction in oratory, stage presence, debate, and the arts of persuasion. Television talk shows, political campaigns, and news broadcasts have taken their place.
— Association of American Colleges (1985, p. 17)

We have examined two forces of change so far—the undergraduate reform movement, and the communication revolution. Since the mid-1980s, communication and media education reformers have been proposing a variety of curricular and philosophical reforms designed to meet the challenges and opportunities created by these changes. Taken together, we see these proposals as a New Professionalism paving the way to two broad, interrelated constructive outcomes.

The first outcome would be greater diversity of undergraduate media education programs than now exists. More individually distinctive, integrated communication and media education curricula would replace the rigid, nationally enforced and prescribed industrial- and occupational-based sequences that have dominated media education curricula for the past 40 years. Under the New Professionalism, faculty members would not be restricted by outside, vocational demands. Instead, they would develop curricula in the context of community values, their vision of the university tradition, and the mission, uniqueness, resources and "geographical destiny"

("Planning for curricular change," 1987) of their college or university. The second outcome would be the elevation of the communication and media programs into the campus academic and intellectual mainline. The new perspective of the emerging discipline would provide for all students, in George Gerbner's words, "a fresh approach to the liberal arts." It would contribute to a New Liberal Arts, through critical and analytical understanding of "the cultural environment of the information society" (p. 40).

Before these outcomes can be achieved, however, there are at least two major hurdles facing media educators. The call for diversity based on a rational, integrative perspective belies the fact that the study of communication at many schools is splintered. The call for integration belies the fact that media educators have generally refused to take responsibility for the development of media courses and programs designed for the general student.

ACADEMIC HURDLES TO REFORM

Fragmentation Within the Field

Currently, the general field of communication education is suffering from a bad image. Critics joke that academic communicators cannot communicate. Motion pictures, such as *Moonstruck,* portray an unsympathetic, even pathetic, communication professor who is inept at interpersonal communication. Whereas these and other images may be unfair, there are substantial problems in programs associated in various ways with communication and media education.

Although "the concept of communication science is not yet an established, operating reality" (Berger & Chaffee, 1987, p. 119), an academic discipline in communication has been emerging and is establishing the conceptual groundwork for a convergence and integration of the field in both research and teaching (Rogers, 1986, pp. 109–110). But the full potential of integration and convergence is being retarded by the existence of two oppositional realms within communication and media education—at once intellectual and political. These two subfields are mass communication (many of which are "journalism and/or mass communication") and interpersonal (or "speech") communication. Each of these has its own history, campus turf, professional associations and academic journals (see Ball-Rokeach, 1985; Benson, 1985; Berger & Chaffee, 1988; Delia, 1987; Dervin & Voigt, 1984; Gumpertz & Cathart, 1982; Hawkins, Wiemann, & Pingree, 1988; Lowenstein & Merrill, 1990; Rogers & Chaffee, 1983; Wiemann, Hawkins, & Pingree, 1988). What was once positive healthy pluralism is now damaging fragmentation.

Mass Communication Versus Interpersonal Communication. The separation of the two subfields has intellectual roots. Interpersonal communication can be traced to classical times and oratorical tradition, "from the tradition of noble virtue" (Hudson, 1988, p. 11) and, more recently, to psychology, social psychology, and linguistics. This intellectual heritage has generally found a home in speech departments. The roots of the mass communication study can be found in the empirical tradition, "from the natural rights principles of freedom and justice" (p. 11). More recently mass communication has drawn "more directly from sociology, and political science, and was driven more heavily by policy concerns" (Reardon & Rogers, 1988, p. 289). As research in this sphere began to grow, it took up residence in departments of journalism, broadcasting or mass communication departments that were offering vocationally based instruction.

Amplifying their different origins, the two traditions in the 1940s adopted "a somewhat mistaken conception" of the Shannon-Weaver model of information theory (Rogers, 1986, p. 85; Reardon & Rogers, 1988, p. 288). The paradigm "encouraged a *feeling* of universality among communication scholars" (p. 288; italics added) "at a time when [c]ommunication researchers were emerging from the ghetto of trade-school education, and straining for the intellectual respect of their academic colleagues" (Rogers, p. 84).

However, each subdiscipline took a different path because the model provided each a conceptual rationalization to examine the communication process through its own channel—interpersonal or media. "At a time when the field of communication science had little identity," Reardon and Rogers reported, "the concepts of interpersonal versus mass media channels seemed to provide an acceptable means of dividing this field of scholarship" (p. 289). Interpersonal channels became mainly face to face, involving two or a few persons, whereas mass media communication became mediated messages affecting large audiences. Integration was abandoned, and a potentially universal conceptual model, upon which a unified science could have been built, "was sacrificed for a bifurcation in the pathways of development of the communication field . . . in favor of what may have been a premature need for identity" (p. 289).

The intellectual separation was reflected in the political realm with separate departments on campus and separate national and regional academic associations and scholarly journals. The major associations for communication and mass media studies scholars are the International Communication Association (ICA), the Speech Communication Association (SCA), and the Association for Education in Journalism and Mass Communication (AEJMC). The ICA has approximately equal numbers of interpersonal and mass communication scholars. The SCA, with about 6,700 members, includes all speech, including interpersonal and related fields. It also has a growing mass communication division. The AEJMC, with about 2,800 members, includes no interpersonal or speech representation and is almost exclusively a mass communication representation with divisions in newspaper, mass media and society, advertising, public relations, minorities, theory and methodology, magazine, radio and television, media management, history, visual communication, secondary education, law, international, qualitative studies, research, and so on. The Broadcast Education Association (a practitioner-academic hybrid), the Film and Video Association and other specialized national and regional organizations have further fragmented the media component of the field. All of these organizations have many active and influential divisions and committees, reflecting a variety of media and academic orientations (see Stacks, Rosenfeld, & Hickson III, 1989).

Analyses of the major communication and mass media education journals have demonstrated consistently that, indeed, "communication researchers do not communicate" (So, 1988). Interpersonal and mass communication scholars rarely consult or cite each other's research (Reardon & Rogers, 1988, pp. 291–293). "The subfields of interpersonal and mass media communication not only represent a real dichotomy in the communication field," authors of a comprehensive study of journals in the field concluded, "but also exhibit inbreeding . . . at least as reflected in citation patterns from 1977 through 1985 (Rice, Borgman, & Reeves, 1988, p. 276). Chief among scholarly journals they cited include *Central States Speech Journal, Communication Education, Communication Monographs, Communication Research, Human Communication Research, Journal of Broadcasting and Electronic Media, Journal of Communication, Journalism Quarterly, Public Opinion Quarterly,* and *Quarterly Journal of Speech*.

Inbreeding and division on campus is equally apparent to administrators, students, and faculty in other disciplines. For all to see and hear, there are competing, sometimes warring departments, schools or divisions of speech, journalism, broadcasting, telecommunications, mass communication, communication arts, theater, film, or a variation of the above (Blanchard, 1986, 1987b, 1988b, 1988d, 1988e; Blanchard & Christ, 1988a, 1988b, 1988c; Christ & Blanchard, 1987). The negative consequences of these intellectual and political divisions and fragmentation have become so apparent that rapid reform cannot be far behind.

As we describe in chapter 2, a "single electronically based, computer-driven mode" of the modern information age is emerging ("Planning for curricular change," 1987, p. 49). This includes machine-assisted interpersonal communication (Dominick, 1987, pp. 11–12) "that has qualities of both mass media and interpersonal channels yet is different in several important ways from either one" (Rogers, 1986, p. 3) — the long-ignored telephone and newer technologies such as teleconferencing networks, electronic messaging systems, computer bulletin boards, and interactive cable television. Neither interpersonal communication nor mass communication alone has the methodologies or models to adequately examine or explain the processes of interactivity or the individualized, de-massified, and asynchronous nature (lack of time-boundedness) of the new media and communication systems (p. 7).

This is because, as we already have suggested, the Shannon-Weaver model was interpreted and applied to communication as linear and unidirectional, with either person-to-person channels or media-to-audience channels going from sender(s) to receiver(s). Concepts of subjectivity and interactivity through both interpersonal and media channels were ignored. This is in spite of the fact that these elements were suggested in the model and were central in another well-known (Wiener, 1950) communication model. But, as Rogers argued, these feedback and dynamic aspects were overlooked "because a linear model . . . more conveniently fit the one-way nature of the mass media (newspapers, radio, and television) that communication scholars were studying at the time" (Rogers, 1986, pp. 88–89).

New integrated theory is needed to make sense of the new technology and there is hope that the interpersonal and mass communication researchers will begin collaborating more than they have in the past. In the first place, researchers in both fields have almost always focused their research on emerging, new media (p. 68); if they follow this pattern, they will converge along with the media they are studying. Second, the growing economic, social, and political importance and consequences of new communication technologies should attract scholars from both fields (Rogers, 1986, pp. 6–7). And, finally, scholars in the two realms of interpersonal and mass communication already are beginning to recognize how artificial the distinctions between the fields have become. A wealth of literature recognizing the problem has appeared. (See bibliography in Reardon & Rogers, 1988.)

The Corn-Hog Cycle. We have suggested that mass communication curricula have been organized around specific occupations—such as public relations, journalism, or advertising—or specific technology of delivery systems—such as newspapers, magazines, television, radio. The first mass communication programs were newspaper training programs established before radio. When radio and television came on to the scene, the established journalism programs generally rejected or ignored each. Speech departments and programs took up instruction in broadcasting (Dennis, 1988b; Dressel, 1960).

As enrollments grew in the 1960s and 1970s, demands grew in journalism schools for other media-related instruction. Additional sequences, "curricular wings," were established by the journalism schools in advertising, broadcasting, graphics, photojournalism, and public relations. Lately, some speech departments have been developing public relations and mass media studies programs around their offerings in interpersonal, group, and organizational communication (Dennis, 1988b, pp. 15, 18).

Fragmentation and specialization in media programs seemed to make sense when media and related occupations were relatively few and unchanging. But, as we describe in chapter 2, media delivery systems have increased greatly to create an interconnected media system in which "the old divisions between print and broadcast are mostly irrelevant and immaterial . . . [because] . . . they are governed by the same forces and subject to many of the same pressures" (Dennis, 1987, p. 1). And traditional distinctions between news and advertising are blurring as editors, news directors and other news people find they cannot succeed without understanding audience data, market penetration, circulation problems, and related industry-wide aspects (Dennis, 1987).

> Meanwhile, on campus, the communication and media study faculty are seemingly comprised of members of a discordant tribe, with each individual representing a particular interest and little holding them together except the obvious connection to the communication industry. . . . [P]rofessionally oriented teachers who teach the more practical skills courses often find little in common with research-oriented teachers . . . [of] conceptual courses that sometimes seem far afield from professional issues and problems. ("Planning for Curricular Change," 1987, p. 80)

Because they have been "fragmenting their efforts by rapidly multiplying the areas of study and subsets of industry," the communication and mass media studies programs have "a peripheral role . . . instead of providing coherence in understanding the media" on campus (p. 61). The costs of fragmentation are amplified by what economic theorists informally identify as the "corn-hog" cycle. Douglas Gomery (1986) applied the theory to the academy:

> The more popular the major, the more graduates; the more graduates, the lower the wage necessary to hire one; the lower the wages, the fewer new majors; the fewer new majors, the higher the wage needed to be offered to new graduates, and so on. . . . [As students] flood into one major and then . . . jobs, the supply . . . increases and . . . wages fall. Frustration sets in and the "word" goes out to find another major. (p. 4)

The corn-hog cycle creates two problems for communication and media professional programs—one campus-wide, the other within the department or school. Campus-wide, the internal organization of the university does not allow for the flexibility of response that a corporation has to the shifts

3. A BLUEPRINT FOR RENEWAL

in enrollments in the corn-hog cycle. Labor intensive, operating under rules and regulations based on custom and tradition, managerial authority in the university is divided. A department's standing and prestige among academic and professional colleagues has as much, even more, to do with allocation of resources as enrollment. Gomery wrote:

> While prestige is a difficult concept to define, it is closely correlated with such variables as the research accomplishments of faculty members and the strength of graduate programs. . . . [T]he maximization of prestige presents a unique problem within the study of the mass media. For traditional academic departments, the study of the mass media is seen as something frivolous, not a truly serious inquiry. (p. 5)

Fragmentation and lack of curricular coherence has contributed to the relatively low status and low intellectual rigor and research productivity that communication and media study programs have represented on most campuses. At the very least, it has been used by university administrators as justification for underfunding—"until you people get your act together." One of the great economic facts of life shared by nearly all media study programs has been the squeeze between, on one hand, rapidly expanding enrollments during the 1970s and 1980s and, on the other hand, the lack of university resources to serve those enrollments.

Other agricultural metaphors have been used by journalism program administrators to describe this dilemma. Those from midwestern land-grant universities, especially, have been heard describing their programs as the campus "cash cows" because they generate large enrollments from which departments with lower enrollment draw their resources. At the same time, their departments or schools have been kept "down on the farm" or "sucking the hind tit" when it comes to receiving adequate resources to support the increased enrollments.

Compounding the campus-wide lag of resource reallocation has been the "corn-hog" cycle within communication and mass media studies. Although overall communication and media study enrollments have increased, there have been dramatic shifts of enrollments among the media-based subdivisions. Thus, although enrollments in the print journalism sequences have increased slightly, enrollments have increased greatly in advertising, in public relations, and, to a lesser degree, in broadcasting (Hirschorn, 1987, p. A36; McCombs, 1988, p. 104). In 1975 and 1976, advertising and public relations accounted for 24.4% of all bachelor's degrees awarded in communication and media study programs. In 1986, public relations and advertising students accounted for 44% of the students in the nation's journalism and mass communications programs, up from 37% 2 years earlier (McCombs, 1988, p. 102). These shifts have created shortages of faculty in advertising and public relations and in some areas of broadcasting. Although print journalism faculty are underutilized, the program administrators are faced with having to attract qualified advertising and public relations faculty with extraordinary salaries or underqualified faculty for modest salaries, or a combination of these (see chapter 7).

In short, the 40-year-long efforts of media study programs to offer varieties of subspecialities, in response to student and media practitioner demand, have been fragmenting and sapping limited resources. Instead of absorbing new applications of fundamental skills and knowledge, building interdisciplinary linkages, and redeveloping existing faculty, they have been creating new labor-intensive, specialized sequences to reflect new media delivery systems and occupational subspecialities to serve industry demands for cheap labor.

Apparently the lesson still has not been learned by some journalism and mass communication administrators, according to an Oregon Report ("Planning for curricular change," 1987) survey:

> Several [administrators] who responded . . . insisted that schools . . . must establish cable, direct broadcast and other specialized electronic sequences. The possibilities for almost unlimited expansion of highly specific programs seem very real, and it is likely that some industries will provide financial incentives to guarantee that this happens. It would lead to continued fragmentation, instead of coherence. (p. 49)

If, as the corn-hog cycle theory predicts, enrollments in professional media programs decline or shift once again, what will happen to those programs that have invested heavily in the sequence-fragmentation curriculum strategy? Judging from their apparent lack of respect for such programs, we would assume that university administrators would jump at the chance to make, understandably, substantial reductions in communication and mass media education budgets.

The University Tradition and the Corn-Hog Cycle. As we have suggested in chapter 1, and argued so far in this chapter, communication and media programs should shift their emphasis. They should move away from specialized education that serves the short-term, narrow needs of the industry and its related professions and move toward more general professional education and mass media studies linkages to the traditional disciplines that serve the long-term needs of all students and society. There are at least two arguments, one philosophical one economic, that support the call for New Professionalism.

In chapter 1, we describe Boyer's identification of two powerful, but contradictory, traditions in the undergraduate experience in America—

individuality and community. There are strong student-parent and industry-practitioner pressures for the pursuit of individual goals. The result is fragmentation, diversity, and potential selfishness that comes from narrowly formed specialized education. In view of this, Boyer expressed a widely held position that undergraduate education for the benefit of the community "must be vigorously affirmed" to balance the privatistic ethos.

Using James W. Carey's analysis, we extend and apply Boyer's analysis to professional education generally and communication and media education specifically. Carey's eloquent exploration of the inherent tensions between the "university tradition" and the professions, including media professions, has resonated through the field since he first expressed these views in 1978 as president of AEJMC. Carey's plea for the university tradition originated from Canadian economist and historian Harold Innis, who in 1944 expressed "concern about the professions and their attempts to capture the university by turning its attention to practical matters, to narrow its interests in life, and make it a spokesman for professional interests" (Carey, 1978, p. 847).

The inherent tensions between the university tradition and the professions can be viewed as a microcosm of the contradictions between individualism and community existing throughout our society. Individuality prevails, especially in this era of high educational costs. This tradition is rooted in the view that education, especially higher education, is an investment in human capital. Following that logic, in the short term, employers-as-consumers expect well-trained graduates who are ready to perform without much or any in-house training skills in organizations as they are presently equipped and structured. For parents- or students-as-investors, this means well-paying, entry-level jobs immediately upon graduation (Gomery, 1986, p. 5). A survey by *Change* magazine found that "parents increasingly seek practical benefits from a college education. Short-range thinking seems to rule most investors' decisions in America today—parents investing in their children's education are no exception" (Krukowski, 1985, p. 25).

From Boyer's point of view, this narrow, short-term, privatistic perspective should be balanced in the baccalaureate—for the good of society, the "community"—with broader education that "focuses on the society and culture as a whole, a sense of civic and social responsibility and on what individuals can contribute to the larger society of which they are a part" (Boyer, 1987, p. 68). This is especially important for professional education and, we argue, media education.

As we reported earlier, May (1986) argued that in addition to "cultivating the well-rounded person . . . and training the skilled person," the university professional programs "must pursue what the ancient Greeks saw as a fundamental purpose of education, . . . the cultivation of the civic self or the political self—the self as it readies itself for public affairs" (pp. 23–24).

Likewise, Carey reasoned that communication and mass media studies professional curricula should also go beyond individualistic and narrow professional needs and reflect community needs in the university tradition, as we see in chapter 4.

Returning to Gomery's economic perspective, we would agree with his suggestion that a broader based, more general component of the professional curricula has practical benefits. The corn-hog cycle results in either too many graduates going after too few jobs—which makes the employers happy and parents/students, who are caught on the downside of the cycle, unhappy—or the reverse can happen.

In either case, the highly specialized professional programs lose. When the former students are unhappy, the word gets back to incoming and new students who seek other subjects. Enrollments in the out-of-fashion specialized programs go down. When employers are unhappy, they blame the professional programs for not "producing" enough quality graduates and eventually withdraw their support. Gomery (1986) reasoned that this economic perspective supports those who advocate less specialized and more general education.

> Wage maximizing individuals and captains of industry certainly would like universities to train individuals who can step right into productive careers. However, [especially in media training], this is very expensive. . . . Specific training is always more expensive and prone to being out-of-date. Recognizing this, why not educate students so they can adapt to whatever real world they enter and let businesses teach the specifics? (p. 5)

Gomery understated it when he said that businesses "would like to avoid" the full cost of training graduates for their specific entry-level jobs, "but society should benefit in the long run since generally trained citizens can switch jobs more easily and are less likely to be stuck in the one career for which they were trained" (p. 6).

If Boyer's and Carey's calls for civic virtue are not enough to inspire reform in communication and mass media studies, perhaps Gomery's economic arguments are. "Educational policy," observed Arnold Ismach (1987), who succeeded Dennis as dean at the University of Oregon, "has a way of coming to terms with the nobility of the budget" (p. 5).

Leadership Default

The second hurdle facing the outcome of media education reform is the apparent unwillingness of leaders in the field to develop courses and curricula in communication and media for the general student or nonmajors; they are reluctant to embrace the role of sense-makers of the information society.

Journalism departments "were well situated to embrace the new medium [of television] . . . to provide leadership," wrote Everette E. Dennis (1986a), a pioneer for curriculum reform in mass communication education. "On this score they failed. They viewed the new medium reluctantly, even with hostility, and for the most part shrugged it off" (p. 23). Speech and rhetoric departments took up television instruction, as they had taken up radio instruction, because the journalism programs were not interested and because of lagging student interest in their traditional subjects. Dennis added:

> These developments led to a fragmented, bifurcated view of electronic media that erected barriers to the holistic study of communications. . . . My reading of history is that much of journalism education failed to assume leadership for broad-based communication studies and in the process failed higher education and American society by refusing to be a major force for learning and the advancement of knowledge about mass communication in a manner useful for all citizens. Consumer education took a back seat, while professional education was proclaimed premier. (p. 23)

Dennis believed that the mass media studies subdiscipline, more specifically the journalism and mass communication field, should not make that mistake again. Faced with another great opportunity provided by revolutionary changes in the modern information society, the field should reject "sluggish and unimaginative" leadership that in the past has reflected "limited goals and a hod-carrying mentality" (Dennis, 1986a, p. 24). It should take the lead in the development of the discipline, both in instruction and research. If it doesn't, others will. "Speech-communication programs, business schools, library science programs and other university departments" Dennis said, are "moving steadily into education for the information society, often taking bolder leadership" ("Planning for curricular change," 1987, p. 4).

We agree that the mass communication subfield has advantages because, to a greater degree than speech, it spans both professional and academic/intellectual spheres. It also has stronger traditions in and greater familiarity with technology, public policy issues, and industry linkages. In short, as the Oregon Report ("Planning for curricular change") concluded, ". . . the journalism and mass communication unit must be the principal focus of the university's teaching, research and service activity in this field, because journalism/mass communication schools and the discipline have the strongest and most comprehensive traditions in these areas" (p. 1).

However, in light of the convergence of interpersonal and mass commu nication, effective leadership in undergraduate reform must actively include both media and interpersonal subdisciplines. This means that a journalism and mass communication or mass media studies department, seeking to "take the commanding heights" of the discipline and to become "a leading player in the modern information society" (Dennis, 1988b, p. 18), must reach out to include the departments and programs that house the interpersonal subdiscipline. And those in speech departments should accept offers of collaboration, for time is running out for the discipline, as Dennis (1986a) suggested:

> The leadership of higher education [is not] willing to give the communication field a central role in the university, let alone a fair share of university resources. Change comes slow to universities, and with so many journalism schools presenting a fragmented face to their university colleagues, it is little wonder that they don't inspire confidence as genuine leaders in the information society. (p. 24)

THE ENRICHED MAJOR AND BEYOND

Moves toward both diversity and leadership start with a careful look at the field's major. We recall the three components of a liberal education presented in chapter 1 — study in depth, or the major, the integrated core, and the electives. Reformers find that "liberal arts" or a liberal education does not reside exclusively in any one of these. Rather, all three components of the baccalaureate, taken together, can add up to a liberal education. The New Professionalism is presented in this context, for communication and media education can and should contribute to all three. Furthermore, the New Professionalism itself reflects a liberal education trinity of its own, consisting of a conceptual core, a conceptual enrichment component, and an experiential learning capstone that emphasizes familiarity and understanding, rather than practitioner proficiency, with media technology.

In an undergraduate education, the major is the students' speciality area, where their *individual* contrasted with *community* aspirations, interests, and goals are pursued. As suggested in chapter 1, the traditionalists and reformers are in rare general agreement that there is too much specialization, vocationalism, or occupationalism in undergraduate education and too much student time, effort, and interest spent preparing for entry-level jobs at the expense of broader, enduring knowledge and community values.

But that is about where their agreement ends. The traditionalists, most of them representing the inherited academic disciplines, recommend reducing or eliminating professional programs or just adding "more liberal arts." They are less willing to acknowledge that there is little liberal arts in their "there" — that fragmentation, specialization, and vocationalism have developed in their own disciplines during the past 30 years.

Reformers argue, citing substantial literature, that the *way* content is presented is more important to liberal learning than *content* itself. Furthermore, they recognize that historically preparing for careers has always been a chief, or sole, purpose of undergraduate education. They also recognize the futility of ignoring legitimate student and public demands for undergraduate study of subjects related to modern technology and institutional systems; that, like many of the professional programs, the "traditional" disciplines have also become overspecialized and fragmented; and that there are substantial "liberal components at the base of professional education" (Marsh, 1988, p. 12). Their solution is more coherence and integration in undergraduate majors, regardless of the subject matter. Above all, "the heart" of the reformers' curriculum proposal is that, "rather than view the major as competing with general education, we are convinced that these two essential parts of the baccalaureate program should be intertwined" (Boyer, 1987, p. 110).

Communication and media education also is torn between traditionalists and the reformers. As we see in chapter 4, major media practitioner associations assume that communication and media education faculty and programs have nothing to do with liberal education. Most practitioners support the fragmented, sequential, vocational training mode, and oppose the development of what they pejoratively label theory.

The reformers propose a curriculum concept that is called variously "generalized or generic" ("Planning for curricular change," 1987, p. 56), "foundational" (Ward, 1987, p. 3), or "holistic" ("Planning for curricular change," p. 61). We call it the New Professionalism because it affirms the role of communication and media education programs in undergraduate education while responding to the challenges and opportunities of change in American undergraduate education, in the communication industries and professions and in communication theory. New Professionalism responds to the New Liberal Arts because it joins and balances the individual pursuit of depth and speciality in the major with the community goals and breadth and unity of knowledge of general education.

Again, the New Professionalism would have three components — the conceptual core, a conceptual enrichment component, and an experiential learning capstone or media workshop emphasizing familiarity and understanding with, rather than technical proficiency in, media technology. While these are similar to the recommended curriculum in the Oregon Report ("Planning for curricular change," pp. 48-62), we add some elements drawn from other reformers and attempt to link them in a preliminary way to broader undergraduate reform concepts presented in AAC, NIE, Carnegie, Michigan, and Syracuse reports.

The Conceptual Core

A universal core for the major (Blanchard & Christ, 1985, p. 29) parallels the baccalaureate "integrated core" concept proposed for the bachelor's degree by Boyer and others. At the onset of their exposure to the field, students would be introduced first to essential knowledge and literacy skills "common to all forms of mass communication work, rather than on the nuances of particular industries" ("Planning for curricular change," 1987, p. 57). Second, the students would be familiarized with connections among the subdisciplines in communication and media studies. Depending on the nature and mission of the university or college, this core could include both interpersonal and media subject matter, or be limited to an integrated mass communication core.

Depending on the quality of the students, particularly the level of their language and writing skills upon their admission to the program, the core might include some communication literacy skills. But overall the emphasis should be on conceptual perspectives and knowledge, reflecting Boyer's criteria for the enriched major—the field's history and tradition, social and economic implications, and related ethical and moral issues (Boyer, 1987, p. 110). These include:

1. a preliminary sketch of, or introduction to, the "conceptual map" ("Planning for curricular change," 1987) for the major and communication industry, an inventory for understanding interpersonal, group, and organizational communication and comparative communication systems in the context of broader historical, legal-ethical, institutional, social, economic, and other social systems;

2. technological literacy—understanding of visual, aural, and computer "grammar and phenomena" in media; and

3. information gathering and media writing and speaking capability, including the ability to gather and present information systematically in written and oral form. At some institutions, these capabilities are strong or at least sufficient when the students are admitted and the capabilities are enhanced by common curriculum courses that include research, writing, and oral delivery. Depending on its resources and role in the college or university, the communication and media unit might participate in that process (see chapter 6). A unit that chooses or is required to devote most of its introductory efforts to "weeding out" students or to teaching high school writing, research, and oral skills may be destined to remain a vocational program. We discuss this problem in chapter 4.

The "conceptual map" sketch usually consists of one or two introductory courses that have multiple, overlapping functions—introduction and orien tation to the discipline and the program; preview of advanced work to follow; linkages with traditional disciplines (e.g., political science, psychology, sociology) and what they say about communication and media; as well as an overview of fundamental knowledge and concepts common to human communication and media industries and professions.

Consistent with the concept of integration, both skill and conceptual components, whenever possible, should be combined in individual course offerings. Information gathering, writing, and speaking, for example, could be integrated into all conceptual courses, with students assigned individual or group reports on substantial subjects that require library and field information gathering and written and oral report presentation.

Hands-on practice with video, aural, and computer technology, as we see in later chapters, should be preceeded — as does the application of technical skills by practitioners — by conceptualization. The core would concentrate on the development of critical analysis and awareness of common aspects of information gathering and presentation and their possible media applications. This would include the "implications for content presentation, volume, display, image, editing, and perception represented by the various technologies and their interactions" ("Planning for curricular change," 1987, p. 38).

Emphasizing conceptualization-before-application in the core is an important lesson. Most media educators are aware of the educational and cost-benefit limitations of unsupervised, amateur "play-pen," "doing my thing" applications of technology in academic settings. Idea-before-use, in fact, is at the heart of the distinction between trade or occupational school and the New Professionalism baccalaureate education, a distinction all communication and media educators should want to make emphatically clear both on and off campus.

Although the occupational employee and the professional use the same technology, "the tradesman [sic] unimaginatively performs relatively routine tasks at the behest of another person" (Dressel, 1960, p. 87). The New Professional with a "liberating" education, on the other hand, sets goals and, with an "awareness and understanding for the capacities and differences of . . . media" ("Planning for curricular change," 1987, p. 38), conceptualizes the most effective message with which to achieve those goals, and selects the appropriate technology to manufacture and distribute the message. "In doing so," wrote Dressel, the professional "demonstrates initiative and assumes social responsibility" (p. 87).

Conceptual Enrichment

Regarding the social responsibilities of practitioners, the second component — conceptual enrichment — links the New Professionalism major to broader ethical, social, economic, and political contexts. It fills in with more detail the "conceptual map" sketch introduced in the core. It includes the theoretical underpinnings of the emerging discipline, an overview and history of the United States' and other media systems, and structural relations with other social, especially political and economic, systems.

This component, more significantly than the others, responds to the Carnegie Foundation's concept of the "enriched major" as an antidote to "rootless vocationalism," or the idea of what the Syracuse Experiment identifies as *embeddedness*. Embeddedness is the opposite of the "distorting tension caused by the *extraction* of each profession and discipline from immersion of the totality of things"; that is, no discipline or profession is an island in society (Marsh, 1988, pp. 24, 93, italics added).

The enriched major is designed to encourage "students not only to explore a field in depth, but also . . . put their field of special study in perspective." Similarly, the Syracuse Experiment emphasized the importance of recognizing "the historical and conceptual roots and sociocultural embeddedness" that all disciplines and professions have and the dangers of their being bypassed in undergraduate programs "as an impractical luxury." According to Marsh (1988), "This 'luxury' is essential to liberal education, and it is indispensable to sound understanding and performance in the professions" (p. 23).

Boyer's criteria for the enriched major are suggested in three essential questions: What is the history and tradition of the field? What are the social and economic implications? What are the ethical and moral issues to be confronted (1987, p. 110)?

The conceptual enrichment component would expand on the distinction between vocationalism and the New Professionalism introduced in the core. The "values professionals bring to their work are every bit as crucial as the particularities of the work itself," Boyer wrote, adding an illustration from mass communication: "A television set is a complex instrument, but producing high-quality sets in large numbers is much easier than producing high-quality programming" (p. 111).

Boyer described professional curricula that he believed illustrated the enriched major. Among them is one in journalism and mass communication:

> We found at a large state university a journalism major in which students are being offered breadth in a field that is often considered narrow. In this program there are courses on the history of communication and the ethics of journalism. The dean said, "I feel strongly that an undergraduate program is for people who are not experienced enough to be sure of what they want. Not all of the students here are primarily interested in journalism as a career. We have at least fifteen a year who go to law school. We do not owe a student just a ready-made formula for career training." (p. 113)

Experiential Learning

"Hands-on" instruction, using new media and information technology, is essential for media education programs. One learns by doing. But, as we note in our idea-before-use discussion of technology, practical training in the baccalaureate must be linked carefully to the values, knowledge and perspectives of the core, and conceptual enrichment components of the curriculum if it is to be more than rootless vocationalism. The Oregon Report recommended that the preparation of professionals in particular areas take place during the senior year of study or in graduate school, a fairly common practice in most programs ("Planning for curricular change," 1987, p. 57). We believe that familiarization with technology and application of fundamental writing, speaking, and production principles should begin as soon as possible, even the first year.

For the New Professionalism, we believe programs in communication and media education have two options in experiential learning. One is the media *workshop,* which is analogous to the Oregon Report's "media laboratory." Both the media laboratory and the media workshop are preferable to the common practice in most programs of investing valuable faculty and other resources in junior-level, rigidly structured and thinly veiled "weeding-out" remedial writing or production courses. These occupational boot camps foster some of the more archaic personnel and management practices of industrial-based mass media industries. As we see in chapter 4, some media practitioners encourage this vocational approach because they recognize it as more an occupational screening, socialization, and indoctrination service than an educational enterprise.

We hope the word *professional* will not be abdicated to those occupationalists who abuse its broader meaning and we seek to develop *professional* to its full potential. Similarly, we do not abdicate the powerful concept of *laboratory* to what we believe are limited, workshop applications of its potential. The media *laboratory* would provide for systematic investigation and experimentation with purposeful challenging of media content and forms. Reflecting the liberal ethos, it would go beyond the replication of contemporary, management and occupational hierarchies, as useful as they might be. In chapter 6, we describe specific applications of the media laboratory—a vision for the future in which we hope it will be the standard in experiential learning for the New Professionalism.

A *workshop* is a more limited concept. (But it is preferable to the rigid approaches we describe in chapter 4.) It is what some of the better media programs have been offering for years. Generally, it fosters on-campus apprenticeship experiences that consist largely of informal instruction by peers—on the student newspaper, radio station, television station. It ranges from informal instruction from advanced, faculty-supervised student media management internships to apprenticeships with experienced campus-media student practitioners with no formal media training or supervision. At its best, it provides intermediate and advanced experience that involves some formal faculty instruction for students whose interests and abilities enable them to survive and thrive at the supervised apprenticeship level.

The apprentice-to-advanced prescription implies the existence of facilities, technology, and staff. As we have suggested and as we shall see later, a workshop is probably more efficient than attempting to keep up with changing media delivery systems and shifting occupational modes through individual course offerings. In an on-campus workshop, for example, fundamentals of information gathering, media writing, elementary technological familiarity, and legal and ethical aspects could be at once integrated, reinforced, and amplified in an all-student theme production, such as the desk-top publication of a newspaper or magazine, an audio or video documentary, or the conceptualization and execution of a public service promotional campaign. The production could be devoted to a controversial issue, such as student drug use or individual sexual orientation. This would involve—to name a few—matters of taste, libel, credibility, accuracy, access to and protection of sources, and related issues in the context of potential institutional or organizational pressures not to report these issues on campus, to reveal sources, and so on.

Happily for media programs that have been offering workshops, and for others seeking to establish them, liberal education reformers in the 1980s discovered and elevated experiential learning to new heights of pedagogical respectability. The National Institute of Education's Study Group on the Conditions of Excellence in American Higher Education, for example, found that "student involvement" is "perhaps the most important" of three conditions necessary for "improving undergraduate education" (NIE, 1984, p. 37).

> There is now a good deal of research evidence to suggest that the more time and effort students invest in the learning process and the more intensely they engage in their own education, the greater will be their growth and achievement, their satisfaction with their educational experiences, and their persistence in college, and the more likely they are to continue their learning. (p. 38)

The NIE Study Group recommended intensified efforts in the undergraduate curriculum to create more student involvement in learning. Their recommendations included activities already operating in many media education programs, such as encouraging internships and other forms of carefully monitored experiential learning, involving practitioners as visiting teachers, and developing simulations in appropriate subjects (see chapter 6). They proposed increased support for "existing cocurricular programs and activities for purposes of maximizing student involvement," such as student media (pp. 40–42).

The Carnegie Foundation, exploring "creativity in the classroom," urged that all students be asked to do something frequently asked of students in professional media education programs "to participate in collaborative projects, that they work together occasionally on group assignments, that special effort be made . . . to create conditions that underscore the point that cooperation is as essential as competition in the classroom" (Boyer, 1987, p. 151).

Media educators should exploit these new attitudes espoused by influential groups supporting workshop instructional methods. Media programs for years have had practicums, newsrooms, radio and television stations, visiting practitioner programs, and other forums for student involvement. Media educators should seek workshop modernization and maintenance with renewed vigor and optimism. Programs that do not have them should seek support to establish elementary media workshops, or link experiential learning programs with facilities available elsewhere on campus or in the community. Hands-on experience is now fashionable, as it should be, in the emerging undergraduate reform ethos.

But, because of the swiftness with which media technology is changing, a serious challenge faces professional programs regarding the uses and objectives of their media workshops. Sound advice on how to meet this challenge was provided by the Oregon Report, which found it essential that every professional media education program have a facility where "some practical familiarity" with media hardware can take place. The report implied, and we would amplify the point, that a flexible media-familiarization center for all students could replace most media-specific, technologically based skill courses, which have drained professional media program resources for so many years. As George Gerbner summarized it:

> Existing undergraduate departments and schools can best update and diversify their offerings by creating comprehensive media laboratories in which both majors and non-majors can be exposed to a great variety of media literacies, skills, internships, and other practical experiences. These laboratories would be designed more for exposure and familiarization than for vocational or professional training. ("Planning for curricular change," 1987, pp. 37–38)

Their objective "is to explore the implications for content presentation" in order to "heighten sensibilities to possibilities and constraints," not to produce polished, "finished products." The laboratory would provide a "sampler of representative equipment that the student will need to know and understand to 'survive' in the modern communication industry." It does not have to be "state-of-the-art so long as it demonstrates the basic functions of the various new technologies" (p. 38). The Syracuse Experiment report on professional and liberal education also found that "the very rapidity of technological advance" requires that more effort be made on students "grasping the underlying theories and principles" of technology "than to master current practice" (Marsh, 1988, p. 9).

A modern, even modest, media workshop could be a more comprehensive and flexible alternative to expensive, separate media-specific courses. It could provide centralized information, scheduling, equipment, maintenance, and instruction. The workshop should be equipped with essential, if rudimentary, technological components and information that would be linked to more advanced and comprehensive resources elsewhere. Like an executive management team, the program's faculty would establish policies and procedures to be carried out under their general supervision by knowledgeable, "user-friendly" professional and technical support staff or, if resources are limited, advanced student work-study or volunteer mentors.

The media workshop should include a student management hierarchy whose members are selected by the faculty on a competitive basis for previously observed apprenticeship and intermediate professional performance in the media and information workshop. It should reflect, where possible and appropriate, the organized activity and ethos of two or three information media companies with enlightened personnel and management policies. It should be an environment where students — carefully monitored and based on their level of competence — individually and in groups from a variety of programs and courses, can carry out assignments, test their skills through systematic practice, probe possibilities, apply ethical principles though an "ethical dialogue" (Lambeth, 1986, p. 159), and execute the full process of a media production.

Along with an illustration of the media laboratory concept, we provide examples in chapter 6 of how some programs have addressed the media-skills, experiential learning challenge with media workshops.

MEDIA EDUCATION IN THE NEW LIBERAL ARTS

We have discussed how the New Professionalism is a call for more diversity among media education programs. This diversity, developed within the context of each institution's mission and destiny, is the first step toward making media education a central part of each institution's academic and intellectual offerings. We now examine how the New Professionalism can become part of the New Liberal Arts.

If we were forced to rely on one general definition of liberal arts, without a specific list of outcomes, we would choose George Gerbner's definition and its implied liberating effect:

> The liberal arts [are] those skills and concepts that liberate the individual from an unquestioning dependence on the local and immediate cultural environment. . . . Liberal education today is the liberation of the individual from the necessity of drifting with the swift cultural tides of our time and the preparation for such self-direction as may be necessary and possible. ("Planning for curricular change," 1987, p. 40)

In the context of this definition, and because of the increasing centrality of communication media in our culture, the role for communication and media studies is very clear. It is, Gerbner said, to "move communications to the center of academic life" in order to provide a "fresh approach to liberal arts" by bringing every student "an analytical and critical approach to the everyday cultural environment" (Gerbner, 1984; "Planning for curricular change," 1987, p. 40).

As we have said earlier, this means that media education programs, which have concentrated almost exclusively on the major, must move beyond that to contribute more to the general education and the elective components of the baccalaureate. Communication and media education should be "part of a process which is redefining knowledge and the structure of the academy. . . . With this in mind, [the field] has a reason for being besides the need to train professional communicators" ("Planning for curricular change," 1987, p. 40).

Contributions to General Education — The Integrated Core

In exploring ways that communication and media education might contribute to general education, we begin by applying the Carnegie Foundation's "integrated core" categories, although we recognize that each college or university has its own version of them.

The Carnegie study found in its nationwide survey of general education that, despite their statements of support for general education, faculty were engaged in "curriculum tinkering rather than [in] genuine reform" where, for example, "narrowly focused courses in English, science, and history often were renamed 'general education,' " and "protecting departmental turf often seemed more important than shaping a coherent general education program" (Boyer, 1987, p. 87).

On the other hand, the study found that, although students were primarily interested in pursuing personal career goals, they were enthusiastic about general education courses "where great teachers link learning to contemporary issues" (p. 85). Repeatedly throughout the Carnegie and other reform reports, the theme for general education is the need for "a new breath of life," to relate general education "to the lives of students and to the world they are inheriting" and "to the application of knowledge to life beyond the campus" (pp. 90-91).

The other consistent theme is for integration of the disciplines in general education where students can begin to make connections and see relationships, "how the content of one course relates to that of others," and in so doing "gain not only a more integrated view of knowledge, but a more authentic view of life" (p. 92).

We believe communication and media subjects, because they are both contemporary and interdisciplinary, can and should make meaningful contributions toward the achievement of those general education reform goals. Just how they might do this depends, of course, on the nature of general education reform formulations.

The goal of liberal learning, Boyer maintained, is to help students see both sides of their existence, their isolation and their connections to each other. In their essay, *Quest for Common Learning,* Boyer and Arthur Levine (1981) identified universal experiences that shape the lives of every individual and every community—"shared use of symbols, shared sense of history, membership in groups and institutions, relationship with nature, and shared activity of work and leisure" (p. 35).

They suggested several "areas of inquiry" that should relate the general education curriculum "to experiences common to all people." Three of these, which are also discussed in Boyer (1987, pp. 93-101), have potential for the discipline's involvement in the integrated core—shared *language and symbols,* shared *institutions,* and shared *work and leisure.* Where appropriate, we would include the nature and function of media technology in each of the three.

"The impact of mass communication should . . . be examined," Boyer and Levine (1981) wrote. "Students urgently need what might be called 'tube literacy,' to help them see how visual and auditory signals reinforce each other, how ideas can be distorted, how thoughts and feelings can be subliminally conveyed, and how the accuracy and reliability of messages can be tested" (p. 37). The Association of American Colleges also noted that "television is so much a part of our lives that it is foolish simply to deplore its weaknesses and its bad habits." The study of television communication is included as part of its core curriculum recommendation for "literacy—reading, speaking, listening." Students should "learn how to look and listen to . . . television . . . critically, with as much focused intellectual energy as they are expected to apply to other experiences that call on their ability to listen and see intelligently" (AAC, 1985, p. 17).

Clearly, the discipline can play a role in the formulation and execution of this component of the integrated core, guided by such questions as: "How do symbol systems shape the values of a culture?" and "What are the possibilities and problems introduced by the information revolution?" (Boyer, 1987, p. 93).

At this point, we would ask this question: Who on campus is more qualified than the communication and media studies faculty to address these and similar questions about contemporary language in our culture? An exemplar course in this area is "Signs and Communication," offered at Cornell University, "that investigates how language relates to particular cultural codes. . . . The goal is to examine the symbol systems human beings use and investigate how language differs from one culture to another. . . . There is . . . study of literature, television advertising, computer language, and architectural signs" (p. 93).

In another area of inquiry, "Institutions: The Social Web," the role of the discipline, particularly media education, is manifest. Because institutions "make up the social fabric of life . . . no integrated core has been successful if it has not acquainted students with the major institutions . . . that make up our world" (p. 95). We would agree and would offer communication media institutions as among those to be included for special consideration. At the very least, the impact of media on all other institutions should be included in this area of inquiry.

Professional programs in general would seem to be appropriate contributors to the area of inquiry the Carnegie report identified as "Work: The Value of Vocation." Because, "except for a handful of individuals, no one can choose not to work" and because most students are enrolled in a college or university to prepare for work, this seems to be an appropriate area of inquiry to get students' attention. The difference between work in our modern information society and work in the industrial age is a topic to which the communication and media studies discipline could make a contribution.

Contributions to University Electives

Reformers remind us of the vital importance of the elective component in the baccalaureate. As we note in chapter 1, they have distinct, often serendipitous advantages and relevance to liberal education. Electives, for example, enable students to sample offerings, professors, and experiences to which they might not otherwise be exposed. They allow for students to acquire or enhance skills that might not be taught in required subjects; to develop interests and talents in "performance" areas such as drama, studio art, music ensembles, athletics, and, media message making; as well as to satisfy curiosity about unfamiliar subjects and to learn new things. These and similar functions contribute to the overall liberal education of the student (Carnegie Foundation, 1977).

For those reasons, students not majoring in communication and media education should be invited to explore *both* the media workshop/laboratory and conceptual offerings in communication and media studies. Students majoring in the discipline should also be encouraged to explore extra conceptual enrichment offerings in their field as part of their baccalaureate electives, especially those that enhance liberal outcomes and provide what the Oregon Report calls "linchpins to the liberal arts and sciences" ("Planning for curricular change," 1987, p. 57).

As noted earlier, the discipline has grown a great deal in 40 years and the trends identified then have further evolved. Most of the conceptual enrichment areas we have defined earlier have direct, manifest linkages with traditional disciplines and assumed liberal outcomes such as economics (economic aspects of the media), history (history of communication) and political science (legal and regulatory aspects, international communication systems), philosophy (philosophical aspects), and sociology and psychology (communication theory). To the extent that the content of traditional academic disciplines is assumed to be liberal arts, most of these communication and media-oriented conceptual enrichment areas are, too. Students majoring in communication and media courses can benefit greatly from the connections they make between the discipline's conceptual courses and related courses in the traditional disciplines.

In this context, we would argue that students majoring in the discipline should not be unduly restricted to the number of extra courses they elect in this category by arbitrary accreditation, university, or department rules designed, ironically, to require "a liberal arts education" (see comments on accreditation in chapter 8). Taken within the requirements of the major, these courses enrich the major. But, beyond that enriching function, additional courses elected by the students are not only "liberal" because of their content, but because they contribute to liberal outcomes. The total number of courses communication and media studies majors may take in their department should be no less than limitations placed on other disciplines, such as history or philosophy. Such limitations are usually established on a college- or university-wide basis and range from 42 to 60 semester hours of a 124-hour baccalaureate.

While nonmajors can derive the same liberalizing benefits from the conceptual enrichment courses, they also should have access to the liberalizing potential of "skills" or "craft" courses in media writing, speaking, and production. These courses or workshops could enhance the liberal outcomes reformers associate with experiential learning, especially if these courses are integrated into the media workshops where students gather and evaluate information and manufacture and disseminate messages about contemporary issues.

The New Liberal Arts project, funded by the Sloan Foundation, reported

(Kanigel, 1986) how work with media technology revitalized liberal education in Wellesey College, where there is no professional program. A course entitled, "Television, Technology, and Social Impact" combines study of the fundamentals of television technology, analysis of commercial broadcasting, hands-on experience with the use of video equipment, and the study of television's impact.

> One student team investigated the popular notion that MTV—short, stylized story segments that act out typically violent or sexual fantasies to an incessant rock beat—may have peculiarly powerful impact on the adolescent mind. . . . The students had to conceive an experiment to test their hypothesis, prepare questionnaires, edit video segments for showing . . . set up equipment, analyze the results, and write them up—all activities making them more at home with the workings, both physical and intellectual, of technology. (p. 30)

The course "was not intended to make engineers of the students," but the rudiments of the technology "got attention," including workings of video cameras, how television is broadcast, how color is transmitted. As one student concluded: "I'd like to make a film or a video some day. I don't want to make a better lens or a better phosphor." But she knew what a phosphor was (p. 30).

Work with new technology is not the only fresh approach to liberal arts that communication and media offerings can provide. Recall our discussion in chapter 1 about the distinction between "liberal arts" content and the method in which knowledge is presented. Liberal arts proponents Woditsch, Schlesinger, and Giardina (1987) presented a compelling argument for the superior and enduring values of a liberal education over professional education. But, after careful examination, they joined most authorities and reformers in questioning whether the traditional disciplines are, in fact, providing any more liberal an education than professional programs. Because they valued liberal pedagogical processes over content, they looked for them wherever they could find them, and they were not above looking at professional programs—where, indeed, as we see in chapter 1, they could find them. They offered their generic prescription for the liberal teaching process:

> Students encounter the distinctive behavior of the intelligent mind in their own familiar realms: sports, pop culture, and political and social issues that touch them. Good teachers entice them, in these familiar realms, to act in unfamiliar ways; to attend selectively, to analyze issues thoroughly, to make telling comparisons, to propose solutions and tease out their consequences. They go to the student's realm not to pass the time pleasantly, but to awaken and whet such skills. With their skills whetted, the students are taken back to the discipline. (p. 57)

We see in the authors' prescriptions more liberal learning potential of communication and media education programs—such as the relationship of the discipline with many aspects of our mass-mediated contemporary culture. As David Sidorsky (Fletcher, 1988) suggested, a liberating attribute such as freedom of choice, in an increasingly technologic society, "requires liberal education to include mass and popular culture" (p. 29).

The AAC observed that television talk shows, political campaigns, and news broadcasts have taken the place of classical and traditional oratory, stage presence, debate, and the arts of persuasion (AAC, 1985, p. 17). Regardless of whether or not this is a desirable development, students need to learn about television and other new technologies, which are performing important cultural functions.

Jay Rosen (McCall, 1988) reported that a number of traditional disciplines have been integrating modern media.

> Convinced that TV is too important to be ignored, academics have come to the box in search of a secret passageway to the American mind. . . . If they can understand TV then they'll be closer to what's really going on in the country. Academics who study television have thus rescued themselves from a marginal existence. (p. 35)

4 The New Professionalism and Media Practitioners: A Blueprint for Reconstruction

> *Media industries . . . are getting a good deal. As long [as] they can count on a steady supply of cheap labor . . . why should they change the system? A handful of media companies and foundations generously support journalism education, but most are Uncle Scrooges.*
> —Dennis (1988b, p. 19)

> *Most editors want someone who can come into the newsroom and be immediately productive. They are not all that concerned about how productive he or she may be in five years. . . . I think the single most influential group pushing toward the craft approach [in journalism education] and away from the liberal arts is the editors in this country.*
> —Gerald D. Sass (Dennis, 1988a, p. 92)

James Ottaway, Jr. is chairman of Ottaway Newspapers and senior vice president of Dow Jones and Co., Inc. He is a thoughtful, concerned, and active analyst of journalism and mass media education in the United States. The major complaint about journalism and mass media education expressed by his fellow publishers and their editors, he said during a roundtable discussion with educators, was that graduates' "lack basic skills." The solution to this widespread problem, he suggested, had been found at a southeastern state in a university course called "Grammar Slammer": "You're put in the Grammar Slammer until you pass basic spelling, writing, and grammar tests. You may take it 10 times over four undergraduate years, but you don't get your B.A. in journalism until you've gotten out of the Grammar Slammer. We need more of that essentially remedial work in journalism schools" (Dennis, 1988a, p. 88).

Later in the roundtable discussion, Everette Dennis, who was chairing, attempted to suggest a broader purpose for communication and mass media education:

> Everybody here is agreed that the journalist needs both a strong liberal arts background and—*for expediency's sake*—some knowledge of the craft. But what about knowledge of the media industry itself? Many leading schools do

not teach the history of journalism, for example. Do potential employers and industry leaders care whether the journalists they hire know anything at all about the history and economics of the field or, say, of communication theory? (p. 92, italics added)

[Sharon] Murphy, [dean of the College of Journalism at Marquette University, answered that] "there might be some lip service paid to it, but I really don't think they do." Ottaway [responded]: "Well, let's be candid, if you have only so many hours of education available, I give that lower priority."

Murphy: "But the reporter's history background ought to include a history of our communications system."

Ottaway: "No doubt, but if pushed I would say that *most kids today pick up a great deal about the electronic and print media by osmosis. I would give up something in that area if I had to.* (Dennis, 1988a, p. 92, italics added)

This clash of educational priorities expressed between the publisher and the educators is a pervasive and familiar one, expressed in varying degrees of intensity. Unlike Ottaway's, the language of many practitioner complaints and proposed solutions is much blunter and confrontational when expressed to educators at the grassroots levels—at state or city press association meetings, for instance.

A growing number of educators, especially administrators, are beginning to question grammar-slammer and similar approaches and the educational agendas they imply. More and more educators suspect that courses designed to weed out students with narrow basic-skills certification functions may also eliminate the more independent, brighter students. Although these courses may improve the grammar of the surviving students, the more powerful subtext of their pedagogy is inculcation of an unquestioning dependence on narrowly applied technique, obedience to directions from above, and adherence to arbitrary rules and procedures. In sum, the grammar-slammer approach to education is seen by an increasing number of educators as an artifact of archaic, industrial-age personnel management policies with which they would rather not be associated.

But the craft versus concept clash is only the tip of the iceberg. More fundamental are questions about relationship between media practitioners and educators. Unfortunately, the long-standing, underlying assumption in this relationship has been that mass media programs were established and exist primarily, or exclusively, to serve the media industries. Basically, it has been a one-way relationship, characterized recently by impatience on the part of the practitioners when presented with concepts of the New Professionalism.

MEDIA MANAGEMENT AND CURRICULUM REFORM

As Dennis implied, educators and practitioners seem to agree that mass media education should include both "liberal" and "professional" components. The source of conflict between practitioners and educators is not that the educational "outcome" of a professional curriculum should be a "liberally educated professional," but rather, it is about how to define "liberal" and "professional," what the proportion of each should be in the mix, and the degree to which the communication and media education curriculum is devoted to liberal, rather than vocational and occupational, education.

To address the issue, then, we start with the question: "What is a liberally educated media professional?" First, we would advance two overlapping attributes—a self-directed cultural self-consciousness and a high degree of control over one's field. A liberal education, George Gerbner reminded us in chapter 3 enhances "self-direction" (see chapter 7) by liberating the individual "from an unquestioning dependence on the local and immediate cultural environment" and "from the necessity of drifting" with contemporary "cultural tides" ("Planning for curricular change," 1987, p. 40). Professions, Douglas Birkhead added, are generally accepted to be "occupations whose members have achieved a high degree of control over their fields of work" (Birkhead, 1986, p. 37; see, also, Birkhead, 1988). As we explain later, the distinction between *profession* and *occupation* is an important element in our definition of a liberally educated professional.

We would submit two other attributes to the stated outcomes of the New Professionalism, both of which are antidotes to the excesses of the old professionalism. They are *dedication to public service* and *an ethical commitment*. "The ancient Greeks saw as a fundamental purpose of education . . . the cultivation of the civic self or the political self—the self as it readies itself for public affairs" (May, 1986, pp. 23–24). This is the community, public service dimension that Boyer and other higher education studies, discussed in chapter 1, believe is essential to a reformed undergraduate curriculum.

Despite substantial occupational, organizational, and societal pressures, the liberally educated professional has the ability to reason independently and possesses a capacity for "moral imagination" to get around major constraints and act on principle, rather than to rely unthinkingly on occupational or company conventions, policies, and rules of procedure (Lambeth, 1986). Consistent with these attributes of the liberally educated professional, a reformed undergraduate professional program committed to liberal education is empowering its graduates with the knowledge, skills, and perspectives that would enhance their development as ethical professionals with a high degree of control over their field of work. In the case of communication and mass media programs, this means, among other things, replacement of "unquestioning dependence" on the culture of the market-driven communication industry and related occupations with a concern for public service (Rudolph, 1984, pp. 15–16).

The degree to which programs meet this ideal should be the measure by which they are either primarily *occupational* or *professional.* Programs teach best by example. Empowered programs are designed and taught by self-directed teachers dedicated primarily to the university tradition; who are skeptical of and even challenge the power-knowledge (Jansen, 1988), the perspective, advanced by the industry; whose teaching and research are intellectually competitive on campus; and who challenge graduates to become self-directed professionals.

Occupational programs, on the other hand, exhibit little "self-direction" or liberation from "unquestioning dependence" on the culture of the market-driven communication industry and related occupations that they serve (see Gerbner in "Planning for curricular change," 1987). And, as we argue later, they do so at the expense of the students and the public.

James Carey, Everette Dennis, and other reformers remind us that most communication and media education programs fall short of engendering the liberal ethos in its graduates. Rather, they emulate the occupational culture. The norm is to duplicate in the classroom the occupational culture of the newsroom and other media "shops." Graduates are being prepared to move into the communication industry as refined and standardized cogs, rather than professionals committed to disinterested public service (see chapter 7). This soon becomes apparent to many graduates, as Birkhead (1986) found:

> [There is] the growing realization among practitioners that their moral prerogatives are preempted by how they work, how they are trained and educated, how they perceive their very identity as professionals. They are coming to realize the limitation of their influence over the policies and ends of the organizations they work for. . . . Journalists are beginning to comprehend how extensively their expertise and understanding of news, championed by journalism schools as hollowed knowledge, also happen to serve so fastidiously and efficiently the industry that profits from their services. (p. 43)

Communication and media education professional programs are not alone. Frederick Rudolph (1984, p. 17) found that "what business or engineering major means to an employer is that the young man or woman in question has not been . . . subverted by the liberal ethos." And, although it may be too late for colleges and universities to break away from entanglements with corporate America and professions, "it is not too late," the higher education historian concluded, "to recognize how these alliances have visited upon higher education a paralysis of will and confusion of purpose."

The Management Connection

The state of media education, explored in chapter 3, is due in large part to the paralysis and confusion Rudolph described. The discipline is caught between the ideal of the liberal ethos of the New Professionalism and the imagined imperative of the occupational ethos. A major theme of this book is that the discipline's dilemma cannot be resolved and reform cannot take place without an affirmative, purposeful shift from industrial and occupational and individualistic values to liberal university traditions and community priorities.

The New Professionalism may be a switch in time for the industry as well as for the discipline. For we agree with the reformers who believe that the modern information and communication industries increasingly need employees who can think and act independently and who can help media companies eliminate their internal rigidities (Grow, 1991). But personnel cogs that many occupational-ethos programs "produce" are for industrial-age needs, not appropriate for emerging, horizontally organized information companies (Lavine & Wackman, 1988). When graduates have been prepared to exercise authority to shape the nature of their own work they will be better employees for the information society.

John Lavine and Daniel Wackman, in their pioneering textbook on media management, reminded us that new technologies have "eliminated whole categories of skilled workers" in the communication and information business. They have "provided those who gather and develop messages with increased control over their work," have "created new categories of highly trained employees," and have "expanded the possibilities for less skilled or less heavily financed people to start their own media ventures" (p. 13). The best way of "fending off job transfers and raids," they advised, "is to recognize that the motivational needs of [information] . . . staff members are likely to be . . . self-actualizing needs: desire for autonomy, a chance to practice their craft, and the opportunity to face a challenge" (p. 212). Curricular reform should provide for the anticipation, identification, and monitoring of these trends.

More so than any other reform goals, then, preparing graduates to exercise the authority to shape the nature of their own work extends the reformers' mission—The New Professionalism—to the industry. It, in effect, would transform the communication and mass media programs from industry followers to active collaborators and participants in the formation of new policies for the recruitment, hiring, and retention of employees. Instead of reactively adjusting their curricula to fill short-term and perpetually changing occupational fields, the New Professionals would promulgate broader reforms of media personnel recruitment and management policies and practices more consistent with the modern information society. This is the management connection and, as we see in this chapter and chapter 6, it is a two-way street.

Cheap Labor for Uncle Scrooge

Broader personnel and management reforms are long overdue in the media industries, which, in general, treat their younger employees badly. Although media leaders "denounce and denigrate journalism schools," they "eagerly hire their graduates" (Dennis, 1988b, p. 4).

Consistently, newspaper and broadcasting managements have been "seriously remiss" in their "commitment to people," according to Dennis (1986c). "The failure of many media organizations to invest in their own people both diminishes the quality of journalism in America and, in the long run, is also very costly for these cost-conscious organizations." Deficiencies include salaries that are "low in comparison to those paid in other professions and occupations that demand high-quality, creative work from people," a lack of opportunities for professional development and mid-career advancement, and "the failure to actively invest in the best and brightest young Americans who want to have careers in newspapers and television." The result is "an alarmingly high dropout rate," with young people "leaving the news business for other endeavors." This is costly for the organizations that employ them and "quite stupid from a management perspective" (p. 95).

Dennis also found newspaper and television executives "incredibly arrogant" about their recruiting and hiring practices.

> Many of them, at the highest levels, say that all young people must pay their dues before they can be admitted to the quality centers of American journalism. . . . This is truly one of the media's self-inflicted wounds. . . . [In contrast,] law students are courted by the great firms, not because they have adequate experience or any great immediate value, but because they represent the future. The young person, whether a journalism major or not, rarely finds such suitors. (p. 95)

Media firms are losing young people because they are "opting for other fields that are more caring, more humane, and more concerned about them as people and as professionals" (p. 95). And, recalling the two-way nature of the management connection, these short-sighted management policies are damaging to curricular reform efforts. Gerald D. Sass, vice president for education at the Gannett Foundation, has suggested that narrow media hiring criteria that emphasize "craft" or occupational attributes work against the development of liberal attributes (Dennis, 1988a, p. 92).

Management Resistance to Reform

Media managers are getting a "good deal" and see no need for change. But this is a bad deal for communication and media education programs, faculty, and students. How and what should they do to change the relationship? In order to overcome the discipline's paralysis and confusion, reformers should seek to understand "the system," especially practitioners' views and motivations about education and the market and social forces that reinforce them.

As we have already suggested, there is strong resistance to curricular change in many practitioner circles, especially among the middle-management and representatives of organizations and associations of journalists, broadcasters, and advertising and public relations specialists. These include, but are not limited to, the American Society of Newspaper Editors, the Public Relations Society of America, the American Advertising Federation, the American Newspaper Publishers Association, the National Association of Broadcasters, the Radio-Television News Directors Association and their regional, state, and local chapters, and those of other occupational associations.

Even allowing for their high-powered profit motives and personal and business eccentricities, we would expect that media communication executives and pioneers would grasp the significance of the New Professionalism and recognize it as an enlightened, integrative, liberating curriculum for future media professionals. Their successes, after all, are based at least in part on their vision and capacity to understand the fundamental linkages in the information and entertainment business, which transcend particular media delivery systems. Ideally, it is to this part of the "practitioner fraternity" (Birkhead, 1988) that education reformers should address reform proposals. Unfortunately, the successes of media executives and pioneers also may be due in part to their capacity not to concern themselves with issues—such as the undergraduate experience or the role of professional education in U.S. universities—that do not appear to directly impact on their more tangibly profitable activities. Thus, it is the middle-management level and occupational association and organization bureaucrats and careerists to whom such matters are delegated, and it is they who are most vocal about and influential in industry personnel policymaking.

Media practitioners and their occupational associations exhibit what Carey (1978) termed *confounding* characteristics typical of what he calls *excessive professionalism* and what we term *occupationalism*. (Except for direct quotations from Carey, we use the term *occupationalism* to describe excessive professionalism and *occupationalists* to describe those who are excessive in their professionalism.) Occupationalists create and exist in their own, narrow "moral universe," which is less ambiguous than that of the rest of society. Occupationalists, Carey reminded us, "are able to treat as matters of principle what most of us must struggle with situationally and in terms of fine gradations of ethical judgment." They "are so busy standing on principle that there is no room left for the rest of us to stand" (p. 850).

Middle-management and trade association media practitioners tend to hold a narrow view of liberal arts. In what is more genuflection than reflection, many practitioners profess their unyielding support, even defense, of liberal arts. Yet, their operational views of education are embedded more in their economic and occupational priorities than in societal or intellectual roots. Often, the occupationalist's definition is similar to what Syracuse Experiment found prevailing among some of the traditionalists in the academic community: Liberal arts is a slogan or "little more than a tautology" promoting "lingering evaluative connotations that associate liberal education grandly with thought and professional education crudely with skills" (Marsh, 1988, p. 12; see also Jankowski, 1986; Sitton, 1986).

This practitioner/occupationalist perspective reflects little awareness of the occupationalization of the traditional disciplines, discussed in chapter 1, and the existence of or potential for the development of liberal components in professional studies, particularly communication and media education. At the same time, practitioner/occupationalists support fragmented sequences in communication and mass media programs, especially when sequences are named after their occupation or media fields, such as journalism, public relations, advertising, technical journalism, agricultural journalism, photojournalism, magazine journalism, radio, television, and so on (Dennis, 1988b, p. 15).

Middle-management and occupational spokespersons reject, as merely impractical "theory," suggestions for integration of media subfields in the discipline, even though convergence and integration are occurring in the "real world." They ignore that unity and integration of knowledge is the essence of undergraduate liberal education (discussed in chapter 1). Asking these type of occupational practitioners to see how teaching of general media skills and knowledge can be adapted to the needs of a specific industry or media "is asking for trouble," the Oregon Report found. "Professionals [occupationalists] rarely address generic concerns, except for matters of literacy" ("Planning for curricular change," 1987, p. 31).

A national survey of editors in 1989 (Ismach, 1990) found that graduates of journalism schools are considered by editors to be *weaker* than graduates of other disciplines "when it comes to knowledge of current events, broad perspective, capacity for leadership, problem-solving ability, and capacity for hard work." While editors gave high marks to journalism schools "for training students in writing and news gathering," they gave low marks in some specialized skills such as graphics and photography and "analysis and problem-solving, and understanding issues." Yet, as Ottaway suggested in his comments during the roundtable discussion, they listed courses in "mass communication" and "newspaper history" as least useful (p. 3).

To Arnold Ismach, dean of the School of Journalism at the University of Oregon, the survey results reflected "an unbecoming anti-intellectualism that, regrettably, has always been a part of the newsroom culture." He added:

> [Editors] dismiss courses in journalism history, theory, research and mass communication as unimportant, yet those are precisely the courses likely to develop the critical skills of analysis and problem-solving so highly desired [by them]. They stress the importance of a broad liberal arts education, yet want journalism schools to emphasize professional skills courses in classrooms dominated by media professionals who lack training in much else. (p. 3)

Ismach's observation is consistent with the Oregon Report's surveys, which found that "some of the professional criticism of journalism/mass communication curricula smacks of anti-intellectualism" with a "strong disdain for some of the conceptual course offerings . . . even though these courses are vital linchpins to the liberal arts" ("Planning for curricular change," 1987, p. 32).

Media practitioner/occupationalist opposition to the integration of liberal and conceptual studies within the communication and media education programs reflects a variety of concerns. One concern already suggested is that reformed programs probably would not be titled with occupation-specific names like public relations, journalism, advertising, broadcasting, and so on. The implication is that reformed programs would dilute whatever legitimatization, prestige, or recognition that the organizations believe they enjoy by having a college or university program named after their specific occupation or industry.

Another concern, (although they probably wouldn't express it this way either) is that reforms would eliminate or dilute occupation-specific programs that narrow students' perspectives and options—early on in college. Occupation-specific programs—such as sequences in public relations and advertising—teach specific skills and knowledge that are less valuable outside their narrow occupational environments. This is because they are taught—to recall Bell's (1968) distinction between liberal and non-liberal education—"as . . . doctrine or fact . . . an aspect of specialization and technique" rather than taught "with an awareness of its contingency and the conceptual frame that guides its organization" (p. 8). To divert the students further away from a liberal education and commit them to a specific occupation, each media academic sequence (i.e., radio, television, public relation, newspaper) has its trade association clone student chapter—Society of Professional Journalists, Public Relations Student Society, and so forth; together, they worship a narrow occupational icon, imparting the occupational ethic under the guise of higher education.

Practitioners and many faculty rationalize that all of this is to meet student demand. This is a myth. In the first place, students are attracted to sequences because they are there—because they exist in the catalogue. In the second place, students are responding to parental, peer, and other short-term social and economic pressures to answer the question: "What are you going to do after you graduate?" Sequences help give them an easy answer. Students perceive, or want to believe, that they are committed to careers in a specific field. This gives them a sense of security, something that the occupations would exploit, but that the academy should not.

In such narrow systems as the "sequence" major, most students are not aware of a variety of options in information work unless these options are presented to them by faculty. Or they find that out for themselves, two to five years out of college. At that point, most seek other jobs or careers because they have reached a dead end in their jobs, which often do not extend beyond the entry level. When they leave, the media company is ready to hire another newly minted, narrowly prepared graduate to fill the vacancy. This process benefits the company, as the management sees it, because it does not have to invest in all or most of its personnel for longer than a few years. This keeps salaries and other personnel-development costs down.

Students are not the only ones paying the costs of specialized, occupation-specific university programs directly serving the entry-level needs of media companies. Any communication and mass media administrator who has survived in the position of chair, director, or dean for several years becomes aware of the waste, duplication, and inherent inefficiencies in sequences or even in separate occupational departments under the umbrella of a college or school of communication. The current "shortages" of faculty in public relations and advertising, for example, have been created by curricular overspecialization, aggressively promoted by alliances of educators and practitioners. The growing enrollment in these fields, as discussed in chapter 3, will eventually decline, leaving programs with underused, tenured, specialized faculty.

Even more fundamentally, though, the sequence-occupational approach places the priorities on craft over concept, and practice over analysis. As Dennis (1990a, p. 9) described:

Unlike other fields which have happily delegated legal or business education to scholars and teachers instead of practitioners, the communication industry still harbors the belief that emulating the norm of professional practice is highly desirable. In such a world view there is little time for critical analysis or instruction about professional ideals. Such a view relegates the communication school to the position of industry handmaid rather than independent analyst or leader. Journalism and communication schools are thus light-years from the relative maturity of schools that train future legal or business talent, for example.

In other words, another price paid by the communication and mass media programs for their fragmentation of sequence-type, occupational training is their second-rate status even among the other professional programs on campus. Communication and media educators become painfully aware of this when they compare the extent of resources, esteem, promotions, salaries, and productivity of their programs with business programs, for instance. Business schools long ago eliminated industry-specific approaches, replacing them with generic cross-industry subjects such as accounting, management, finance, and marketing (Dennis, 1988b, pp. 20–21).

Despite their liberal arts rhetoric, then, many in the fraternity of practitioners do not want communication and media education programs to engender the liberal ethos. They like programs that are limited. They want programs designed and named to imply to students that they must make an occupational commitment and investment by majoring in a limited field, such as newspaper or broadcast journalism, public relations, or advertising.

In an integrated, cross-industry professional, non-occupational curriculum, as we have described the New Professionalism earlier, the students are preparing for more general communication or information work that can be applied on the job. Depending on the program's mission, students take a few integrated conceptual core courses and engage in some experiential learning that emphasizes familiarity and experimentation with, and understanding over technical competence of media message-making technology. But they devote most of their communication and media academic work to intellectually challenging conceptual studies of mass media and communication that provide bridges to the behavioral and social sciences, arts and humanities. They explore consciousness-raising perspectives that in turn, enhance rather than narrow their independence and options in the market. Applying Bell's (1968) criteria again, the New Professionalism calls for the presentation of professional subject matter "with an awareness of its *contingency* and of the *conceptual frame* that guides its organization . . . [so] . . . the student can then proceed with the necessary *self-consciousness* that keeps" his or her mind "open to possibility and to reorientation" (p. 8, italics added).

In the New Professionalism, students are encouraged and offered opportunities to obtain familiarity with and understanding of media technology, either in the media workshop environment or other media centers or organizations on or off campus. Occupational training is neither mandatory nor the center of the curriculum. It does not absorb a great deal of faculty time and effort, and only a little of it, if any, is for academic credit; it is mostly co-curricular. Students seek this experience on their own extra-curricular, "rest and recreation" time. By so doing, they demonstrate their interests, initiative, and motivation—attributes that cannot be taught in required, lock-step courses but that media practitioners profess to prize so highly. In fact, we would suspect that students from sequence-occupation programs, whom media managers find so ill prepared, have not taken the initiative to seek out demanding practical experience at the expense of their campus and off-campus social schedules. Instead, we imagine that they "grammar-slammer" their way through a paternalistically conceived sequence of required craft and occupational courses, a route they are led to believe will prepare them for professional, rather than merely occupational, work.

The New Professionalism—the cross-media, liberal, integrative program—is consistent with broader undergraduate reform efforts. The danger to intellectual growth in professional programs, reported the Association of American Colleges, is the "excessive structure and overprescription of training in currently fashionable technique, ephemeral information, and obsolescent technology" (AAC, 1985, p. 17).

Addressing the Grammar Slammer Issue

We contend that many media managers believe the occupational programs should, above all, provide two services for the industry—the screening and socialization of students in the occupational ethos for the occupational culture. In chapter 3 we briefly describe the screening and remediation approach, where students are conditioned to adhere to a set of standard occupational practices and procedures. We compare that with a more efficient and humane media workshop in which students are encouraged to develop their abilities to reason independently and to apply principles to organizational realities with "moral imagination" (Lambeth, 1986).

But the remediation imperative is more tangible and it has a nice ring to it, especially when it is expressed by the more enlightened practitioners like Ottaway. Practitioners' expressions of concern about writing and grammar are, on the surface, compelling. How can anyone argue against literacy? It is difficult for educators to respond without becoming defensive and made accountable for every misspelled word or incomplete sentence attributed to one of their graduates—or to any graduates. Like liberal arts, the concept of literacy among media practitioners is more symbol than substance.

Basic skills is the practitioners' code for the functions of mass screening and socialization and indoctrination for the occupational culture they expect programs to perform, if not exclusively, above all other priorities.

The only appropriate response from educators is to point out that their programs emphasize writing and other communication skills more than other disciplines on campus and recite the major curricular commitments, resources, and priorities devoted to basic, but generic, skills. After that, educators should follow the example of the late Dean Richard Gray of the School of Journalism at Indiana University who told practitioners to "check with faculty members instead of hiring indiscriminately" and "stop rationalizing . . . poor management skills by lashing out at journalism education when [journalism graduates] don't work out" (Gray, 1983, p. 13).

Ottaway's casual and unreflective comments about history-by-osmosis represent not only an ingenuous view of education, but also a direct challenge to media educators' aspirations to join the mainstream of undergraduate education through such vehicles as Boyer's enriched major, as discussed in chapter 3. In the emerging ethos of a reformed undergraduate curriculum, the enriched major would be the requisite distinction between a trade or occupational school and a professional program worthy of baccalaureate status. Ottaway's challenge is also a direct threat to educators' aspirations for the discipline, as expressed to editors by Gray (1983, p. 13):

> [If I were a media practitioner] I would spread the word that if journalism education is to hold its intellectual place on a university campus, it must be more than vocational training. I would recognize that the press—one of democracy's most crucial social institutions—deserves scholarly attention and research just as do the courts by law schools and the Congress by political science departments. . . . I would encourage teaching and research about journalism's history, law, philosophy, ethics and process.

"EXTIRPATING" THE OCCUPATIONAL SPIRIT

How, then, do media educators turn the tables on this unproductive relationship with practitioners? First, they should recognize that the twin functions of screening-remediation and socialization-indoctrination represent the excesses of the "professional spirit" or occupationalism, which, as Carey (1978) recommended, should be "extirpated" from academic programs (p. 854). Indeed, reevaluation of practitioner relations and their motivations for opposing curricular reform should lead faculty and administrators to a thorough questioning of their curricula. They should ask, above all, "how much of the communication and media education curriculum reflects the occupational, rather than liberal, ethos?"

Because the media occupations and industries constitute quasi-public institutions, communication and mass media reformers should also seek to counter the intrusion of excessive professional, or occupational, values in public life as well as in the academy, for the primacy of liberal over occupational values on campus can be achieved only when public values reign over excessive professional values in society. Reformers in communication and media education would seek to, as Carey expressed it, put "a harness on the ideology of [excessive] professionalism which in its extreme manifestations destroys the conditions of an effective press *and* public" (p. 855, italics added).

What are these extreme manifestations? Simply put, the excesses of any profession (including those of an academic discipline) occur when the profession becomes too far removed from, and places its own values above, the society from which it arose. Each profession "inhabits a particular moral universe, peculiar unto itself, in which the standards and judgments exercised are those not of the general society and its moral point of view, but of a distinctive code" (p. 851). When it becomes too autonomous, its values—however originally well intended—become narrowly supportive of the profession at the expense of broader public or community values.

We have reported some of the reformers' concerns about the excesses of professionalism in the academic community. These excesses have resulted in the decline of coherence in the undergraduate curriculum and its teaching mission. "Too many teachers of liberal subjects," Rudolph (1984) found, "are so far gone into specialization . . . that the challenge of teaching, of bringing students into a humanistic relationship with their subjects, are beyond their interest or capacities" (p. 41). The principle of this decline of the teaching function is the mark of professional excess—when professionals are, as Carey (1978) said, "far more concerned by the way they are viewed by their colleagues than with the way they are viewed by their clients"—in this case, students (p. 851).

The power of the excessive professional is based on the dependency of the client. "The professional-client relationship," said Carey, "is one in which the professional dominates and in which typically and perhaps inevitably . . . the professional feels justified in treating the client in a paternalistic and manipulative fashion." There is "little reward" in the professions for re-examining the intellectual basis of professional practice. "The lawyer is rewarded for winning a case, not thinking about the law, the journalist for getting a story . . . not mediating on the nature of truth, the doctor for treating the patient, not thinking about the nature of health" (p. 851).

Carey believed that excessive professionalism promotes the primacy of client-professional relationship and resists, even attacks, attempts to establish public scrutiny of their realms. For this reason, professional knowledge replaces public discourse "as the reigning model of rationality." The result is the erosion and eclipse of the broader "moral basis of society" and the concept of the public and public discourse (p. 854). Carey suggested, as many others have since found, that this segmentation of society by professions is reflected in our political discourse, or lack of it, which has become a babel of political action and interest groups while the broad interests of the society are ignored.

As we have noted earlier, Carey (1978) challenged communication and media education programs to rid excesses of the occupational spirit from their curricula and "reassert the university tradition . . . the general ethical and intellectual point of view. . . ."

> We must recognize that we are not merely training people for a profession or for the current demands of professional practice, but for membership in the public and for a future that transcends both the limitations of contemporary practice and contemporary politics. . . . Above all, this means freeing ourselves from the tyranny of the present, of today's headlines, in order to take a longer view of things, in order to assert the scholar's tradition of concern with what is beyond our nose. That is, we must be concerned to teach, above all, the limitations of journalism as a practice. (p. 855)

The client of communication and media education programs, he suggested, is the public more than its consumers or the professions.

ROOTS AND RESTORATION

What do communication and mass media educators offer in their curricula in place of the instruction that feeds the extreme manifestations of professionalism? We have been suggesting that what is good for the academy is good for the media businesses. After all, the new commercial information and communication industries, shedding their old industrial characteristics, are becoming more like universities and colleges, which always have been in the information business (Blanchard, 1987c).

Although their missions are not the same, media businesses and universities are being held to more accountability and efficiency. Colleges and universities are being asked to come up with a bottomline, not with dollar profits, but with measurable "value-added" education and tangible proof that attending college makes a substantial difference in the outcomes of student graduates. The Association of American Colleges found that "one of the most remarkable and scandalous aspects of American higher education is the absence of" a means of "social accountability" (see chapter 8). In a free economy and society "where survival and growth are the only tests of virtue, colleges and universities have paid too little attention to the measures appropriate to an assessment of their performance" (AAC, 1985, p. 33).

Media and information companies, on the other hand, are being asked to justify the special treatment—their "franchise"—guaranteed by economic advantages, protective laws, and constitutional privileges. Lavine and Wackman (1988) found that the more enlightened media executives understand that short-term actions that ignore social responsibility and obligations "undermine the media's public support" of the privileges the media enjoy. The primary goals of media companies should be to serve both their markets and themselves by serving the public and society as a whole while making "adequate" but not excessive short-term profits. This approach positions the companies for long-term success (p. 381).

Reforms in both realms should reduce the excesses of professionalism and the occupational ethos, making them both humane and "ethically efficient" (Lambeth, 1986, p. 159), "user-friendly" institutions for their information workers, their clients, and the public. Communication and media educators, who become active collaborators in the preparation of liberally educated professionals, would be serving both their students' and new media management needs. Seeking what is fundamental in all communication and media processes and engendering their students with community values and self-direction is consistent with the needs of modern information and communication companies.

The practices and policies of the academy and industry will become increasingly more common as the academy reforms its undergraduate curriculum for the benefit of students and the public and as commercial information companies adopt more enlightened personnel management practices and assume greater social responsibility. We would argue that this emergence of public virtue and enlightened self-interest in the two institutions is not a revolution, but a restoration to common and more liberal roots and purposes.

Oratorical and Natural Rights Heritage

The commercial communication and information industries and the academic communication and mass media discipline profess a major, common purpose in society—to advance clear, accurate, responsible expression in the public service. Historically and philosophically, it is a unifying theme within communication and media education (because the expression ranges from interpersonal to mass communication channels) and with traditional liberal arts theorists (Birkhead 1986; Carey, 1969; Hudson, 1988; Schudson, 1978). Stewart Hudson argued that both the early Greek orators and the English natural rights empirical philosophers emphasized the primary importance "to speak well and think right in the service of civic virtue" and he traced this priority in early journalists and the drafters of the U.S. Constitution (p. 10).

Athenian orator Isocrates represented "the oratorical affirmation of absolute moral truths and of education in the service of civic virtue [which remained] at the core of liberal arts educational philosophy well into the nineteenth century." And, although the rationale was different, "the early English empirical philosophers had a parallel faith in universally accepted civic virtues or moral absolutes—based, in their case, on natural rights, and enlightened self-interest" (Hudson, 1988, p. 11; Kimball, 1986, pp. 35, 165–168). The journalism of Addison, Steele, and Dr. Johnson "was one of the fruits of the empirical enlightenment," and "American constitutional theorists, who followed Hobbes and Locke, affirmed the importance of accurate use of language." Both Jefferson and Madison emphasized the importance of a free press to insure a free flow of information from which citizens could arrive at worthwhile conclusions and policies (Hudson, p. 11), and this, of course, is reflected in American law and custom, including the First Amendment.

The starting point, then, for new media industry–academic relationships is to establish and maintain their common, long-term priority of advancing clear, accurate, responsible expression in the public service. Through their joint efforts, the new priority would replace the media system's short-term and short-sighted "commercial culture" (Bogart, 1991) and "marketing culture" (Christians, 1989, pp. 3, 13) that now pervade the media industries and professions.

The Ethical Trump Card

Critics have argued that excessive professionalism, especially in journalism, poses a threat not just to the media, but to the very foundations of democratic society. To counter this, Carey (1978), a John Dewey disciple, urged scholars to take up the daunting and long-term task of conceptually restoring "the idea of the public and public life." Specifically, for example, he urged media educators to help "the media in restoring the public as a real rather than a fictive part of American politics" (p. 854).

We believe the New Professionalism would be a big first step in that long journey. We emphasize again that a liberal education for future professionals starts at home—in the major—where the occupational ethos is not duplicated or emulated, but exposed for what it is; in its place the alternative, liberal ethos is given meaning.

Alleviating the liberal ethos means more than a freestanding and often token course on ethics. We agree with an early journalism educator reformer, Joseph Pulitzer, who insisted on ethics as a cornerstone of his proposed College of Journalism: "Everybody says that ethics must be taught. But how? I have expressed myself poorly if I have not made it clear that here is the heart of the whole matter. . . . There will naturally be a course in ethics, but training in ethical principles must not be confined to that. It must pervade all the courses" (Christians, 1989, p. 13).

An example of the broader view of ethics can be found in the subject of history. Through it, we can see the development of the commercial and marketing cultures (Bogart, 1991; Christians, 1989) in the occupational ethos. The history of mass communication and journalism in the United States identifies, as William F. May (1986) expressed it, "two effective sources of a press," which "produced two different definitions of the reader." The Constitution, on one hand, "chiefly orients to the reader as a *citizen*," while the marketplace orientation of the media, which began with the Penny Press, relates to the audience as a *consumer* (p. 27, italics added). Whereas these two concepts of audience are not mutually exclusive and can often be creatively synthesized, they are more often in conflict. Rather than presenting a relativistic "balanced" view in which both audience concepts are "equal," the reformed curriculum would focus on the audience-as-citizen.

This principle could be reflected in media case studies. For example, most news media either do not bother to make corrections publicly to their reporting errors, or they "bury" them. Although the error may have been significant enough to appear on page 1, the injured party finds the correction on page 33; usually the space or time is needed for newer stories, which command more attention from consumers. "Clearly," May (1986) argued, "the founders of the nation did not have the amusement of consumers but the deliberative life of citizens in mind" when they gave the press special constitutional protections. "For this reason, the ideal of 'accuracy, accuracy, accuracy' should trump other considerations in professional practice" (p. 27).

Another case in which the occupational could be replaced with the liberal ethos is in alerting students to unwritten occupational codes and practices in journalism that are often contrary to the public good. Philip Meyer (1987) found, in a national survey of editors conducted for the American Society of Newspaper Editors, five "hidden rules" that newspapers practice. Although the rules are not always contrary to the public good or ethical journalism, they lead to problems just because they are hidden and "escape analysis" (p. 33). The rules reflect the excessive professional drive to construct a "particular moral universe, peculiar unto itself, in which the standards and judgments exercised are those not of the general society and its moral point of view, but of a distinctive code," to recall Carey's (1978) characterization (p. 851).

4. A BLUEPRINT FOR RECONSTRUCTION

Meyer described a variety of problems, many of them harmful to the public good and contrary to the ideals of good journalism, created by such "folklore precepts" as (pp. 24–33):

1. "A story originated by another medium is never as newsworthy as one originated by one's own paper." This often leads to media "blackouts" or "boycotts" of information that should be widely disseminated to the public.
2. "Newspapers are written for other newspaper people, not for the general reader." This reflects another characteristic of excessive professionalism where practitioners — to again recall Carey's (1978) characterization — are "far more concerned by the way they are viewed by their colleagues than with the way they are viewed by their clients"; in this case, the readers (p. 851).
3. "Newspapers avoid directly admitting a mistake." This is an extension of the previously discussed case of "burying" errors, reflecting a lower priority for accuracy than for fresh news.
4. "Always publish, regardless of the consequences or costs to individuals or institutions."
5. "If it involves money, it is probably bad."

Rules 4 and 5 are not entirely wrong, but following them religiously can inflict serious damage in some cases. Substituting "a knee-jerk . . . reaction for analysis and reflection can prevent a newsperson from recognizing those exceptional cases" (Meyer, 1987, p. 33). Although this example is from the news business, institutional studies of other types of information companies could generate hidden rules observed by their employees.

The work of scholars in communication and mass media history and ethics is being applied by Christians (1989), Lambeth (1986), Meyer (1987), and others in instructional materials to deal the ethical trump card. In the reformed communication and media education classroom, to restate what we have said earlier in this chapter, the occupational ethos is neither duplicated nor emulated, but *exposed for what it is*. At the same time, the New Professionalism founded on liberal ethos, is given meaning. We believe that this is not only the best preparation for students seeking careers in information and media work, but also it is best for the information and media professions and industries. Above all, it is best for our democratic system. In the next chapters, we explore how these ideals and principles are being applied in some exemplar communication and media education programs in the United States.

11 BUILDING FOR REFORM

5 Frameworks for the Enriched Major

It is very important . . . that an organization recognize that the least effective response to increased demands is business as usual. A conscious, flexible response, difficult to undertake because the pressures themselves reduce the time to think, is crucial.
   —Hampden H. Smith, III, from Washington & Lee University

Ideas that cannot be implemented are of limited value on the front lines of educational reform. What's doable? Part II investigates key parts of the curricular equation: the major, general education, electives, links to academics and practitioners, teaching strategies, and accountability and accreditation. Throughout this section quotations from administrators are used to illustrate key points. Unless otherwise noted, these quotations are taken from personal correspondence, which includes both letters and literature collected during a survey conducted by the authors in the summer, 1990 (see Appendix A).

Our call for diversity has not been an apology for the status quo. Far from it. "Business as usual" is impossible, not only because the "business" to which many units are linked is being transformed, but because media educators need to redefine and/or reaffirm the business they are in. Are they in the "business" of training people to fit into an industry? If so, what is the industry? Are they in the business of educating people to challenge the status quo? If so, what links should there be to the industry? How do the different forces play out in the rough and tumble of a unit's decisions about courses, curricula, and faculty hires?

This chapter looks at a unit's major; the importance of articulating mission statements and philosophical orientations; the need to develop a small, carefully thought-out core of courses; the rejection of rigid, industry-oriented sequences in favor of flexible, functional approaches; the acceptance of innovative, capstone experiences as ways of integrating a variety of media functions and perspectives; and the affirmation that a unit's culture or ethos, as understood by students, is a strong indicator of a unit's success.

MISSION STATEMENTS

Mission statements are "political" documents that can be used to clarify or obfuscate a unit's reality. They can accurately mirror a vision or simply reflect a pipe dream. In a recent survey distributed to 258 member schools of the Broadcast Education Association, less than 56% of the large schools' departments and less than 50% of the medium and small schools' departments were identified as having mission statements (Warner & Liu, 1990). This is a surprisingly small number.

Apparently, many schools do not think explicit mission statements are needed. Departments might argue that they have implicit mission statements or that no matter what the mission statement says, it is the faculty, courses, and facilities that define a program. Though there is merit in this argument, explicit mission statements should be at the center of curricular discussion. Well-conceived mission statements provide vision and focus for a department, establishing a rationale for the allocation of limited resources. If taken seriously, they can be guideposts that remind people where a program's been and firmly point the direction in which it is going.

Russell Ackoff (1986), from the Wharton Business School, wrote that a mission statement should have five characteristics. First, *"it should contain a formulation of the firm's objectives that enables progress toward them to be measured.* To state objectives that cannot be used to evaluate performance is hypocrisy" (p. 39). It is important that the objective's of a mission statement are not simply a string of "operationally meaningless superlatives such as *biggest, best, optimum, and maximum*" (p. 38). The Missouri School of Journalism's multifaceted mission statement, provided by Charles Warner, is an example of specific, measurable objectives (these have been abbreviated):

1. *to teach students the principles and techniques of journalism,* which we define as current, reasoned reflection, in print or telecommunications, of a society's events, needs and values;

2. *to serve, improve and provide leadership to both the university and the journalism, telecommunications and advertising professions* through a variety of activities and services such as workshops (etc.);

3. *to create for the students, faculty, administration and staff of the School of Journalism a challenging, intellectually stimulating, professionally rewarding, cooperative, participative, secure, supportive and collegial environment* that encourages risk taking and the creation of new knowledge through research and creative activity;

4. *to be sensitive and responsive to the needs, concerns and interests of our multiple stakeholders:* students, parents, faculty, administrators, the curators, staff, alumni, professionals, media, potential employers of students, supporters, suppliers, government, educators and community; and

5. *to maintain, enhance and promote the reputation of the School of Journalism.*

These five statements fit Ackoff's first mission statement "characteristic" because each can be used to evaluate the University of Missouri's program.

Ackoff's second point is that *"a company's mission statement should differentiate it from other companies.* It should establish the individuality, if not the uniqueness of the firm" (p. 39). Not all units see their schools or themselves as unique. As one person wrote us: "I am not sure there is any particularly distinctive element of our program. We are a small- to medium-sized exclusively undergraduate program at a mid-sized comprehensive state-assisted university. We are over enrolled and under funded." Others have been able to use their distinctiveness as an asset. James Webster, School of Speech Communications at Northwestern University, wrote:

> Northwestern is unlike most universities that offer programs in media studies. In some ways it makes us unlike other Big Ten schools. NU is relatively small . . . private and enterperneurial. It is in close proximity to a major media/telecommunications market. . . . In many ways, we're more like Ivy League schools, a group of universities conspicuous in their indifference to media studies. Judged against these universities, NU's president concluded that media and communication studies were areas of "competitive advantage" for Northwestern.

Ackoff's third point is that *"a mission statement should define the business that the company wants to be in, not necessarily is in"* (p. 40). It is true that the business of the academy in the United States is varied. From technical schools to liberal arts and sciences colleges to major research universities, from teaching programs to research mills, the "business" of education is diverse and is, at least partly, determined by the philosophy of the unit.

The importance of Ackoff's third point is that mission statements should be statements of vision. Not only should they clarify a unit's objectives and distinctiveness, but they should illuminate a unit's potential. For some units this has meant moving from journalism programs to programs of journalism and mass communication; from broadcasting programs to programs of broadcasting and electronic media; from radio, television, and film to communication, mass communication, telecommunication, or information sciences.

Of course, we believe we are in the business of studying communication: how it is produced, funded, and legislated; its impact and effects; its potential for good and ill; and its historical and aesthetic dimensions.

Ackoff's fourth suggestion is that *"a mission statement should be relevant to all the firm's stakeholders. . . ."* The mission should state how the company intends to serve each of them . . ." (p. 41). Missouri's School of Journalism listed 15 shareholders. Based on the philosophy of the school this list might shrink, expand, or change. For many public schools the "government" shareholder has mandated at least part of the mission statement. For example, Pennsylvania State University's School of Communications' mission statement stated:

> As an academic unit within a major land-grant university, the School of Communications has a threefold mission:
>
> 1. To educate people for careers in the media and in the academies of the Commonwealth of Pennsylvania and the nation.
> 2. To further research and creative work in the field of communications. The research dimension includes both professional and theoretical/critical approaches to the media, while the creative dimension includes works of the highest imaginative, artistic, and ethical standards conceived within those media.
> 3. To improve general understanding of the workings of modern mass media among the University community and the population of the Commonwealth through instruction, continuing education opportunities, conferences, workshops, and publications. ("Pennsylvania State University School of Communications," n.d.)

Penn State's self-perception as a land-grant institution drives the thrust of its program.

The last characteristic of a mission statement, according to Ackoff, is of greatest importance: Finally, and of greatest importance, *"a mission statement should be exciting and inspiring.* It should motivate all those whose participation in its pursuit is sought. . . . It does *not* have to appear to be feasible; it only has to be *desirable . . ."* (p. 41). We would add a sixth point to Ackoff's five characteristics. Mission statements should accurately reflect the educational philosophy of the unit. As Douglas Anderson, Arizona State University's Journalism and Telecommunications, wrote, their mission was "driven by a variety of factors: accreditation requirements, professional orientation, intellectual pursuits of individual faculty, location in a metropolitan Sun Belt area, enrollment management, financial support and facilities." But the bottom line is that these factors converge in the philosophy and ethos of a unit. As Anderson wrote in a Director's Statement in the school's literature, "The primary mission . . . is to prepare students to enter positions in media fields" (Anderson, n.d.).

PHILOSOPHICAL ORIENTATIONS

Earlier in the book, we presented a rationale based on outcomes that breaks down distinctions between liberal arts and professional education. For many, however, the distinctions continue to be real.

In mass communication education, what has been called the liberal arts versus professional debate goes back many years. In 1947–1948, Judge Justin Miller, President of the National Association of Broadcasters, called a meeting between leaders in broadcast education and industry representatives. The consensus on basic premises included: "(1) that an overemphasis on the trade, or skill, aspect of broadcasting was undesirable; (2) that a sound liberal arts program should constitute the heart of the degree program" (Head & Martin, 1956–1957, p. 41). In other words, broadcast education was expected to be true to both the industry's needs and liberals arts education. This attempt to straddle the philosophical fence between professional training and the liberal arts may account for why as Niven (1961) reported, 32 of the 41 schools that responded to a 1961 survey question on philosophical approaches put themselves in a category that called for a "broad liberal arts background plus professional training for first job skills and a basic knowledge of the industry" (p. 248).

In a recent study developed by the Broadcast Education Association's (BEA) Courses and Curricula Committee, respondents were asked to select their "department's orientation" based on the following scale: "Professional (5) (4) (3) (2) (1) Theoretical" (Warner & Liu, 1990). Forty-six percent rated themselves more professional than theoretical ("5" or "4"), 38% rated themselves in the middle ("3"), whereas approximately 15% rated themselves more theoretical than professional ("2" or "1") (see also Kamalipour, 1990; Rosenbaum, 1991).

Still, it is not always clear what these terms mean. Perhaps units can be defined by the amount and type of courses that fit into one of the three following categories: (a) courses that train students for "entry-level" positions in the trades (e.g., broadcast news, newspaper journalism, video and audio production), (b) courses that study the industry so that students can "fit into" the industry (e.g., communication law), and (c) courses that critique the industry so that students can be an informed public, informed consumers (e.g., mass media and society courses). Perhaps it is the mix of these three types of courses that reveals a program's philosophy. Of course, faculty may see their courses fitting into more than one category (e.g., a video production course that stresses concepts, critical thinking, and criticism). How courses ultimately are categorized should be determined by the faculty at the departmental level and guided by each program's mission. Media units do not exist by themselves. They are housed in broader administrative configurations. Where a unit is housed will have an impact on its mission, philosophy, what it teaches, and its ethos or culture. Following are six types of common department-university programs (see also "Planning for curricular change," 1987, pp. 8–10).

The Trade School Program

The "trade school" program locates the professional unit within a professional or trade school environment. There is no question that the mission of this unit is job training. Many 2-year schools or community colleges fall into this category as do some 4-year programs. Many do an excellent job of training people for entry-level positions in the trades.

The We-Train-Them-You-Educate-Them Program

Here the professional unit is located in a 4-year college or university, "liberal arts" environment. Accreditation (see chapter 8), by assuming that the liberal arts component of education comes from disciplines outside the unit, applies this "we-train-them-you-educate-them" perspective to mass communication academic units that want to get accredited. Courses are limited in the "professional" major so that the students can get their "broad" education from other disciplines. This mutually exclusive philosophy was represented by Walter Bunge when he was the Director of the accredited Ohio State University School of Journalism: "Whether your goal is print journalism, broadcast, public relations, or advertising, we believe that you should receive a sound liberal education *in addition* to your professional training in journalism" ("Journalism at The Ohio State University," n.d. p. 20, italics added).

We have argued on numerous occasions (cf. Blanchard, 1987a, 1987b, 1987d, 1988a, 1988c, 1989; Christ & Blanchard, 1985, 1988) that "professional" programs should take a more critical, more systematic stance toward the study of the media and see themselves more as preparing a literate public and self-directed (cf. Grow, 1991) professionals than training practitioners. Unfortunately, accreditation standards do not take into account any liberal arts component in mass communication study or even a linkage or integrative function. Although we disagree with their conclusion, programs that espouse this model might consider themselves as being liberal arts programs because they offer strong professional courses in their department *but require* "liberal arts" courses outside the department.

This combining of professional programs within a liberal arts university can be seen in such diverse programs as Eastern Illinois University's Department of Journalism and Washington and Lee University's Journalism and Communication Department. Eastern Illinois University's Department of Journalism's literature suggests that its degree "effectively joins professional and liberal arts education to provide flexibility, breadth and depth of educational experience" ("Journalism at Eastern Illinois," n.d.). This is linked to the mission of the school: "Eastern's primary mission is to provide a comprehensive undergraduate program of liberal studies as a foundation for all students as they seek degrees in arts and sciences, business, teacher education, and other professional programs . . ." (Mission and goals of Eastern Illinois University, n.d.)

According to Hampden H. Smith, III, of the Department of Journalism and Communications at Washington and Lee University: "W&L is a liberal arts college with two professional programs, the commerce school and the journalism department. They both are distinctive among liberal arts colleges, and the administration and faculty generally recognize these programs are major admissions drawing cards."

The We-Educate-Them-You-Train-Them Program

In this model a "liberal arts" unit is found within the professional or trade school institution. English or speech departments sometimes have mandates to provide the liberal arts "component" within the trade school environment. We have not heard from any mass communication programs that describe themselves with this mission.

The Ivory Tower Program

Here, the "liberal arts" unit is housed within a liberal arts and sciences college or university. This department might see its mission as less concerned with preparing people for the trades and more concerned with a "studies" approach of the media. The University of Pennsylvania's Annenberg-East fits this model. Its literature read:

> The general purpose of an Undergraduate Major in Communications is to offer a scholarly and systematic approach to the understanding of communicative acts and the symbolic environment, through which all members of a community become enculturated, socialized, and "humanized." This approach combines the insights of social science with those of the humanities and the arts. ("Major in communications," 1990, p. 1)

In the communication unit at Annenberg, with 200 junior and senior majors, no undergraduate courses are offered in writing, production, or management. Instead, they have organized their courses and congruent courses from other departments along eight "thematic" clusters:

1. Communications and Culture: Anthropology, History, Cultural Studies, Folklore, and American Civilization.
2. Communications and Politics: Political Science, History, International Relations, and Urban Studies.

88   5. FRAMEWORKS FOR THE ENRICHED MAJOR

3. Communications and Language: Linguistics, Psychology, Folklore, Philosophy, and Education.
4. Communications and Policy: Political Science, Economics, Legal Studies, and Urban Studies.
5. Communications in Society: Sociology, Anthropology, Political Science, History and Sociology of Science, and Urban Studies.
6. Communications and Art. Art History, Folklore, Design of the Environment, Comparative Literature, Music, Theatre Arts, and Fine Arts.
7. Communications and Literature. English, Comparative Literature, Theatre Arts, and Folklore.
8. Communication and Commerce: Management, Marketing, Economics and Legal Studies. (p. 3)

An example of the philosophic differences between the professional orientation articulated by position 2 (the we-train-them-you-educate-them program) and a position that may be reflective of position 4 (the ivory tower program) was articulated in the mid-1960s in a dialogue of articles that developed in the *Journal of Broadcasting* between John H. Pennybacker, who at the time was Executive Secretary of the Louisiana Association of Broadcasters, and Assistant Professor of Speech at Louisiana State University, and Charles M. Woodliff, then Assistant Professor in the Department of Radio-Television-Film at the University of Denver (see also Carroll, 1987).

In his articles, Pennybacker (1965a, 1965b, 1965c, 1965–1966) perceived a direct link between the broadcast industry and broadcast education. He ended his first article by quoting one of the primary goals of the former Association for Professional Broadcasting, "encouraging and maintaining in colleges and universities professional broadcasting education that will produce such men and women as can command the respect of the colleges that graduate them and the industry that employs them" (1965a, p. 187). As might be expected, this is similar to the present Broadcast Education Association (1990) goals that include, "We hereby establish the Broadcast Education Association, declaring our intent to encourage and maintain in colleges and universities professional broadcasting education that will produce such men and women as can command the respect of the colleges that graduate them and of the industry that employs them" (p. 1).

Woodliff's (1965) heated answer to Pennybacker was that as teachers in the university "our professional obligation is to breed dissatisfaction with the status quo among our graduates. We must *widen* the academic gap between commercial broadcasters and the schools" (p. 329; see also Davlin, 1965; Woodliff, 1965–1966). Though Annenberg does not offer writing, production, or management skills courses, they do have an internship

PHILOSOPHICAL ORIENTATIONS   89

program. An Ivory Tower program is not excluded from teaching writing, production, and/or management courses. As Hudson (1988) pointed out, the oral tradition in the development of media studies is strong. Performance, long a tradition of speech departments, was also an early tradition of many journalism and broadcasting programs. We agree with H. H. Smith of Washington and Lee University, when he said that "surely, one-tenth of their journalism education must not be learning to use PageMaker or dBase IV or Lotus 1-2-3." However, we also agree with Samuel Becker of the University of Iowa who wrote when asked, "how do you answer critics who say that teaching skills courses at the university level is not appropriate?": "We do not waste time answering critics with such foolish views. It is obvious that some skills, such as writing and speaking, should be worked on throughout one's lifetime. The skills of production need to be taught for the development of better and better film and video artists. Computer skills must be taught for a wide variety of purposes. Language and statistical skills are important for scholars to learn. Etc., etc., etc."

We also agree with Robert Moore of Elizabethtown College who wrote: "Skills are an important part of the curriculum—but not an end product. Even in courses where production is an emphasis, societal implications and ethical considerations are a focus. Additionally, students spend significant time in looking at message design and aesthetic presentation." (For a discussion about how a "skills" course might be taught within a liberal education see Christ, 1975; Lawson, 1983; Williams, 1992.)

The Hybrid Program: Dual Tracks

Probably most programs see themselves as hybrid programs. Even those programs cited earlier might argue that we have drawn the distinctions too finely. Within the hybrid programs there are those programs that try to explicitly offer both the practitioner and studies perspectives within their major and those that try to integrate both perspectives.

How a hybrid program grows can be seen in Val Limberg's history of the program at Washington State University:

> In 1964, two programs were merged into a Department of Communications: Broadcasting from the Speech Department and Journalism from the English department. In 1968, Advertising and Cinema options (or sequences) were added to the department. A few years later, Public Relations was added as a sequence....
>
> In 1984, the Speech/Communication programs came out of the Speech Department and joined the Communications Department, making it expand across the various areas of communication (speech, interpersonal, rhetoric,

etc.). It has worked out quite well, giving the department a broad theoretical framework but building in the various professional structure needed to prepare students to work in the professional world. In April 1990, the Department became the Edward R. Murrow School of Communication. . . . This further gave the direction of media, reporting and ethics as a part of the School's orientation. The faculty of the School is now working on the duel goal of better preparing students as professionals and as future academicians.

Donald Brod, Department of Journalism, Northern Illinois University, pointed out: "Some schools have gone to a two-track system—one track for students planning to work in the media and a general mass communications track for those who aren't. By allowing the students to make choices, we have, in effect, set up two tracks in one curriculum."

Although the concern of this book is with undergraduate education, an example of this "two track" idea can be seen at the University of North Carolina's new M.A. program that provides for three professional sequences and one mass communication sequence:

> The primary role of the School has been and continues to be the education of young people for professional careers in the mass media of North Carolina, and most especially for newspapers of the state. (Cole, 1989, p. 22)

> In 1988, we introduced a major revision of the M.A. program. The new program comprises four distinct sequences: news-editorial, advertising, public relations, and mass communication. The first three sequences are professional; after completion of coursework, students may write a traditional thesis or prepare a professional project. The mass communication sequence is academic and is designed for students who want to enter a doctoral program, prepare for a research career, or study the mass media without becoming a professional practitioner. (Cole, 1989, p. 15)

The Hybrid Program: Integration

At Trinity University, there are no tracks or sequences. Students who major in communication take core courses and select from a variety of courses in three functional areas: media studies, media message making (production/writing), and media management (including advertising and public relations). These courses bring to bear on media issues both industrial and critical perspectives. A student's program is built around his or her needs and the strengths of the university. This reflects a view of the learning process expressed by Samuel Becker from the University of Iowa: "Our faculty—at least most of them—do not believe that any particular area or course is *essential* to our program. What is essential is some combination of breadth and depth that ensures, insofar as possible, that students learn to think, to pose and solve problems, and to communicate well in different ways."

DePauw University has a variation of the hybrid program. DePauw's program combines a variety of communication perspectives to build a program that integrates study and performance, theory, and application. Jeffrey McCall, Chair at DePauw, wrote:

> DePauw's mass communication courses, by design, are housed in the broad-based department of Communication Arts and Sciences. The department also offers coursework in rhetoric and public address, interpersonal communication, theatre, and voice science. This approach recognizes the roots of communication study as a liberal kind of study. It also focuses the department on an overall process of communication, with provisions to study this process in varying contexts. . . . Students who wish to focus on mass communication and perhaps enter a media-related field can benefit from this liberal sharing within the department. . . .

But this does not mean DePauw offers only study courses. McCall argued:

> Students interested in advertising can benefit from courses in persuasion theory. Students interested in on-air work can benefit from performance-based theatre classes. Future scriptwriters can make use of courses in dramatic form or playwriting. Students in an organizational communication course can take the opportunity to study the organizational structures of media organizations. An interpersonal course can be essential for a student in media sales, who must develop client relationships, or for an on-air announcer, who must relate individually with the audience on a para-social basis.

The DePauw program permits substantial flexibility but, like the Trinity program, does not require the same highly prescribed structure for everyone.

CORES AND SEQUENCES: PUTTING YOUR RESOURCES WHERE YOUR PHILOSOPHY IS

"Most of us would argue that our discipline is basic. But can we explain what is basic about our discipline?" (Blanchard & Christ, 1985, pp. 28–29). Between the extremes of dictating every course or requiring no courses is a large gray area where most programs reside. Within the "major," issues of breadth and depth are often played out in a unit's approach toward core courses and sequences.

The Core

There are three interrelated factors a unit considers when developing a core. The first is to decide whether or not to have a core (cf. Moore, 1990;

Quenzel, 1990). The second is to agree on the kind of core (e.g., universal or sequence; practitioner or studies). The third is to agree on the courses, experiences, and outcomes of the core.

To Core or Not to Core? Core courses are one way of putting your resources where your philosophy is, of demonstrating what is basic and fundamental to the discipline. Requiring core courses is one way of working toward outcomes that are stated or implied by mission statements and philosophical orientation (for a discussion about what is essential to the broadcast curriculum, see: Blanchard & Christ, 1990; Dates, 1990, 1991; Finney, 1990; Fletcher, 1990; Guterman, 1991b; McCall, 1990; Potter, 1991; Renz, 1991; Tucker, 1991; Walcovy, 1991; Wood, 1992).

In the survey conducted for the BEA Courses and Curricula committee, Warner and Liu (1990) noted that "more than half of the 128 schools offer between two and six core courses. This situation is especially the case with large schools (67.3% required between two and six core courses). There was great diversity in the number of required core courses and no pattern in the data was discerned" (p. 7). They found that 35% of the schools required "Introduction to Media," whereas over 25% required "Media Law & Regulation" and "Introduction to Broadcasting."

Building Bridges or Walls: The Universal versus Sequence Core. We believe that bridges need to be built among the different areas of communication. Media education should provide an integrated perspective, a foundation from which to understand media's impact from a variety of viewpoints. If core courses are one way of ensuring this outcome, then a "universal" core, a core required of all communication students, should be the norm. It is not.

For example, the School of Communications at the Pennsylvania State University, which offered five undergraduate majors, did not have a universal core. Its "programs are designed to educate students for entry-level positions in communications—newspapers, radio, television, magazines, cable, advertising, film production, research and public relations" ("Curriculum guide for students/advisors 1990–1991," 1990, p. 1). There were "core" courses within each sequence, but there was no core course that transcended sequences. These "sequence" cores provided common knowledge to all advertising students but not to all advertising and journalism students. Advertising students took different core courses than journalism students, who took different core courses from broadcast/cable, film/video, and mass communication students.

A more integrative core existed at Arizona State University. Instead of five majors, Arizona State University had two: journalism and broadcasting. Each major contained three areas of emphasis and a core of between 15 and 18 hours. The journalism core consisted of: introduction to communication, newswriting, reporting, editing, communication law, and visual communication or history. The broadcasting courses included: introduction to communication, fundamentals of radio-television, radio-tv writing, production techniques and communication law. This program was more integrative at the core level than Penn State because two courses were required of all majors: introduction to communication and communication law.

Programs may require courses of all their majors but not be integrative in the sense we mean because their majors are limited to one area of mass communication. For example, the California State University-Fresno Telecommunications degree required 14 units including Media Problems and Practices, Writing for the Media, Media Audiences and Effects, Broadcast Regulation, and Proseminar in Media Issues. We would consider them integrative if they included both print and electronic media issues in their "media" courses. Michigan State University's Telecommunications department listed ten program emphases with a core that included five courses: Telecommunication Processes and Effects, History and Economics of Telecommunications, Basic Telecommunications Technologies, Basic Audio and Video Production, Basic Telecommunications Policy. Because the department was "only" telecommunications, the core courses would not be performing the function called for in earlier chapters (cf. chapter 3).

The University of Michigan's Department of Communication appeared more integrative at the core level because it required three courses of all majors: Media of Mass Communication, Freedom of Expression, and Information Gathering. Their "major" courses included such diverse areas of study as persuasive communication, film analysis, ethics of journalism, and radio/TV directing.

One of the most explicitly integrative core configurations was found at the University of Iowa, as explained by Samuel Becker: "We operate under the assumption that there are a limited number of things that are basic to a liberal education: students must learn to ask questions and must acquire the skills to answer those questions in a variety of ways." The University of Iowa ("Communication studies," 1988, p. 2) required four core courses of all majors "although in two of the categories they have a choice between two different courses" (p. 2): A course in broadcasting (Mass Media and Mass Society), communication (Communication Theory in Everyday Life), film (Intro to Film Analysis or Survey of Film), and rhetoric (Persuasion in Society or Communication & Contemporary Culture). It is this kind of integrative approach that builds bridges not only among different *mass* communication disciplines, but among speech, film, broadcasting, and communication theory. This is not to say that Penn State and others do not build bridges among different areas of their curriculum. It is just not explicitly evident in the core courses.

A Practitioner Versus Studies Core. Writing is a strong part of most journalism programs. Many in journalism education would agree with Walter Bunge, The Ohio State University, when he wrote, "Our basic philosophy for communication education is that writing ability is the underpinning for all other journalism/mass communications courses." It comes as no surprise then that in each of OSU's four sequences (news-editorial print, broadcasting, advertising, and public relations) writing is one of their required core courses. They required "Basic Reporting and News Writing," "Development of the Mass Media in America," "Mass Media Research and Theory," and either "Law of the Press, Radio, and TV" or "Mass Media, Society, and Basic Issues." "International Communication and the World Press" is an option for those going into the news/editorial print and public relations sequences.

Writing, and specifically science writing, was the focus of the journalism department at Oregon State University, which "has as its primary mission the education of 'Renaissance journalists' — writers and reporters who can compete in traditional journalism but who have in-depth knowledge of science and technology" ("Department of journalism," n.d. p. 1). They had five options in their program: science writing, science information, photojournalism, technical writing, and broadcast journalism. Their core consisted of 25 credits: "News Writing," "News Writing II," "Wordcraft for Journalists," "News Writing III," "Editing and Layout," "Reporting," "History of Mass Communication," and "Mass Media Law." Jon Franklin, Professor and Chair of Journalism at Oregon State University, argued that, "our core courses all have a science-in-society, C. P. Snow emphasis."

Where their unit core stresses writing, they also required (24 credits) a nonjournalism core, which presented the student with such varied topics as computers, history, philosophy, and economics: "Computers: Applications and Implications," "Politics and the Media," "History of the United States," "Principles of Economics," "History of Science," and "Critical Thinking."

This emphasis on requiring courses outside of the major in other content (e.g., history, political science, and economics) or skills (e.g., computers or statistics or typing) areas was also evident in other journalism programs such as Indiana University's School of Journalism. In addition to such entrance requirements as being able to type 35 wpm, proposed required courses for graduation included literature or art history/appreciation, United States history, United States political institutions, statistics, United States minorities or ethnic studies, and economics. Indiana University's core consisted of Communications in American Civilization, Writing for Mass Media, Visual Communication, Communications Law, The Media as Social Institutions, plus one reporting and one editing class.

As is evident above, even the strong "practitioner" programs usually have elements of "studies" courses in their cores. There are, however, programs that stress studies in their mission and their core. Annenberg-East required students to take two core courses out of three that are offered: Introduction to Mass Media and Society, Introduction to Political Communication, and Visual Communication. No writing classes were required. As we noted earlier, no writing classes are offered.

Based on the mission of the university and the department and the strong background of the students who enroll, Trinity University's Communication Department, in 1990, moved from five core courses to three as it moved closer to a "studies" perspective. The original five core courses included an introduction to the media, an introduction to applied media aesthetics, a media writing course, communication law, and a media issues (new technology) class. Both media writing and communication law have been eliminated as required core courses, whereas the aesthetics course has been reworked as a message theory class. Writing, production, and management courses are still offered in the department but are not required as part of the core.

Core Outcomes. A core should communicate to students, colleagues, administrators, parents, and legislators what a unit thinks is central. How units want to be perceived will be partly a function of curricular decisions made about the core. Do units want to be known because they teach skills, concepts or some combination of both? Our position is that the students at Trinity are best served with courses that provide conceptual maps to the field. In the core, we have moved away from industry-oriented courses like media writing to broader, studies courses.

Care and Maintenance of the Core. It is not easy to maintain and sustain core courses. Entropy is probably no more evident than with core courses. Many times faculty do not want to teach the courses, students feel unfairly obligated to take them, and administrators sometimes regret having to staff all the sections. Questions that need to be answered in all courses somehow seem exaggerated for core courses. There are, for example, philosophical questions, with respect to what should be in the courses. There are pedagogical questions about how should the courses be taught. Should the same text be required for all sections? And, there are administrative questions with respect to who should teach the course. Should all the lectures be on television? Answers to these questions come partly from establishing the centrality of the core. If the core is central to all mass communication students, then a unit's best resources should be aimed at developing the best core possible. This is not easy, but it is possible and ultimately desirable.

Again, although core courses provide unique challenges to a unit, they are one way of defining student outcomes. They are a way of taking philosophical positions and mission statements and making them explicit. Opposition to any core course is partly based on the idea that students should have the freedom to choose whatever they want. Although popular at the end of the 1960s and through the 1970s, this philosophical approach to course selection has been modified by many as the criticism of higher education has grown. Our feeling is that there should be a limited number of courses that are required of all those who are majoring in communication.

Sequences: From Here to Eternity

One of the more controversial developments coming out of the Oregon Report was the rise of the "generic" curriculum, a curriculum that looked less towards rigid specialization and more toward a broad-based emphasis for undergraduate education (cf. Christ & Blanchard, 1987; Ishmach, 1987; Ward, 1987; Winston, 1987). As is clear from earlier chapters, we are dead set against inflexible sequences from philosophical, pedagogical, and practical perspectives. There are those that disagree with us.

Again, turning to Walter Bunge of the Ohio State University's School of Journalism, whose program has four sequences: "I am not convinced that a generic communications curriculum is the correct way to train future communicators. My experience is that the practical training of a professional sequence brings the student up to speed more quickly and with more willingness to work hard. The student in a 'track' feels pride and commitment to her/his specialty and usually works a bit harder than the "generalist" in a professional program."

Developing curricula that will facilitate student pride, commitment, and motivation is an important consideration. We find that student motivations emerge in many different ways for many different career possibilities. "Forcing" motivation through practitioner sequences seems too high a cost in time and resources, too restrictive a perspective for the challenges media educators face.

There are schools that have modified the traditional sequences to include some aspects of the "generic" curriculum concept. Brian Winston, School of Communications at Penn State, wrote:

> We have abandoned the traditional sequences but we have done so in what I like to think is a rather clever and conservative manner. That is to say we

have not opted for courses in such things as media writing. Rather we have altered the structure of the degree forcing, for instance, all journalism students (whether they see themselves as print or broadcasters) to take both the beginning writing courses (of course) as well as the beginning electronic news gathering course. We have also redone the curriculum of this latter so that it too is writing intensive—i.e. radio. Our ambition was to break away from having industrial considerations over-determine our curricula, because obviously the industries are changing; but not to throw the baby out with the bath water. That is to say we wanted to continue to teach proven courses but to reorganize them, trying to achieve the maximum reconfiguration at a degree level with a minimum amount of alterations at course level.

This is certainly one way to encourage integration: require a variety of courses that reflect traditional ways of carving up the field. Because there is so much potential for overlap among basic courses, it is our feeling that integration is important at the course level.

An example of a program where this is taking place is at the University of Minnesota. It has made alterations at the course level by instituting such "generic" courses as media writing and information gathering. These are courses that cut across old sequence configurations like print and broadcasting. It is this integration that we think best suits the present day communication student.

And, not only large programs like Penn State and Minnesota are grappling with how best to teach our students. Robert Moore, of Elizabethtown College, discussed his program's move from sequences to concentrations:

> Twice in the past 10 years, the Communications curriculum has undergone major revisions—in 1983 and 1990. The focus of the change was to develop a more balanced professional communications program within a liberal arts institution. . . .
>
> In both revisions, the goal was to eliminate "sequences" in speech, radio, television, theatre and develop a more integrated approach to educating the "well-rounded" communicator. The terminology used was to graduate a well-educated generalist rather than a communications specialist.

And, this from Donald Brod of Northern Illinois University: "The NIU undergraduate curriculum has no sequences, but it allows students to specialize *if they choose to*. On the other hand, they can obtain a broader, more general major if that is their choice." Interestingly, Brod continued: "Our no-sequence curriculum is new. After the first year, it looks as if most of our students still choose to specialize. (I'm sure it has something to do with the job market.)"

And, this:

> Instead of separate majors in print news, broadcast news, public relations, and photojournalism, the new program offered simply a journalism major. With the blurring of distinctions between and among the media, the new curriculum reflected the new reality. Still, because of the wishes of professional organizations and students who were concerned about jobs, the courses were arranged in such a way that students could specialize just as they had done with sequences. But the beauty of the new curriculum is that students are not *forced* to specialize. Our hope is that more of them will choose to "mix and match," to build a more general program that will provide them more options than narrow specialization does.

Like other units, Northern Illinois University is feeling pressures by internal and external forces. The need to provide a program that allowed students to specialize was partly a function of pressure from practitioner organizations: "The concerns of professional organizations (such as the Northern Illinois Newspaper Association, the Illinois News Broadcasters Association, and the Chicago chapter of the Public Relations Society of America) and a number of students prompted us to provide a way to specialize for those students who felt the need to do so."

At Trinity, students are able to build their own "programs," their own sequences of courses with guidance provided by faculty advising. The three required core courses (see earlier) are followed with a course in one of each of three main areas: media studies and theory, media message making (production and writing), and media management (advertising and public relations are included here). This leaves the student with 12 to 18 hours of electives. We think this balances the need for students to get a firm conceptual map of the field and to experience a variety of media areas, and at the same time, it gives students a major say in their own education.

Capstone Experiences: Experiential Learning

Experiential learning, as discussed in chapter 3, is such an important component of undergraduate education that we think it should begin as early as the first year of higher education and continue through the senior year. At the upper division level, capstone experiences are one way of pulling together students' education. Whether they take the form of senior theses or projects, internships, or a combination of the two, they can provide an important integrative function in a student's education.

In chapter 6, we describe how the media workshops and laboratories at Trinity University provide introductory experiences in media message making, management, and critique. For advanced students the workshops and labs can provide an integrative function.

Media Workshop. Each workshop (e.g., television, radio, print) has student leaders who are asked to participate in a faculty-administered board. Students are expected to apply their message making, media management, and media studies concepts and skills in solving problems facing the centers. This type of experiential capstone learning experience challenges students to move from theory to policy; from appreciation to application; from self-doubt to self-direction.

Media Laboratory. Although in its infancy, the media laboratories are seen as places where students will come together to challenge the forms and content of present day practitioners. Instead of replicating the management and practitioner hierarchies of the media center, the media laboratories reflect the entrepreneurial, democratic liberal ethos at its best (see chapters 3 and 6). Advanced students can use the laboratory experience to experiment with ideas that are not normally associated with mainstream media communication. They integrate their interests, skills, and insights to creatively address a variety of communication challenges. The point is capstone experiences are another way of building in an integrative function in the New Professionalism.

A UNIT'S CULTURE

"What I thought was great about Trinity was that we got to use all this great equipment" (Louanne Walters, 1990 Trinity graduate). Sometimes a student's perspective can be humbling to curriculum reformers. When talking about mission statements, philosophical orientation, cores, and sequences, a unit's ethos or culture may be more "telling" than its philosophy. And, how can a unit's culture be observed? One way is by observing and talking with students. The faculty and administration have certain perceptions about a program, but the students live the program. It may be that "things" are being unintentionally communicated. Media educators may think the strength of a program is the faculty or the innovative curriculum while the students think it is the equipment (cf. Porter & Szkolka, 1991).

One way of understanding a unit's culture is to determine who gets rewarded. Are the student stars the "worker bees" of the media workshops (i.e., the television, radio, or print centers) or are they the ones who win undergraduate and graduate paper competitions? Or, are both kinds of students rewarded? Are students moved by the enduring questions concerning the media and their impact on society or questions about the latest sound effects library? What drives the students? What interests the faculty? How does a department want to spend its precious teaching time?

A second way of understanding a unit's culture is to ask not only journalism and mass communication (JMC) administrators (cf. Weaver & Wilhoit, 1988; Whitfield, 1982) but central administrators of universities housing JMC units. Tan (1991) found that his study of central administrators confirmed "our worst fears: we do not have a good image in the academy" (p. 16). He suggested that, "This study provides strong evidence that university and college administrators generally evaluate their JMC units less favorably when compared to other departments in their universities, particularly on research/scholarship criteria. JMC units granting the PhD tend to be evaluated more favorably, but these units still get relatively poor ratings on research productivity" (p. 16). Another way of interpreting Tan's data is to suggest that many JMC unit cultures clash with the university's culture. The New Professionalism is a move toward placing media studies in a central position in the university; central within the university culture. How a unit's culture can impact on the New Professionalism is discussed more fully in chapter 7.

As is clear from the examples in this chapter, curricula have been developed from a variety of perspectives. Those that stress integration, bridge building, and clear vision have the best chance of thriving into the 21st century. In the next chapter we discuss building bridges within the academy and with enlightened practitioners; building bridges for the New Professionalism.

APPENDIX A: REQUEST CIRCULATED SUMMER 1990

Part 1: Please send us a catalogue and/or supportive material.
Part 2: Tell us something interesting about your program.
Part 3: In 750 words or less, answer ONE or more of the "global" questions below.

1. During the 1980s, a great deal of criticism has been forced on higher education. As a result of this criticism, and for other reasons, some schools have been through extensive undergraduate curricular revisions. Has your academic unit revised its undergraduate curriculum over the last 10 years? What forces motivated the revisions? How much were the revisions based on internal (administrative, etc.) pressures and how much on external (perceptions of professional needs, etc.) pressures?
2. Undergraduate education has been under pressure to get "back to the basics" of liberal education. How has your program defined itself in terms of what is basic or fundamental to a liberal education and what is basic and

fundamental to our discipline? What kind of commitment has your department made to the liberal education of all students?

3. Although it is difficult to generalize, we are interested in your approach to new hires. What are the trade-offs you make between professional experience, research expertise, and teaching; trade-offs between those coming out of a practitioner's background and those coming out of an academic background? Of course actual hires depend on lots of intangibles like personality and availability of candidates, but we are interested in what you look for when you begin looking through resumes.

4. How is your academic unit perceived on campus by the faculty and by the administration? Are you considered intellectual leaders in communication and media studies? Are you considered leaders in the liberal arts? Do you consider it important to be considered campus leaders in media studies and/or the liberal arts?

5. Both the Carnegie Foundation and the Association of American Colleges reports outline desired outcomes for undergraduate education. Labeled, in one case, "essential undergraduate experiences" and, in the other case, important "capacities," they are authoritative guidelines of what undergraduate liberal education should "produce" in its graduates. Have your faculty developed outcomes for the student who majors in your academic unit? If so, what are they?

6. Specialties and subspecialties can be developed ad infinitum within an undergraduate curriculum. But, there are limited resources. How do you balance the breadth and depth issues within your curriculum? How do you ensure that undergraduates have an understanding of the scope of our discipline while giving them the opportunities to develop expertise in specific areas? Which areas, courses, or experiences do you think are essential to your program?

7. Communication and media studies programs exist in the world of the academy while being linked to an industry and profession. How does your program balance the world of the academy and the world of the practitioner? Does your program fit in one world more than the other? What kinds of professional ties does your academic unit nurture? If the job preparation function of your curriculum were taken away, which courses would remain? How does the professional versus research-oriented faculty controversy play out in your academic unit? Or, if that's not an issue, how does the professional versus liberal arts controversy play out?

8. New technologies and the new uses or re-configurations of older technologies continue to change the content and processes of mass communication. This challenge creates opportunities for re-defining what we teach and how we teach it. How are these changes addressed in your curriculum? Which new technologies should be taught? What is it about communication technologies that should be taught and learned? Have you developed new

courses, new sequences, new orientations? Have you re-named yourself lately? Which kinds of courses (e.g., writing courses, production courses, etc.) are most impacted by the technological revolution and how have they been impacted?

9. Due to the integration of communication theory where intrapersonal, interpersonal, and mass communication are seen as integral parts of the same on-going process, what bridges are there among the various communication departments on your campus (e.g., speech, broadcasting, journalism)? Has the bridge building worked? What are the pedagogical and political strengths and weaknesses of such linkages?

10. How do you do *one or more* of the following:
   a. Give your students a "conceptual communication map" that places intrapersonal, interpersonal, group, organizational and/or comparative communication systems in the context of broader historical, legal-ethical, institutional, political, social, economic, and other social systems?
   b. Present media writing and speaking capability
   c. Present information gathering
   d. Present technological literacy—understanding of visual, aural and computer "grammar and phenomena" in media.
   e. Present the history and tradition of the field, the field's social and economic implications and the ethical and moral issues to be confronted?
   f. How do you answer critics who say that teaching skills courses at the university level is not appropriate?

+ +

IF YOU DON'T LIKE ANY OF OUR QUESTIONS, WE'D STILL LIKE TO HEAR FROM YOU! Tell us something about curriculum that you would like to see as part of the national debate. If you've heard of a program or an aspect of a program that you think works, tell us about it. If you only want to answer parts of one question, do it. We'd like to hear from you.

Thanks!

6 Building Toward the New Professionalism

> *Journalism [media] schools can become professional problem-solvers and public sense-makers. There is still time for them to become the architects of the information society rather than their own chief mourners.*
> —Dennis (1988b, p. 22)

As a media education unit reforms its mission and curriculum, building bridges within the academy and with practitioners will need to be addressed. This chapter describes a variety of ways media educators can build bridges within the academy and to practitioners.

Within the academy, general education is seen as central to a unit's mission and a primary way of making media studies accessible and fundamental to students' education. Minors and electives, practica and internships, and the use of internal resources are all seen as ways of building bridges to colleagues and with students who are nonmajors.

Also addressed is the use of external resources, the pros and cons of practitioner associations, and the potential of practitioners to "use" media educators.

BUILDING BRIDGES IN THE ACADEMY

Intellectual leaders. Sense-makers. Bridge builders. Media educators have the opportunity and responsibility to teach a future generation about the power and impact of mediated communication. As we have argued before, this does not mean simply preparing people for occupations. It means reaching out to the nonmajor; seeing media courses as central to students' general education; building bridges among departments and disciplines; and providing extra- and co-curricular activities for the academy as a whole.

This reaching out is good for both majors and nonmajors alike. As Samuel Becker from the University of Iowa wrote: "Our undergraduate program is designed for students who want a liberal arts education. This is one of the reasons we do not restrict any of our courses to majors; we want our students to interact intellectually with students from history and psychology, literature, political science, and economics." Bridges allow for the flow of ideas from both sides, and that is why one of the jobs of media educators is to build bridges.

General Education

Boyer and Levine (1981) argued that: "Each general education revival moved in the direction of community and away from social fragmentation. The focus consistently has been on shared values, shared responsibilities, shared governance, a shared heritage, and a shared world vision. To us, this is an important point. It suggests that the ebb and flow of general education is, in fact, a mirror of broader shifts in the nation's mood" (p. 17). If media are as essential and important as has been argued then media studies should be part of every student's general education. Like core courses, general education courses require a commitment of time and resources. As with core courses, many programs do not have the will, the resources, or the inclination to commit their overworked faculty to the general education of nonmajors.

Lack of resources, for example, is one reason Walter Bunge of the Ohio State University, gave for not involving more nonmajors in their program: "We have very few nonmajors involved in our program because we aren't staffed to accommodate them. . . . Eventually, when we have control of our enrollment, we'll encourage the university to include our introductory mass media course in its list of core courses. For the present, it's only core for our majors."

Having a separate unit committed to general education is a reason Douglas Anderson of Arizona State University gave for not having to offer university-wide service courses: "because there is a separate unit on campus (the Department of Communication, with approximately 1,000 majors, plays a large service role to the university with its interpersonal, intrapersonal and organizational approaches) that relieves us of a major university-wide service responsibility."

Other units have tried to balance the needs of nonmajors with majors. Jo-Ann Albers of Western Kentucky University wrote: "Anyone who is not a journalism major may take up to 12 hours of journalism courses under our new department admissions policy. The policy was adopted in part to ensure that our majors were not pushed out of classes by nonmajors."

Units committed to general education have developed courses that fall into two broad categories: skills and studies courses.

Skills Courses. As discussed in chapter 5, there are schools that see their mission as including or emphasizing the practice of journalism. "Journalism" writing may be a skill brought to the general student that celebrates accuracy, clarity, and precision.

Jo-Ann Albers of the Department of Journalism in Western Kentucky University wrote that her University's basic reporting course is part of general education: "Despite the university's counting of JOUR 202 Basic Reporting as a general education course, we do not consider it as anything other than a skills course." Colorado State University's David G. Clark of the Department of Technical Journalism, noted: "We have three service courses for nonmajors. A technical writing course is required of some 30 out of 54 university major programs. A business communication course is similarly required by the more business-oriented majors. And a course in professional writing is part of the university's general core requirement in reasoning and communication skills."

Requiring writing of students as part of their general education is common, although English departments that stress rhetoric tend to have political control over many of these programs.

Writing, like speaking clearly and forcefully, is central to communication, and because these skills are central to educational achievement, programs that feature writing in their major should move to integrate their writing courses into the general education program. Equally important—we would say more important—is the need for mass communication units to make media studies central in the academy.

Studies Courses. As media sense-makers on campus, media educators should be providing media studies courses for the general student—in the social sciences and the humanities; in theory, economics, history, criticism and effects—that integrate disciplines and methodologies. These courses should reflect the best a unit can offer students.

It is one thing to say that there should be an "Introduction to Mass Media" course, it is another thing to decide what that course should contain. Earlier we argued that it is not so much the specific subject matter of one course that matters, but a total approach that moves students towards becoming active, self-directed, critical thinkers (also see chapter 7). An Introduction to Mass Media course can be taught in a variety of ways depending on the strengths and interests of the faculty. The outcome of such a course should see the student developing an understanding of the powerful impact of the media and the challenges facing democratic ideals as the new information technologies change the way we live and organize our lives. We would expect this course to address historical, economic, political, and social issues.

Communication models can be useful when organizing introductory courses. For example, Lasswell's (1948) model, even though it is incomplete and rudimentary, provides five areas around which to organize a "Media and Society" course: the source, message, channel, audience, and effect (see Sandage, Fryburger, & Rotzoll, 1988).

The source. Who are the people and organizations who control the media industries and creative processes? What are the financial and regulatory constraints on the production process? How did these media organizations develop?

The message. What is the content being communicated? What does it say about our society and culture? How do issues of power, status, race, class, and gender get played out in the messages?

The channel. How has technology had an impact on how and what we communicate? Who controls the communication channels and how does that have an impact on what we know and learn?

The audience. Who is the audience? How is the audience defined? What does it mean to define ourselves demographically, psychologically, and behaviorally? How many audiences are there?

The effects. What kind of effects are there? Short term? Long term? Short lived or cumulative? Pro or antisocial?

Courses can be developed that tap one or more of the areas above. For example, Trinity University has three courses in the university-wide common curriculum. A Mass Media course stresses the need for students to grapple with issues in the following areas: history, industry structure, culture, and effects. Another course centers on new information technology where questions are raised about what it means to be in an "information technological revolution." The third course is titled "Arts Criticism." Students study and apply aesthetic theory while writing journalistic essays critiquing the latest cultural events in San Antonio.

Dennis and DeFleur (1991) acknowledged the challenge of developing an introductory media course that also appeals to the general student. They suggested the use of key topical essays that make linkages between the media and other key disciplines. They suggested, for example, "Noam Chomsky and Why is He Saying Such Awful Things About the Media" to illustrate media ethics from a linguistic viewpoint. Or, "How Children Learn to Buy" to discuss advertising from a consumer behavior, sociological, and psychological perspective. Or, "The Novel as Quantitative Research" to emphasize mass communication research from an English and American literature orientation.

Different schools have developed other approaches to general education courses. For example, some schools like the California State University-Fresno reported one "service" course: "We offer only one course in the University's General Education pattern, TCOM 163, Radio/TV as Popular Culture. It can be used to satisfy a state requirement that 9 units of general education be at the upper-division level and contribute to a pulling together of the lessons of general education—scientific or cultural insights, communication skills, critical thinking ability, etc."

Washington State University offered courses in both the Humanities (Mass Communication & Society) and in the Social Sciences (Mass Media and Public Opinion). Others like Elizabethtown College offered a variety of courses: Com 105 Basic Speech, Com 115 Media and Society, FS 100 Freshman Seminar ("two sections one 'Women and the Media' and 'Persuasive Messages' "). Robert Moore, of Elizabethtown College, wrote, "Plans in the coming year include adding a course in the Power of Language area of Understanding and in Junior/Senior Colloquium."

In chapter 2, we argue that changes in technology would have a major impact on the discipline. We agree with Harlan Cleveland (1985) who argued that the changes in the "information society" should have an impact on general education: "Honing the mind and nourishing the soul are both functional in the new knowledge environment. What we need now is a theory of general education that is clearly relevant to life and work in a context of the information age—a rapidly changing scene in which uncertainty is the main planning factor" (p. 20).

Minors and Electives

The minor, in some ways, is the distillation or essence of the major. It represents a mid-ground between those who want to dabble in the discipline, taking one or two courses, and those who are serious majors. The minor, as much as the major, communicates to the university the scope and orientation of the discipline. It helps communicate the intellectual interests and rigor of a unit. It is a way for those in political science, sociology, English, psychology, art, drama, history, and the sciences to be taught contemporary knowledge about the media. Our own inclination is to use the minor to stress a "conceptual" roadmap or framework for the study of media. At Trinity University, we require three core courses: Mass Media (a study of the media industry), Media Messages (a study of media content; see Johnson & Christ, 1985), and New Technologies (a study of the transformation taking place in our media environment due to changes in how information is communicated and how the transformation is effecting us). We also require an upper division "perspectives" course that changes topics and methodological orientation depending on who is teaching it; and electives from the "studies/theory" course offerings.

As with the development of general education courses, developing minors and electives for nonmajors takes time, energy, and resources. For some schools the tax on the faculty and facilities precludes reaching out to the nonmajor. For others there are fewer restrictions. As Hampden Smith, III, wrote, "We have no prerequisites on any of our content courses, purposely so they are appropriate for all nonmajors." And this from Donald Brod, Northern Illinois University, where they had made a conscious effort to facilitate nonmajor participation:

> Nonmajors are welcomed into many journalism courses. A freshman-level survey course in mass media is specifically for nonmajors. In the past, we required passing our Journalism Qualifying Examination (a grammar-spelling-punctuation-usage test) before taking our basic journalistic writing course. Now, in an attempt to open the course to nonjournalism students who might want one course to help them organize their writing, we have pushed back JQE, making it a requirement for taking any course that has the first course as a prerequisite.

Samuel Becker wrote the University of Iowa also has an open program for nonmajors:

> Nonmajors are involved in our program in all of the ways that our majors are, with two exceptions. Nonmajors are not formally advised by our faculty (although we often do a good bit of informal advising for some of them), and nonmajors may not register for our internship program. (The only reason for the latter is that the two of us in charge of the program have our hands full guiding and evaluating the papers that our majors write at the end of their internships; we do not have the time to take on anyone else.)

Practica/Apprenticeships

The distinction we make between practica/apprenticeships and internships is that practica/apprenticeships take place on the campus under the supervision of faculty and/or staff, whereas internships are off campus experiences. In chapter 3 we wrote that experiential learning is something that many mass communication units have been doing well for a long time. Experiential learning is an important curricular component for those who wish to test theories and participate in the execution of their ideas. Providing practica or apprenticeship experiences are ways of reaching the general student.

The Media Workshop and Laboratory

At Trinity University, as elsewhere, there are media workshops that cater to majors and nonmajors alike (see chapter 3 for a discussion of media workshops). Trinity's workshops, or centers, provide experiences to all interested students through 1-hour pass/fail apprenticeships centering around television, radio, and print production, and management. The workshop concept allows the general student an opportunity to get involved with a variety of media, a chance to "kick tires," and to see how messages are constructed from the inside out. Also, it gives the student the opportunity to hone his/her production and management skills.

DePauw University in Greencastle, Indiana, has recently committed itself to the development of a Center for Contemporary Media (McCall, 1987). The Center is seen as a workshop for non-majors to learn about and experience media production and organizations first-hand. Jeffrey McCall, of DePauw, wrote:

> The Center for Contemporary Media will provide unique opportunities for the students of a small, liberal arts institution. First of all, it will provide a modern facility for student media organizations in print, radio, and television. The campus cable outlet will be housed in the building. In keeping with the liberal arts nature of the campus, the facilities will be open to students of all interests and majors. Students from a variety of majors can capitalize on an interest in the media by involving themselves in the activities of the student media organizations. This involvement can not only be an enjoyable campus co-curricular activity, it can help make a broad range of students more aware of how the media work. Over the years, many students majoring in liberal arts studies other than communication have used campus media experience as a springboard into media careers. No doubt the media industry can benefit from the contributions of philosophy, economics, or political science majors.

At both Trinity and DePauw there is no waiting until the junior year to experience the media. These workshops are open to all students, with the difficulty and responsibility of the positions increasing as students develop their expertise. At Trinity, students who are not majoring in communication frequently have taken significant leadership positions in the workshops.

Perhaps one of our more controversial recommendations is the establishment of a media laboratory that is fundamentally different from the media workshop. Whereas the workshop strives to create an enlightened practitioner ethos so that students can experience some of the trials, tribulations, and challenges facing media practitioners, the media laboratory directly challenges the practitioner ethos as it is practiced at many industrial sites. The media laboratory is seen as a place where students will come together to challenge the actions and ethics of present day practitioners. Instead of replicating the enlightened management and practitioner hierarchies of the media workshops, media laboratories reflect the entrepreneurial, democratic, liberal ethos of the university classroom at its best.

As we discussed in chapter 2, the communication revolution has seen changes in how content is produced and delivered, the kind and quantity of information, changes in communication processes, and the cross use of technologies. Whittle Communications, led by Christopher Whittle, who has been called "media baron for the 1990s" (Reilly, 1988, p. 1), epitomizes a media company that has embraced the challenges of new technology and moved beyond the replication of traditional media forms. These nontraditional forms include Channel One, the controversial, commercial television programming for schools (cf. Dagnoli, 1990; Honig, 1990; Levine, 1990; Stein, 1991) as well as "Special Reports," the linking of magazine and video programming for doctors' offices. "Though Whittle's field is publishing, his real business, he'll tell you, is inventing new forms of media" (Ralston, 1989, p. 31). As with the Whittle company, we see the media laboratory experimenting with new forms.

Whittle Communications has also demonstrated innovative management techniques: "Mr. Whittle has kept the company's divisional structure decidedly low-key. Whittle is based on six free-floating divisions. . . . Each division works simultaneously in magazines, newsletters, videos and wall posters. The only formal structure a division may have revolves around the advertiser" (Reilly, 1988, p. 90). Mr. Whittle suggested, "A company like ours doesn't need managers. What we really need are entrepreneurs" (Gendion & Brown, 1989, p. 39). Applied to an academic setting, the idea would be to create a laboratory experience for students where they could work on a variety of media to communicate "stories" about a number of topics or issues.

Although still evolving, Trinity's media laboratory is taking place in an advanced media message making course. In an attempt to break down preconceived ideas about what it means to "make" news or advertising or public relations, the class is structured around story telling. As Gerbner (1984) wrote: "The best general term for the symbolic construction process is story telling. All our arts, sciences, religions, and statecraft, consist mostly of stories we tell and internalize. That process weaves the seamless web of human cultures defining the world and guiding its social relationships" (p. 10). He goes on to identify three types of stories including those "about how things work (drama and fiction which make the all important but invisible relationships in life visible and understandable); stories about what things are (facts, expositions, descriptions); and stories about what to do about them (stories of action, choice, and value such as sermons, instructions, and commercials)" (p. 10).

The laboratory is seen as a place to experiment with storytelling and not a place to replicate how stories are currently being told by the industry. Importantly, as the discussion of Whittle Communications suggests, this direct challenge of the occupational and enlightened professional ethos will serve students well as they become practitioners and are asked to develop creative solutions to intransigent problems. As we wrote earlier, the New Professionalism should be considered good news for practitioners too.

Interdisciplinary Bridges

Building bridges can take different forms, including close working relationships with other departments. As R. C. Adams, from CSU-Fresno wrote:

> We provide a minor and have students from the School of Business and the School of Agriculture minoring with us on a regular basis. We also work closely with the Departments of Journalism, Speech Communication, and Theatre and Dance, as well as taking on some joint ventures with the Department of Music from time to time. We also provide supervision for the operation of the University radio station and support a student television production organization, Bulldog Video. Both are open to all students in the university and both have led to students from other majors taking one or more of our courses, just as a matter of interest.

At CSU-Fresno, they also "team teach, with the Department of English, INTD 168, Cinema and the Humanities, an inter-disciplinary offering." Mass communication, by definition, cries out for an interdisciplinary approach. This was pointed out in the Michigan State University literature about the subfield of telecommunications: "Telecommunication is an interdisciplinary field where one finds such professionals as producers, managers, financial, organizational and research specialists. Telecommunication includes the diverse areas of broadcasting, cable, telephone, information services and parts of the data communication field" ("Michigan State University's Department of Telecommunications' packet," n.d.). We would say that mass communication is an interdisciplinary field where one finds philosophy, sociology, psychology, political science, history, economics, business, and even, for some, engineering.

In Northwestern University's Master's program, engineering is part of the speech/telecommunication curriculum. James Webster cited three schools and two departments that focus their attention on media/telecommunications/mass communications: the Schools of Speech (Radio/Television/Film and Communication Studies), Journalism and Management plus 2 departments in the School of Engineering. In their Master's program, "Telecommunications Science, Management, and Policy," they have developed a three course core that requires students to cut across disciplines: Introduction to Telecommunication Science (engineering), Information Systems and Telecommunication Management (management), and Legal and Political Dimensions of Telecommunication ("Telecommunications master's program," n.d.). As Webster wrote: "Occasionally I'm struck by what strange bedfellows we (Speech and Engineering) make, but when I consider that digital broadband networks, capable of delivering video on demand, are 'just around the corner,' it makes a good deal of sense. I'm also under the impression that relatively few universities have joint communications/engineering programs in which video artists are talking to electrical engineers."

Some schools, like the University of Iowa, have formalized the interdisciplinary approach to communication. Samuel Becker commented: "One of the most exciting intellectual developments on our campus in recent years is the nationally recognized Project on the Rhetoric of Inquiry (POROI). Among the leaders in this project are four faculty from our department. . . . Our faculty have co-authored or are co-authoring studies with people on campus in such varied disciplines as psychology, English, sociology, botany, journalism, and economics." Although Becker admits that many of the linkages we think are so important occur mostly at the doctoral level, we think they can and should be made at the undergraduate level.

It is not only important to build bridges among mass communication and other disciplines in the academy, but, also to build bridges within the communication discipline, between electronic and print, journalism and mass communication, and speech and mass communication (see discussion of Wichita State University's program in chapter 8).

Intradisciplinary Bridges

We have decried the fragmentation of our field. While some programs have made decisions to fortify the walls, others are trying to break them down (cf. Roberts, 1984). DePauw University's communication department sees utility in a program that puts many parts of the communication puzzle within one unit. As Jeffrey McCall wrote: "DePauw's liberal arts major in communication arts and sciences provides for course work in the areas of mass communication, rhetoric/interpersonal/organizational communication, theatre, and voice science (see also Bohn, 1988; McCall, 1991).

Another program building "intradisciplinary bridges" is at the Pennsylvania State University. This time the linkage is between film and mass communication. Brian Winston wrote:

> We organize the School so that all of the scholarly persons would join together in a central scholarly mass communications department that had the dual responsibilities of both providing chalk and board courses for the four professional majors as well as servicing its own body of undergraduate and graduate students. The dangers here are obvious—we built into the system a divide between the green eye shade and the chi-squared faculty. . . . we for instance are, I believe, the first school to bring some film scholars to the AEJMC. Similarly, we were the first school, I think, to bring a journalism scholar to the Society of Cinema Studies. I see this as extremely important if

we are going to achieve effective synthesis in the next stage of the development of the field. I don't think we ourselves can easily absorb contingent areas of scholarship. However, I think if we speak and talk together we might produce a generation of students for whom these divisions are less apparent than they are to us.

That students are less concerned than faculty about the artificial divisions created within our curriculum is a recurrent theme. Again, from the University of Iowa's Samuel Becker: "Unfortunately, it [the linkage] does not occur as often as it should with journalism—largely for political and philosophical reasons, although students move back and forth between the departments a fair bit and we serve on each other's doctoral committees." Students recognize and search out the interrelationships. It continues to be the media educators' job to help students investigate the intradisciplinary and interdisciplinary nature of the discipline by building bridges, not fortifying walls.

Keeping Media Issues Central

We have illustrated a variety of ways of building bridges with the general student and with colleagues in the academy. Through general education, minors, electives, and practica/apprenticeships and inter- and intradisciplinary initiatives, a variety of means are available to the creative communication unit for making connections and providing media studies experiences for all students. We have also acknowledged that not all units have the resources to develop ambitious, curricular "outreach" programs. This section deals with extra-curricular approaches for keeping media issues central. Although time consuming, they do not necessarily require a great deal of additional resources. Robert Moore of Elizabethtown College provided a useful list for how to keep media issues central on the campus: "Media issues central to institutional discussion are addressed via guest speakers, sponsored all-college assemblies, banquet speakers, debate in the campus media (newspaper) and in departmental media (FM radio, TV, magazine, weekly newsletter), and in presentations at faculty forum."

Guest Speakers. A university's faculty are a rich, accessible resource. Many have studied or thought about the media and welcome the opportunity to discuss their ideas. For example, in a "Media, Advertising, and Society" course that the second author teaches, he has asked a variety of colleagues to tell his classes how they, from their disciplinary viewpoint, would approach advertising. He has had a communication, legal expert discuss First Amendment protection of commercial speech; a philosopher discuss if and how a corporation that has been convicted of a criminal offense could be punished through court-ordered negative advertising; an economist discuss the economic costs and benefits of advertising; a religious studies teacher give a Feminist critique of gender roles in advertising; an art history teacher discuss "Renaissance advertising," the use by patrons of statues and paintings to persuade audiences of their political and/or religious intent; an art teacher discuss art and whether or not advertising is or should be considered art. The point is that guest speakers enrich courses and demonstrate how media can be studied from many social science and humanistic perspectives.

Sponsored All-College Assemblies, Banquet Speakers, and Debates. Assemblies, banquet speakers and debates are three more outreach programs that can be used to keep media issues central on our campuses. Some schools may be too large for all-college assemblies, and holding banquets might be too expensive, but developing campus debates is doable. At Trinity, during the Gulf War, a "teach-in" was developed to discuss the history, politics, and ethics of the crisis. Unfortunately the organizers did not think to invite a media scholar to discuss the implications of the media's role in understanding, perpetuating, and ending the crisis. The point it that the media are central to how people learn about, understand, react to, and appreciate the world. Media educators should have a strong role as sense-makers in this mediated world.

Faculty Forum. In addition to being involved in debates, another way of keeping media studies central is through faculty forums. Students see professors in classes but may not often get to see what intellectually excites professors outside the classroom. Faculty forums or symposia where faculty get to present their research or creative work can help generate excitement for the process of scholarship and productivity. An added benefit is that faculty forums present the faculty as being actively engaged in their work, actively participating in their profession.

BUILDING BRIDGES WITH PRACTITIONERS

Jack Highton (1989, p. 61) wrote that, "From the professional point of view, much of journalism education is worthless." Over the years there have been a number of articles that try to identify either what students want from practitioners or what practitioners want from students (cf. Bolduc & Medoff, 1990; Funkhouser & Savage, 1987; Garland, 1983; Parcells, 1985; Renz, 1988; Rogers, 1982). Although we believe it is not the mission of undergraduate media education to train students for deadend media jobs, building bridges—facilitating the students' transition from the campus to the world of the practitioner and informed citizen—is an appropriate function of the New Professionalism.

This chapter describes how various programs have built bridges between educators and practitioners. Internships that stress a studies component, the use of external resources, and the pros and cons of aligning a program with practitioner associations are discussed. Like the connection between media educators and the academy, the bridge between media educators and practitioners should be a two-way street. However, media educators need to be clear that they are the ones ultimately responsible for the curriculum and the education of students in the academy.

Internships

Jeffrey McCall of Depauw University noted that "most laboratory/ experiential learning takes place outside the traditional course structure." Internships are no exception. Location, of course, determines the availability and variety of internship opportunities, although many schools offer internships (cf. Meeske, 1988). Schools close to or in substantial media markets have many opportunities (see O'Keefe, 1986). As Robert Finney, University of California-Long Beach, wrote: "Our location is really an advantage because of the extensive L. A. professional media market. Internships and special studies are available throughout the academic year and the summer." This does not mean that schools in smaller towns do not have internship capabilities. McCall, Depauw University (located in rural Indiana), indicated that off-campus "experiential" learning takes place during a Winter Term program. He wrote that in addition to the Winter Term, "other students complete internships while studying in off-campus programs sponsored by the Great Lakes Colleges Association. The GLCA, a consortium of twelve midwest liberal arts institutions, sponsors off-campus semesters in New York, Philadelphia, and Washington, DC. Students in GLCA programs typically take two academic courses, and complete a two credit internship with a media organization."

Even in those schools with limited industry affiliations, the internship is often seen as a positive relationship between the academy and the industry. As Samuel Becker wrote: "We believe that our department serves the industry best by not focusing a large portion of our energies and other resources on preparing people for their *first* jobs. Instead, we believe we serve them well by giving them a sound basis for preparation for their *last* jobs, which, in many cases, will be leadership roles in the industry. The only ties to the industry that we nurture are for our internships." Although internships are viewed positively, aspects of the internship experience are often a topic of heated debate (cf. Hilt, 1991). Questions that invariably are raised include: How should interns be evaluated? How much credit, if any, should interns be given? Should interns be paid?

How Should Interns Be Evaluated? When deciding what constitutes a successful internship, a distinction should be made between the industry work and academic study. Faculty usually have little direct supervisory control over on-site interns. Too many times, practitioners are asked to evaluate students based on "job" performance. From those dubious evaluations grades are sometimes assigned by an "internship coordinator" faculty member who acts as a part-time employment and placement agent for the local media (cf. Garrison, 1981).

We think academic integrity and learning are better served when academic credit is granted for work done under faculty supervision. One exemplar is the internship seminar at the University of Pennsylvania. There the Annenberg School of Communication allows credit only for a Communications Internship Seminar, which its curriculum booklet describes as a "scholarly counterpart for student internships" ("Major in communications," 1990, p. 9) at local media organizations. Students, sometimes with tips from faculty but usually through their own initiative, arrange for an internship with a local media organization. The seminar provides "an academic basis for the analysis of news and programming decisions and practices" (p. 9). Credit is given for successful work at weekly meetings and individual conferences along with readings on media-related topics. Students are required to prepare field notes and terms papers integrating readings and discussions with internship experience. In reality, academics have very little control over the internship experience. What academics do have control over is an atmosphere for reflecting on the experience.

How Much Credit? The Zero-Hour Internship. Experiential learning is an important part of a broad-based, balanced, liberal education. As we have suggested, credit for internship experience should be integrated with scholarly work and should be limited to no more than three semester hours, one course, or approximately 10% of the major.

As a rule, students should be encouraged to seek noncredit, off-campus experience. However, media organizations sometimes will not take on any interns unless they are placed "for credit" through a university. Some give bogus reasons for this—that the U.S. Department of Labor requires that interns be "paid" with academic credit in lieu of wages. Actually, the USDL Wage and Hour division has ruled that nonpay, noncredit internships are acceptable as long as they "provide a student with professional practice in the furtherance of his/her college education and the training is academically oriented for the benefit of the student" (Starr, 1989, p. 37). Some media organizations are more candid and say they prefer students being enrolled to motivate them to work, follow orders, not leave in the middle of the internship period, and so forth. To provide for these organizational concerns, real or imagined, and to provide the student interns with official certification, the zero-credit internship is proposed for those universities that have noncredit registration procedures. These internships are noted on the student's transcript for no credit.

The zero-hour internship experience is especially appropriate for motivated students who seek as many internship experiences as they can during the summers and other times. The zero-hour internships solve the problem of limiting internship credit while allowing students to obtain certification. Students benefit by not having to pay tuition for the experience and the media organization is usually satisfied to receive a letter from the academic department or school stating that the student is registered for an internship. We believe this also addresses an ethical question: Students should not have to pay tuition for academic credit that involves little or no participation of faculty or any other university resources or services. When asked, rarely, by media representatives, "How much credit are you giving," Trinity University replies that student transcripts and registration information is confidential, but they can rest assured that the student is registered for an internship.

Should Interns Be Paid? Yes, they should. Will they be? Many times, no. As we said in chapter 4, there is an exploitative side to the academic-practitioner relationship. This is probably no more evident than when a student is given few challenges or opportunities beyond that of a "gopher," someone who "goes for" things that are needed by the crew or staff. If the student is receiving academic credit or has been placed by a university or department, the academic unit is at least an accomplice in this exploitative system. Academics need to explicitly articulate their expectations to the media industry and screen both prospective interns and internship sponsors. For example, at Trinity University, there are three steps to internship placement.

First, the intern must apply to the faculty for clearance. All faculty are asked to review and comment on applicants. Prospective interns are asked to state why they are seeking an internship and what they expect the internship outcome to be. If approved by the faculty, students are assigned to two or three media outlets that have requested interns for interviews. Depending on requests, more than one intern-candidate is assigned to each prospective media sponsor for interviews. It is important that the placement process simulates the job search and placement process, that market forces come into play, and that both the student and media intern directors compete for the best internship match. This process is more open and less susceptible to the criticism that arises when the academic unit or faculty members act as *de facto* placement centers for their media and student friends.

Finally, after the interview between the potential intern and media outlet takes place, each has the option to veto the internship. For "highly prized" interns, payment for the internship is sometimes suggested by the academic unit as an inducement by the media sponsor. Intern candidates are expected to participate in the center, laboratory, or practicum experiences on campus before seeking off-campus experiences. When students cannot find a suitable off-campus internship they are encouraged to continue their campus work until they are competitive enough in the off-campus internship market.

At best, internships can be exciting and useful experiences that build bridges between the academy and the media industry. By providing students with work in media outlets along with the self-reflective, questioning aspects of an academic context, students are able to get first-hand knowledge for evaluating their own interests and passions. It is not uncommon for students to reject media work as a long-term commitment after experiencing a successful internship. Likewise, internships have been known to kindle a life-long "love affair" with media work. (See Garrison, 1981, for major recommendations of the 1980 Internship Committee's report.)

Adjunct Professors and Guest Lectures

Due to limited resources, over-enrollment, specialized courses, or a desire to make linkages with practitioners, adjunct professors are a fact of life for many universities. Reed and Grusin (1989) wrote: "No matter how defined, part-time faculty members constitute approximately 40 percent of all faculty in colleges and universities, and that figure may be even higher for journalism and mass communication" (p. 29).

Unfortunately, hiring adjunct professors does not guarantee that bridges will be built between academics and practitioners. Throughout the book we have argued that the ethos and culture of the academy is different from the ethos of the practitioner. The New Professionalism requires an understanding of the practitioner's world based on study and experiential learning, not on indoctrination (see chapters 3 and 7). Practitioners who are hired because they have a corner on "real world" knowledge can do a disservice to a unit's culture.

Reed and Grusin pointed out that "heavy reliance on part-time faculty can cause problems of orientation, socialization to department practices, coordination of instruction, and continuity" (p. 30). To ensure the positive use of adjunct professors, they recommended a plan:

> This plan should include a policy of hiring part-time faculty well before the first day of classes in time to order texts, consult with department and sequence heads about assigned courses, and generate a detailed and

thoughtful syllabus. The plan should include bringing them into academic deliberations of the department when possible. In addition, it should include requiring credentials appropriate to the classes they teach and faculty visiting their classes to ensure the quality of instruction. (p. 30)

Media practitioners sometimes see the academy's hiring of adjunct professor's as a way of making the academy more rigorous. Waldman (1986) wrote that schools "should depend primarily on working journalists hired on a part-time basis or under short-term contracts" so that it "would prevent journalism schools from becoming retirement grounds for burned-out journalists" (p.54). Fedler, Counts, and Stoner (1989), who studied the grading practices of full-time versus adjunct professors at three universities, discovered that not only do adjunct professors already teach many of the skills courses at the three schools, but "there was no evidence to support the notion that media professionals—adjuncts—are more rigorous than the schools' regular faculty members. Rather, the opposite was true. Adjuncts at all three schools awarded the highest grades" (p. 36). They went on to say, "The finding is important because the journalism schools that limit their enrollments often consider applicants' grade point averages. Thus, the grades given by adjuncts are critically important. Most adjuncts teach introductory classes, and students' grades in those classes may determine whether they are accepted as majors" (p. 36). Even with these caveats, using adjunct professors can be a way of building bridges between the academy and practitioners (see Plumley, 1990).

Using guest lecturers is another bridge-building strategy. Earlier we discussed the wealth of resources available on most universities within other academic disciplines. Many media practitioners are very happy to come to classes and discuss their profession with students. Cloud and Sweeney (1988) made seven suggestions about guest lecturers, including choosing a guest carefully, prompting a topic, dropping hints about such things as speaking extemporaneously, adapting speakers to the course, using recent graduates, recruiting in advance, and asking speakers back. In some instances, practitioner associations are heavily involved in formally providing guest lectures.

Practitioner Associations and Industry Connections

There are two comments that reflect the pros and cons of associating a program with industry organizations or practitioner associations. The first from Donald Brod, Northern Illinois University: "The concerns of professional organizations (such as the Northern Illinois Newspaper Association, the Illinois News Broadcasters Association, and the Chicago chapter of the Public Relations Society of America) and a number of students prompted us to provide a way to specialize for those students who felt the need to do so."

The second comment came from David Clark, Colorado State University:

> Corporations have provided excellent support of late. The IBM Corporation placed an electronic publishing systems laboratory with us 2 years ago. Valued at more than $300,000, the lab is constantly updated with new software and hardware. Hewlett-Packard has just given us $50,000 in computer equipment to establish a faculty/graduate student research lab. Last fall US West Communications gave us a loaned public relations executive in residence for an 18-month period. . . . A gift of $50,000 under the auspices of Media & Marketing, a television consulting firm, has permitted us to establish a national data base of minorities in television news in the 214 U.S. markets. Purpose of the database is to provide stations with up-to-date listings of possible minority employees.

For Northern Illinois University, practitioner associations carried enough weight to guarantee input into the curriculum. This is not uncommon with mass communication units. For Colorado State University, strong ties to the industry have meant strong support for worthwhile projects.

Practitioner associations continue to develop programs that build bridges between the academy and the practitioner's world. For example, the Broadcast Education Association, working with the National Association of Broadcasters, has a faculty internship program that places faculty at media outlets across the country. The Advertising Educational Foundation focuses their work with Higher Education on three goals:

> Goal #1: Conduct research to increase our knowledge of communications. . . . The AEF selects the subjects to be studied and then has the research done by leading professors in major universities, thus uniting the fields of advertising and education in cooperative ventures.

> Goal #2: Provide practical experience for professors of advertising and related fields. . . . In this program college and university professors of advertising, marketing and related subject areas are given up to four weeks of practical, on-the-job experience in advertising. The host advertising agencies pay for their board, transportation and expenses during their internship. The professors see and participate in the development of campaigns and work with the various agency professional groups, including account management, creative, research, media and marketing. They then sit in on presentations to clients and, in fact, follow the advertising all the way to completed production.

> Goal #3: Conduct presentations and discussions for colleges, universities and other leadership groups. . . . ("The new forum," n.d.)

The AEF pamphlet ends by saying, "We hope we can make this a two-way process: mutual help through mutual effort" (p. 4). This is the ideal.[1]

Mutual Help/Mutual Effort

Building bridges means that practitioners can benefit from academics as much as academics might benefit from practitioners. As Dennis (1986d) suggested, "Media research and theory can be sense-makers, and, while almost all research has some value, that produced at universities is less likely to be either adversarial or self-serving for any particular medium and so is potentially of great social value" (p. 12). The Freedom Forum Media Studies Center at Columbia University, of which Dennis is the executive director, has been a place where the two-way flow of information between academics and practitioners has been systematically supported. It continues to be a showcase for demonstrating that academics and practitioners, though ultimately with different agendas and missions, do not have to be adversarial. There are mutual benefits in coming together to build toward a New Professionalism.

This chapter has outlined ways in which media educators can build bridges within the academy and with practitioners. In the next chapter, we tip our hats to teachers: the people on the frontlines of curricular reform.

---

[1] A 1991 publication of "The Freedom Forum Media Studies Center," which was formerly the Gannett Foundation Media Center, is a comprehensive directory of faculty development opportunities: *Pioneering Partnerships: Faculty Development Opportunities That Link Journalism and Communication Education With Media Industries.*

7 Teachers and Students on the Front Line of Reform

> *We do not believe that there is one "right" curriculum. On the other hand, there are good and bad curricula. The good curriculum is one that puts able faculty with important and interesting things to say (and interesting questions that drive them) together with motivated students.*
>
> —Samuel Becker, University of Iowa

We can talk until we are blue in the face about curriculum and program evaluation, but without teachers, without the troops in the trenches following through with implementation, curricula remain vague outlines, skeletons, waiting to come to life. Teachers, like the units they serve in and the curricula they implement, create environments where integration and innovation either flourish or die. The culture of the classroom becomes as important a part of reform as the curricular structure and culture of the unit.

In this chapter we recognize and assess teachers: those largely responsible for the implementation of curricula. This chapter outlines the debate over priorities among scholarship, teaching, and service; discusses how technology can be used in teaching; describes curriculum and classroom cultures and their impact on student outcomes; explores how a unit's philosophy can effect who gets hired; and stresses the importance of advising.

As the dialogue continues about what constitutes the place of mass communication in higher education and the best way to serve students through courses and curricula, it is important to remember that media educators are a diverse group (cf. Christ, 1986; Eastman & Adams, 1986). This diversity is a strength as long as it does not splinter and fracture the study of mass communication into a hundred, unrelated specialities. With all this diversity it is somewhat surprising that in many places of higher education the buzz-words are still "publish or perish."

TEACHING VERSUS RESEARCH VERSUS SERVICE

Barry Litman, Michigan State University, summed up the various faculty tensions: "There is an ever present tension between the faculty but the coalitions change for different issues. The splits occur most frequently between researchers and professional people, mass media and telephone-oriented people, production versus nonproduction, and occasionally young versus old. Somehow fragile consensi are formed or the chairperson makes the final decision."

In many ways, teachers are independent contractors who are hired by the university to ply their craft. One of the appeals of teaching is that teachers, in the classroom, can be their own bosses. Another appeal is that college teaching is only one expectation, with research and/or creative productivity and service being important too. The pull between serving students, especially undergraduate students, and the research and service obligations of the individual teacher is one that is played out differently in different types of institutions (cf. Bowen & Schuster, 1986; Fedler & Smith, 1985; Schweitzer, 1989; Stone & Norton, 1980).

Undergraduate education requires a commitment of resources, including faculty resources. The costs of higher education seem too high, the perceived benefits too small, and the calls for accountability too strident for undergraduate education not to take center stage in the curricular debates of the 1990s (cf. Boyer, 1990; Brimelow, 1990). "In a recent survey of the chief higher education officials in the 50 states, the District of Columbia and Puerto Rico, the quality of undergraduate education ranked as the most important issue confronting academia" (Wycliff, 1990, pp. A1, A9).

Surveys that have asked faculty the importance of teaching to their institutions find the expected: Research institutions put less stress on teaching, especially undergraduate teaching, than 4-year undergraduate institutions. This is seen, as we indicated in chapter 1, as a problem by not only book authors (e.g., Sykes, 1988), legislators, and parents (Footlick, Wingert, & Leonard, 1990), but by university presidents. Donald Kennedy, president of Stanford University (Wycliff, 1990), remarked that there "is a suspicion that we have lost focus in designing and delivering a well-planned, challenging and inspiring education to our undergraduates. . . ." And, "Many of Stanford's best teachers of undergraduates are 'undercompensated and unappreciated,' he added" (p. A1, A9)

The call for innovative, interesting, and engaging undergraduate education will continue, and media educators should take an active role in providing provocative and challenging learning opportunities for the major and nonmajor alike. To do this will require innovative, interesting, and knowledgeable teachers. As Boyer (1990) suggested, this will also mean a change in how scholarship is defined.

Ernest L. Boyer, President of the Carnegie Foundation for the Advancement of Teaching, proposed a four-part definition of scholarship: Scholarship of discovery, integration, application, and teaching. "We strongly affirm the importance of research. . . . But to define the work of the professoriate narrowly—chiefly in terms of the research model—is to deny many powerful realities. It is our [Boyer's] central premise, therefore, that other forms of scholarship—teaching, integration, and application—must be fully acknowledged and placed on a more equal footing with discovery" (p. 75).

In relationship to service he wrote: "The nation's schools, its health care delivery system, and its banking system, for instance, all cry out for the sort of application of knowledge that expert faculty members can provide.... We need scholars who not only skillfully explore the frontiers of knowledge, but also integrate ideas, connect thought to action, and inspire students" (p. 77).

The Scholarship of Discovery

The scholarship of discovery is closest to what is normally known as research (Boyer, 1990). It is a central activity of the academy, but too often it is the be-all and end-all of the reward system. The scholarship of discovery is only one approach to scholarship. "The scholarship of discovery, at its best, contributes not only to the stock of human knowledge but also to the intellectual climate of a college or university. Not just the outcomes, but the process, and especially the passion, give meaning to the effort" (p. 17).

The Scholarship of Integration

Boyer is clear that the scholarship of integration is not a return to the diletantism of an earlier time. "Rather, what we mean is serious, disciplined work that seeks to interpret, draw together, and bring new insight to bear on original research.... The distinction we are drawing here between 'discover' and 'integration' can be best understood, perhaps, by the questions posed. Those engaged in discovery ask, 'What is to be known, what is yet to be found?' Those engaged in integration ask, 'What do the findings *mean?*'" (p. 19).

The Scholarship of Application

This is the form of scholarship that may most directly apply to building bridges from the academy to society. The scholarship of application is not simply the act of doing good, but rather, "to be considered *scholarship,* service activities must be tied directly to one's special field of knowledge and relate to, and flow directly out of, this professional activity. Such service is serious, demanding work, requiring the rigor—and the accountability— traditionally associated with research activities" (p. 22).

As we wrote earlier, bridges allow for the flow of energy and information both ways. So it is with Boyer's conception of the scholarship of application: "New intellectual understandings can arise out of the very act of application—whether in medical diagnosis, serving clients in psychotherapy, shaping public policy, creating an architectural design, or working with the public schools" (p. 23).

And, we would add, in such activities as using media to communicate about important issues of the day, and in interpreting to citizens the impact of media on their lives. Faculty in mass communication units pursue scholarship not only through laboratory experimentation but through the application of their work in a broad range of communication areas. The idea of the scholarship of application is analogous to Dennis' (1990b) idea of public scholarship where he argued that media educators "need to be more effective public scholars in a fashion that links systematic knowledge to public discussion and possibly even public policy" (pp. 6–7).

The Scholarship of Teaching

Teaching is a much maligned profession. The old joke that people who cannot do, teach, suggests that teaching is a "fall-back" position. By equating teaching with scholarship, Boyer transforms the routine of teaching into an active, exciting, frontier-crossing activity that creates an intellectual environment where critical thinking thrives long after the last class is taken (cf. Boyer, 1990, p. 24). "Furthermore, good teaching means that faculty, as scholars, are also learners. All too often, teachers transmit information that students are expected to memorize and then, perhaps, recall. While well-prepared lectures surely have a place, teaching, at its best, means not only transmitting knowledge, but *transforming* and *extending* it as well" (p. 24).

Building bridges within the academy, with practitioners, and society require vision and political savy, a need to take into account where a unit finds itself and where a unit wishes to be. However, when all is said and done, much of curricular reform will depend on teachers. Teaching needs to be placed at the center of the reform process.

TEACHING AND TECHNOLOGY

In chapter 2, we stated that technology is not only having an impact on what we teach but how we teach. Media educators have traditionally been in the forefront of the study and use of technology. From teaching courses in video and audio message making to the use of interactive laserdiscs and tapes (cf. Smith, 1986) and computers in education (cf. Adams, 1987;

Beard, 1991; Behnke & King, 1986; Burkhart, 1988; Butler, 1986; Deppa, 1986; Hanson, 1990; Lester, 1989; Lieb, 1990; Morgan, 1988; Oates, 1986, 1987a, 1987b; Rossow, 1986; Slater, Rouner, & Tharp, 1991; Stallworth, 1987; Thompson & Craig, 1991; Wesson, 1986). Media educators have been developing innovative and interesting ways of using technology in the classroom including the linkage of computers and other media (cf. Smith, 1991).

Stephen C. Ehrmann (1990, 1991) of the Annenberg/Corporation for Public Broadcasting Project summarized how technology can enrich teaching and learning. His (1991) four learning or "conversational" styles are outlined in Table 7.1.

Ehrmann's approach highlighted the importance of technology in transforming the teaching environment. Media educators are positioned to be on the cutting edge of developing innovative ways of thinking about technology and how it can be used to educate students (cf. Deppa, 1989).

CLASSROOM CULTURES

In chapter 5 we mentioned how a unit's culture or ethos creates an atmosphere that communicates what should be important to students: Is it important to fit into industry jobs, to learn about technology, to investigate and critique media industries, to replicate a local news program, to write features, or to write scholarly research papers? No matter what the overall

TABLE 7.1
Supporting the Four Conversations

Type of Conversation	Examples of Traditional Technologies	Examples of Newer Technologies
Study of direct instruction	Lecture hall, textbooks, handouts, overhead projector	Video tape and disc, computer-aided instruction, electronic mail
Real-time conversation	Seminar table: blackboard where student can show how they work on problems	Audiographic conferencing telephone, two-way video, text "chat" on network
Time-delayed conversation with other people	Living near faculty so papers can be handed back and forth	Fax machine, file transfer, computer conferencing, exchange of papers on file server, shared hypertext
Learning by doing (action in realistic situations; reflection)	Typewriter, sliderule; library and its books; laboratory and its equipment; internships	Word processor; statistical software; on-line library; CD-ROM database; realistic situations

culture of a unit, media educators can enhance or thwart the New Professionalism by the kinds of "minicultures" they create in their classroom. These minicultures have an impact on how and what students learn and what they value. We have identified four approaches, four curricular metaphors, that will help demonstrate how different teaching approaches may work for or against the New Professionalism: the metaphors of consumption (teacher as server), production (teacher as technician), growth (teacher as gardener), and travel (teacher as guide) (cf. Christ, 1990; Fox, 1983; Kliebard, 1972, 1982; Riesman, 1980). We believe that, of the four, the metaphor of travel (teacher-as-guide) is the most appropriate for the New Professionalism.

There are other metaphors. Teachers might be talked about as archaeologists digging for and uncovering the truth with their students by their sides. Teachers could be considered film directors motivating their students through the "script" of the class. Similarly, teachers could be considered conductors orchestrating their classes, or coaches preparing their players for the big test (cf. Laakaniemi, 1986; Leaming, 1986; Mann, 1986; Potter & Clark, 1991; Schierhorn, 1991). The important point is that each metaphor carries with it assumptions about the teacher-student relationship and the role of higher education (see Table 7.2). When considering curricular reform, the faculty of each media education program should explore the metaphors as a way to assess the underlying assumptions in their classrooms: the minicultures.

Consumption Metaphor:
Teacher as (Waiter/Waitress) Server

We believe this approach to curriculum and teaching works against the New Professionalism, where a program of study should be carefully planned and where fundamental principles should be stressed over fragmentary occupational whims. Here the curriculum is a restaurant or cafeteria that provides the student with a wide variety of dishes from which to choose. The teachers tend to prepare the meals and then act as waiters or waitresses to make sure they are delivered in a hot and timely fashion. In many ways, this metaphor describes those programs that have fragmented the discipline by offering courses based on the latest perceived student or practitioner interest. Specialized majors in advertising and public relations, or courses in direct mail and videotext, for instance, are created to appeal to the perceived needs of a variety of patrons.

This metaphor helps demonstrate that the teaching function can be broken down into at least three parts: course development, the serving of the course, and advising about which course to take. Teachers who are servers may or may not develop the courses they teach. In some colleges and

TABLE 7.2
Teaching Metaphors

Metaphor Type	Educational Issue	Analogy or Educational Implications
Consumption		
	Curriculum	Cafeteria or restaurant
	Student	Customer
	Teacher	Server (waiter/waitress)
	Status	What's being offered and on ability to deliver "food" in a hot and timely fashion.
	Outcome	Depends on customer's evaluation
	Attributes	Effort is made to make the courses appealing to the eye and the "stomach." Choices, variety, and presentation may be important
	Syllabus	Students are presented with options. Servers work with the students to guarantee a successful experience as defined by the students.
	Positive	Students are empowered to create their own educational experiences. Have the opportunity to try lots of different experiences. Image of serving teacher.
	Negative	Foods may be convenient but not nourishing. Teacher might teach for the evaluation. Teacher may not control the curriculum and/or courses.
	Hallmarks	Student-teacher power relationship is reversed.
	Best Student	Someone who has enjoyed the class and says so on the teacher evaluation (i.e., the "tip").
	Battle cry	"We are here to *serve* people and fulfill their needs."
Production		
	Curriculum	Production
	Student	Raw material
	Teacher	Highly skilled technician
	Status	Technicians get their status from their expertise and their ability to mold students.
	Outcome	Depends on students' willingness, commitment, and ability to "fit a mold" that has been carefully designed.
	Attributes	If means of production are wasteful they are discarded in favor of more efficient ones. The channeling of raw material is very important.
	Syllabus	Explicit, incremental, and timely
	Positive	Teacher is valued for specialized training and expertise and ability to mold students. Product is emphasized over process. Image of competent teacher.
	Negative	Cold and mechanistic with product being emphasized over process.
	Hallmarks	Time is of the essence. Operations of equipment and/or technique is critical. "There is probably one best way of doing what is done."
	Best Student	Someone who is a clone: A person who professes the values we profess, edits tape the way we edit tape, writes news leads the way we write news leads.
	Battle cry	"We are here to *train* people in our image!"

TABLE 7.2 *(continued)*

Metaphor Type	Educational Issue	Analogy or Educational Implications
Growth		
	Curriculum	Greenhouse
	Student	One of a wide variety of plants
	Teacher	Wise and patient gardener
	Status	Gardeners get status based on their knowledge of students and their ability to bring out the potential in each student.
	Outcome	Depends on the inherent qualities of each plant.
	Attributes	The gardener treats each according to its needs so that each plant comes to flower. This universal blooming cannot be accomplished by leaving some plants unattended.
	Syllabus	Variations of projects of their own choosing. Experimentation is celebrated over industry job training.
	Positive	Teacher is valued for ability to bring out the best in each student. Image of caring teacher.
	Negative	Too "flippy-trippy." Not appropriate in courses where there are hard facts and specific skills to be learned. Might be appropriate for kindergarten but not the army.
	Hallmarks	Students need to be celebrated for themselves. Learning is a process of becoming.
	Best student	Someone who develops to his or her full potential. The best students are as varied as the flowers in our gardens.
	Battle cry	"We are here to *nurture and cultivate* people's inherent qualities!"
Route		
	Curriculum	Route
	Student	Traveller
	Teacher	Experienced guide and companion
	Status	Guides/companions get status based on their knowledge of the terrain and on their ability to lead others past hidden pitfalls to gems of ideas, knowledge, and wisdom.
	Outcome	Depends as much on the traveller as the guide and the route.
	Attributes	A great effort is made to plot the route so that the journey will be as rich, as fascinating, and as memorable as possible.
	Syllabus	Students are taken through highlights of the subject matter. Assignments will bring out key issues, ideas, and experiences. It's important that students are there for the trip.
	Positive	Being able to point out critical issues, and so on. Image of adventurous, well-travelled teacher.
	Negative	Trips may be superficial. How can trips and guides be evaluated?
	Hallmarks	Students have a responsibility for their education. Variability of experiences are not only inevitable, but wondrous and desirable.
	Best student	Someone who works as hard as the guide to ponder and understand the lay of the land.
	Battle cry	"We are here to *guide and accompany* students in their quest for understanding!"

universities, the courses and curricula are developed by "experts" in the field such as the Public Relations Society of America, and the teacher is seen as the server of the "food." Sometimes the "expert" is the textbook. Some teachers are better at serving food than others.

This metaphor, like the others, implies an advising function. The server metaphor assumes advising only when asked for by the customer. In your better restaurants, allowing the server to recommend food and drink selection is part of the experience. Students might voluntarily choose to let the server/advisor plan the meal/course selection.

In the cafeteria metaphor, education is a quantifiable transaction: Students pay for their experiences and tip the teachers with their student evaluations. At its best, students are empowered to select exactly what they need to build the kind of educational program that is tailor-made for them. At its worst, education becomes one superficial experience after another, where students' programs have no underlying academic integrity. Or, they become so "major intensive" that students lack a solid breadth of experiences. Ultimately, a course or curriculum that is completely consumer driven does a disservice to the students in the program. We believe this approach works against the New Professionalism.

Production Metaphor: Teacher as Technician

Of the four metaphors this is the most mechanistic approach to teaching and, therefore, the least appropriate for the New Professionalism. In this metaphor, "the curriculum is the means of production, and the student is the raw material that will be transformed into a finished product under the control of a highly skilled technician" (Kliebard, 1972, p. 403). This factory metaphor seems to be a popular one in the age of accountability, where production and end products are valued (e.g., the idea of a university being a research mill).

On the positive side, teachers who are technicians have probably been through specialized training and are valued for their training, degrees, and experience. A negative stereotype of "technicians" is that they are cold, mechanistic, and perfectionistic to a fault and are more concerned with the end product than the process, more concerned with developing students who have specific characteristics than bringing out the unique characteristics of each student. They have reputations for not seeing the big picture, for being less abstract and conceptual, more bureaucratic and narrow visioned.

At best, courses developed using this metaphor would be explicit, incremental, and timely. So-called skills courses lend themselves to this metaphor. Production and writing courses are sometimes seen as occupational "training" grounds for specialized positions in the trades where students go through exercises replicating the different mainstream production forms. For example, in television production, the technician teacher might require students to run through different positions on numerous pieces of equipment. These same students might be graded on their ability to run the equipment during specific exercises (i.e., camera operation grade, switcher grade, audio board grade, etc.). In media writing, it might mean that students practice the different forms of writing.

Teachers might argue that "there is probably one best way of doing what we are doing and that is the way that I learned when I was in the business." *Why* something is done (e.g., pan a camera) may be sacrificed for *how* to do it. As an advisor, the technician-teacher would be expected to dictate what a student should take, requiring specific courses for all specialties and subspecialties.

The downside of this metaphor outweighs the upside. To prepare students for the New Professionalism, classrooms, including production classrooms, need to be for exploration, for challenging and understanding principles rather than for the rote memorization of production positions, content, or forms. In the production metaphor, the best students become clones of their teachers. Students profess the values the teacher professes. They direct the way their teachers direct. They write news leads the way their teacher writes news leads. The outcomes are clear, measurable, and predictable. Because the New Professionalism looks for student outcomes that lead to self-direction and individual initiative, this metaphor is ultimately self-defeating (see Grow, 1990, 1991, and discussion later in this chapter).

Growth Metaphor: Teacher as Gardener

In this metaphor, "the curriculum is the greenhouse where students will grow and develop to their fullest potential under the care of a wise and patient gardener" (Kliebard, 1972, p. 403). The image of the nurturing teacher is an appealing one and as long as it encourages individuality, creativity, and caring, this approach fits into the goals of the New Professionalism. However, as will be discussed below, due to the uneven power relationship between teachers and students suggested by this growth metaphor, it is not the ideal metaphor for the New Professionalism.

The first metaphor assumes that students will come to teachers who will satisfy their appetites. The teachers may not be experts in their fields, but they should be good servers. The second metaphor assumes that students come to teachers to learn what the teachers know, to be molded and shaped into a communication professional. The garden metaphor assumes that students have innate qualities and passions that need to be cultivated and directed. Teachers do not teach people, they facilitate learning. On the positive side, the garden metaphor is a rich, pleasing analogy. Unlike farmers, who are involved in agriculture on a large scale, gardeners appear to be more like amateurs than professionals. They are present not so much to make pronouncements and to profess that everything and everybody should be alike, but to understand and interpret the total picture.

On the negative side, the gardener may be seen as being too "flippy-trippy" in the age of agribusiness. In a time of commodity future's trading where the world's markets are humming 24 hours a day, the gardener metaphor seems somewhat quaint. If it is true that "all plants are nurtured with great solicitude, but no attempt is made to divert the inherent potential of the individual plant from its own metamorphosis or development to the whims and desires of the gardener" (p. 403), then a question arises about the exact role of the gardener-teacher. Why have specialists when all we need are facilitators? In the classroom, the gardener-teacher might suggest that certain projects are due on certain dates but leaves the direction of the project open to the student. Less time is spent getting the student to fit into an industry job description and more time is devoted to letting the students experiment. This approach might get high grades for allowing creativity.

Questions about this metaphor might arise with the idea of evaluation. How do you evaluate students within the garden metaphor? If each plant is unique, then do you grade on "growth," on the potential for growth, or on some idealized conception of what a plant "at this stage in its development" should look like?

A provocative thing about metaphors is that they are both precise, specifying a relationship, and open to multiple interpretations and different elaborations. It may be, for example, shocking to the one gardener teacher that first graders could be getting "Fs" for assignments instead of "smiley faces." Another gardener might argue that good gardeners pull out weeds and keep pests away so that the plants designated as desirable have a better chance of thriving. Here the garden metaphor turns from Kliebard's "students will grow and develop to their fullest potential under the care of a wise and patient gardener" to "*some* students will grow and develop, whereas others must be sacrificed for the good of some ideal." Of course, one person's "orchid" is another person's weed. The New Professionalism celebrates the idea that people are unique with individual strengths and weaknesses. Therefore, the garden metaphor, the idea of creating supportive environments where individuals can flourish under the caring eyes of faculty has great appeal. The media workshops, discussed in chapters 3 and 6, would be an appropriate place for the garden metaphor. The media workshops allow students to "kick tires" and experiment under a low-risk, low-threat environment. Practitioner practices, forms, and content are investigated and used to give an understanding, a perspective, about the media environment in which students live.

Travel Metaphor: Teacher as Guide

Here "the curriculum is a route over which students will travel under the leadership of an experienced guide and companion" (Kliebard, 1972, p. 403). We believe this metaphor best describes the goals of the New Professionalism because it has the positive characteristics associated with the garden metaphor together with an equal power-status relationship in which students are held responsible for their own education.

Developed from the root meaning of *curriculum,* "course," or the course run, the idea of curriculum as a "route" may conjure up images of exotic places, snow-capped mountains, and rain-drenched forests, either superficial visits by tourists to Disney's Epcot Center, or the beginning of a life-long immersion in another culture, another time, and place. Guides get status based on their knowledge of the terrain and their ability to lead others past hidden pitfalls to gems of ideas, knowledge, and wisdom.

In this metaphor, the teacher is not simply a guide but a companion. The teacher is not trying *to do* anything *to* the students. This teacher is pointing out the key landmarks that presumably the student has taken the course to understand. "Each traveller will be affected differently by the journey since its effect is at least as much a function of the predilections, intelligence, interests, and intent of the traveller as it is of the contours of the route. This variability is not only inevitable, but wondrous and desirable" (pp. 403–404). The teaching burden is to lead and point people in the right direction. Whereas the presentation is important for the server, the product is important for the technician, and the plant is important for the gardener, the journey is critical for the guide and companion. The guide, characterized by dispassion, does not change or nurture, but helps students get to where they want and need to be if they wish to be considered expert travellers themselves. But the ultimate responsibility for experiencing the educational trip is the students. The guide-teacher can only do so much and need not be held accountable if the student does not take advantage of the trip. As an advisor, advice is freely given and freely received.

At its best, the guide and companion might be a mentor in a quality undergraduate or graduate program; someone who is still excited by the terrain and the new things to be discovered each time (s)he travels it. At its worst, the guide is a disheartened, weary traveller who no longer has the eyes to see the newness, the heart to feel the excitement. Of course, from the technician's viewpoint accountability is also a problem. What kind of outcomes do we expect from the trip? How is the trip evaluated? How does an outside accrediting body know when a teacher is a poor guide?

Perhaps this metaphor more than any of the others helps us make a distinction between teaching and learning. The server equates teaching and student evaluations: "I know I've been a good teacher because my student evaluations tell me so." The technician equates teaching and learning: "I know I've been a good teacher because it is evident from how well my students do on their tests." For some technicians, the test material and the course material are one in the same thing. They teach for the test. The guide/companion, like the gardener, sees a variety of ways of evaluating outcomes.

The guide and companion knows that teaching is not the same as learning. Students should be in school because they want to be in school. They should be in classes because they want to be in classes. Students should be excited by the journey, to learn what they need to learn. For administrative purposes, the guide tests the students to make sure that they made the journey and noticed the high points, but the real obligation for learning falls back on the shoulders of the student. Education becomes an adventure with no mind-numbing, prescribed, lock-step outcome characteristic of the media occupation or technical sequence. There are outcomes, but there are a lot of exciting and interesting ways of reaching those outcomes, it is the process, that is integral to the education.

It should be noted that the travel metaphor is not a *laissez-faire* approach to education. A guide has an obligation to be prepared and experienced. In a television production course, for example, it might mean structuring the course to hit the high points (e.g., conceptualization, visualization, scripting, camera blocking, lighting, audio) without worrying that each student rotates through each equipment position. It might mean experiencing courses as laboratories where the teacher interacts with the students to experiment about lighting, or audio, or the best way to write an opening to a magazine feature article. Most important, this model acknowledges students' rights, obligations, and responsibility for their own education.

Teaching Metaphors: Power and Status

As suggested, each of the four metaphors suggests a different dynamic between the teacher and student. The production metaphor suggests that the student has very little power or status. At best, the student is positioned as an apprentice. At worst, the student is an "illiterate" cog. Students, for whatever reason, either by choice or by rule or regulation, find themselves in the presence of someone who sees his or her role to mold supple minds. "I'm the expert (i.e., boss) and you're here to learn."

In the garden metaphor, the dynamic continues to be somewhat uneven. At best, the student develops under the eyes of a caring teacher. At worst, the student has to deal with *in loco parentis* where the teacher becomes a surrogate parent. In terms of who has power and status, this parent-child relationship ultimately favors the parent.

The guide metaphor, because of the insertion of the word "companion," assumes more equality than the first two. At its best, the student has "volunteered" for the trip, and the teacher, who has dedicated his/her life to exploring the terrain, wants to show the traveller the high points while avoiding potential dead-end logic and foggy thinking. At its worst, the student is being forced to take the trip (i.e., required course) and resents every mile. In the consumer metaphor, power and status have been reversed. Whereas students respect their technician teachers, love their gardener teachers, or follow their guide teachers, here they demand better service, service that is expected to cater to the numerous fast-food whims of adolescent appetites.

STUDENT OUTCOMES

What should endure from the educational trip? Gerald Grow (1990, 1991) criticized curricular discussion for not emphasizing the need to teach students higher order skills. He made a strong case for a teaching style that moves students away from dependence and toward self-direction. This is consistent with the New Professionalism's goal for developing a liberally educated practitioner. Strong teachers invoking the travel metaphor may use a variety of strategies as they move students toward thoughtful responsibility and self-reliance. Grow (1990, p. 3) suggested, "The teacher's purpose is to match the learner's stage of self-direction and prepare the learner to advance to higher stages." Grow's (1990) four stages are presented in Table 7.3 (from his Fig. 3):

Because schools have different missions, a variety of student outcomes would be expected. Outcomes can be simple and general. For example, Robert Finney of the California State University-Long Beach wrote from their mission statement: "Our basic goal is to turn out graduates who know

TABLE 7.3
Overview of the Staged Self-Directed Learning Model

Stage	Characteristic	Role of Teacher	Method
Stage 1	Dependent	Authority, coach	Coaching with immediate feedback. Drill. Informational lecture. Overcoming deficiencies and resistance.
Stage 2	Interested	Motivator, guide	Inspiring lecture plus guided discussion. Goal-setting and learning strategies.
Stage 3	Involved	Facilitator	Discussion facilitated by teacher who participates as equal. Seminar. Group projects.
Stage 4	Self-directed	Consultant, delegator	Internship, dissertation, individual work, or self-directed study-group.

how to: think, read, write, speak, listen, work with numbers, and investigate and solve problems, as well as have some basic knowledge of the fields of audio/radio, video/television, film." Or, as Samuel Becker from the University of Iowa wrote: "We operate under the assumption that there are a limited number of things that are basic to a liberal education: Students must learn to ask questions and must acquire the skills to answer those questions in a variety of ways." Or, this from an Oregon State University pamphlet: "The journalism department at Oregon State University has as its primary mission the education of 'Renaissance journalists'—writers and reporters who can compete in traditional journalism but who have in-depth knowledge of science and technology" ("Department of journalism," n.d., p. 1).

Some schools have developed very specific goals for student outcomes. Although we do not agree with all their "outcomes," a good example of a program that has developed very explicit outcomes is Southern Illinois University's School of Journalism. William R. Elliott wrote: "We decided to confront the problem of creating a new curriculum by developing a set of goals and objectives that could serve as a blueprint for a contemporary journalism and a mass communication program that could be developed using current resources." Using a variety of sources, SIU developed the following outcomes for students. To:

- develop critical thinking skills through exposure to the humanities, sciences, and social sciences;
- develop oral, written, and visual communication skills through exposure to language and literature, art, and design;
- develop an in-depth minor that complements their journalistic training. ("Journalism goals and objectives," n.d.)

They went on to state "Interpretive," "Gathering, Analysis, and Presentation," "Advertising," and "News-Editorial" Goals. For example, their advertising goals stated:

> The goal of the School of Journalism is to provide its students with theoretical and practical foundations relating to the study and practice of advertising. Students need an understanding of the ethical, legal, economic, and social contexts of advertising as well as basic creative, media, and research skills. Students need broad backgrounds preparing them for entry level positions within any area of the advertising industry. Students specializing in advertising will:
> • master the evaluative, editing, and production skills necessary for advertising professionals;
> • learn to think creatively and to apply creative thinking to writing and speech;

- develop skills in marketing, sales, and media planning. ("Journalism goals and objectives," n.d.)

The assessment of outcomes is, of course, difficult and needs to be thought through carefully (see chapter 8).

WHO GETS HIRED?

Samuel Becker, of the University of Iowa, wrote, "We have a simple-minded approach to hiring. We try to find the smartest people we can who are working on interesting problems relevant to communication." Hiring teachers, like other parts of the instructional package, should fit the needs and *vision* of the educational institution and unit. Faculty recruitment can be used to change units to stress what ought to be. As units try to follow their educational missions, who they hire is one more indication of a unit's ethos or culture. We asked unit heads what the trade-offs were that they made between professional experience, research expertise, and teaching. Actual hires depend a lot on intangibles like personality and availability of candidates. In most cases, schools walked the line between hiring people with industry and academic experience with some leaning more one way than the other (see Peirce & Bennett, 1990).

An analysis of responses suggested three broad stereotypical types of hires: the industry practitioner, the hybrid, and the academic. Seen in another way, a graph might be constructed with industry experience on one axis (Y) and scholarly experience on the other (X). Teaching experience could be a third axis (Z). Without considering teaching experience, people might be located somewhere within four quadrants (Fig. 7.1):

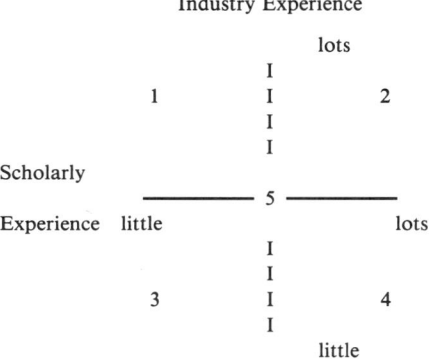

FIG. 7.1 Who gets hired?

The Industry Giant Hire (Position 1)

Those with a lot of professional experience and credentials but very little academic experience or credentials characterize this group. Position advertisements in such trade journals as *Advertising Age* would attempt to attract this kind of person. We would expect industry-oriented programs to have many of these people on their staff. These people are hired for a variety of reasons, one of which is their connections (i.e., placement credentials for the students).

For example, as Douglas Anderson, Director and Professor of the Cronkite School at Arizona State University wrote, "We are a professional program and our hires are consistent with that approach." Relying on their location in Tempe, Anderson noted: "The number of full-time faculty (modest) and the availability of truly first-rate adjuncts (bountiful, largely because of our metropolitan location in the Sun Belt) become variables when we search for new full-time hires." This doesn't mean that all of ASU's faculty could be categorized within one position. Again, as Anderson noted, "The Cronkite School is professionally oriented, but its faculty members increasingly are emerging as respectable scholars in a variety of areas. . . . The Cronkite School of Journalism and Telecommunication strives diligently to balance the world of the academic with the world of the practitioner. . . . Again, because we have a fairly modest full-time faculty base, we seek out faculty who blend professional and academic backgrounds."

The Superperson Hire (Position 2)

Administrators normally covet people who fall into this category. These are the people with years of industry experience plus a strong academic background. Even so, F. Dennis Hale, Director and Professor, from Bowling Green University worried about how the research/industry orientations would play out for his undergraduates: "I do, however, see a continuing conflict between research and professional experience. An active researcher does not have any time to remain active as a media practitioner." So even with the "super hire" it is not clear how effectively the practitioner/scholar can survive the culture of the academy. That is, once hired, they might tilt one direction or the other.

The MA/ABD Hire (Position 3)

A person who has a year or two of professional experience and an MA or is ABD might fall into this category. It is possible that this person is just beginning his or her academic career. In some schools, this might be the "filler" hire. The expectation is that these people will do well until someone with full academic credentials is hired. Although many students are given the advice to finish their PhD before they take a full-time job, this is not always personally or professionally possible. ABDs often come in at lower salaries than their PhD counterparts. This is seen as a plus at some schools.

In some schools, lip-service is paid to the PhD "union card." PhDs are preferred for administrative concerns (e.g., a push by the administration to have the faculty possess terminal degrees), but the orientation of the unit is actually anti-PhD. That is, the unit is anti academic scholarship. The conflict between industry and academic oriented faculty has been referred to as a debate between the "green-eye shades and the chi-squares" (see later in this chapter under "Hybrid Program.")

The Academic Hire (Position 4)

Samuel Becker, University of Iowa, suggested choices are difficult but that ultimately his faculty came down on the side of hiring people with strong academic credentials:

> "Like the rest of the faculty, I want any new hire to contribute to my education, as well as the education of our students. Professional experience is not an important criterion for most of our hires. I regret this at times; all else being equal, it would be good to have more faculty who understand how the industry works from the inside. . . .
>
> We find it almost impossible these days to find faculty members with the intellect and scholarly background and drive that we want who also have meaningful industry experience. And, when it comes down to a choice, we believe the former is far more important for our students than the latter."

The Hybrid Hire (Position 5)

The Hybrid hire was summed up by Robert Finney, Professor from the California State University-Long Beach, when he wrote: "We look for people with professional backgrounds in addition to the academic credentials." These are the people with a moderate amount of professional experience or expertise and a modest scholastic record. These might be new PhDs with three co-authored convention papers under their belt. The hybrid hire is not without its challenges. F. Dennis Hale of Bowling Green observed:

> We have continued to hire hybrid faculty who have some professional media experience *and* a research agenda and who are capable of teaching at the graduate and undergraduate levels. We are facing some retirements of persons

with strong media experience, and I fear that this strategy will eventually weaken the undergraduate program. . . .

My concern is that we can continue to hire a hybrid faculty with modest media experience and a strong research agenda. But this is tilted in favor of the graduate program, which has only 7 percent of our total students.

The Hybrid Program

R. C. Adams, Chair of the Department of Telecommunications the California State University-Fresno, wrote that a two-track hiring policy is the way to go. Some people are hired primarily for their industry experience, whereas others are hired primarily for their academic background: "In our 5-year plan, we have stipulated that we will always need at least two, probably three, faculty who have significant vocational experience in the media professions for which we prepare our students, regardless of whether they have the PhD. Under normal circumstances, we expect to fill all other positions with teacher-researchers in the academic mold."

Pennsylvania State University is another example of a Hybrid Program. Winston wrote: "We organize the School so that all of the scholarly persons would join together in a central scholarly mass communications department that had the dual responsibilities of both providing chalk and board courses for the four professional majors as well as servicing its own body of undergraduate and graduate students." This type of set-up, one that makes a distinction between "professional" faculty and "mass communication/research" faculty, is not without its dangers. Again, Winston wrote:

> The dangers here are obvious—we built into the system a divide between the green eye shade and the chi-squared faculty. However, my feeling was that these people had worked together long enough and that the requirements of the various degrees they were teaching would force them to continue to talk to each other in effective ways. What was less clear to me was that they would talk to their new colleagues from broadcasting and film, etc., etc. My sense of this is that it has worked rather well. . . . I think if we speak and talk together we might produce a generation of students for whom these divisions are less apparent than they are to us.

A theme of the book is the need for program diversity that does not fragment the study of mass communication. As Winston has pointed out, "If we speak and talk together we might produce a generation of students for whom theses divisions are less apparent than they are to us." Whether it is a hybrid program or a program that hires hybrid teachers, the need to present students with an integrated, expansive view of communication needs to be central.

ADVISING

Donald Brod emphasized the importance of advising when he wrote, "The new curriculum requires more careful advising on the part of the faculty. In the past, once students chose a sequence, all they had to do was follow the catalog. Now they have more choices — and need more advice."

As the material from Michigan State University suggested: "A student of telecommunication can premise career plans on the growth of the field as long as the student carefully chooses courses, academic and career directions, extracurricular activities and is willing to spend long hours at complex but highly interesting work" (Michigan State University Department of Telecommunications packet, n.d.). Ultimately, a student's education is the responsibility of the student, but advising can play a key role in enhancing the success of students. Whether the advisor is the teacher, as is found in many small- and medium-size schools, or is a hired staff person, advising is critical for student well-being.

There has been a two-pronged thrust throughout the book. On one hand we have called for diversity and freedom from the rigid, mechanized grasp of sequences or their equivalent. On the other hand, we have called for strong cores and a commitment to general education by providing seminal perspectives about and from the discipline. The balance between a smorgasbord approach to education, the "Consumer Metaphor," and the factory approach, the "Production Metaphor," is not always easy to meet. That is one of the reasons why advising is so important. The "Travel Metaphor," which suggests that the teacher is both a guide and an advisor, is appealing because it promotes the student as being self-directed, yet allows for the important advising and motivating aspects of the educational experience.

Advising, mentoring, teaching. Without interesting, interested, and informed teachers, the potential for any curricular reform, the potential for a New Professionalism, will wither on the vine.

8 Accountability and Accreditation

I think accreditation tends more to discourage innovation and ignore institutional diversity in the application of its standards to the schools. And despite efforts to streamline the process, accreditation is still a heavy burden for schools to bear in terms of time, effort and expense.
—Vernon Keel (1991, p. 4)

Editors dismiss courses in journalism history, theory, research and mass communication as unimportant, yet those are precisely the courses likely to develop the critical skills of analysis and problem-solving so highly desired [by them]. They stress the importance of a broad liberal arts education, yet want journalism schools to emphasize professional skills courses in classrooms dominated by media professionals who lack training in much else.
—Arnold Ismach (1990, p. 2)

Building bridges, integrating disciplines, coordinating and allocating resources, developing teaching and learning strategies—the New Professionalism, like any other curricular perspective, should be subject to evaluation. To alleviate what has been perceived as a major educational problem, as is evidenced by everything from low student test scores to low productivity (see chapter 1), legislatures and institutions alike have turned to outcomes assessment. In this chapter we discuss outcomes assessment strategies and accreditation. We present a rationale for those seeking alternatives to the current accreditation system which, as it existed in the early 1990s, was working against the New Professionalism.

OUTCOMES ASSESSMENT

Outcomes assessment will become more the rule than the exception in higher education. As David Clark, Colorado State University, wrote, "Our state legislature recently mandated 'outcomes assessment' procedures for all schools. We've drafted ours, which are aimed at using accreditation procedures where possible." However, the call of outcomes assessment does not necessarily mean that the procedure will impact at the unit level. As Jo Ann Albers of Western Kentucky University noted, "In recent years we've been asked to develop an outcomes assessment program. That has caused some changes in the way we do things but not in what we do."

Although not always successful, desirable, or clearly defined, addressing outcomes assessment helps a unit focus its attention on its goals. There are many ways programs can perform outcome assessment. As with other areas of the curriculum, our call in this chapter is for diversity.

> "Outcomes assessment" is the term generally applied to methods used to determine the effectiveness and consequences of the formal educational processes in higher education. Encouraged or mandated by politicians and administrators, faculties have been attempting to ascertain the effectiveness of curricula, specific courses, methods of instruction and the accomplishments of their students and alumni in an effort to respond to the calls for accountability in higher education. (Eshelman, 1991, p. 2)

Every time a student takes a test or completes a project, outcomes assessment is taking place. What concerns some is that the outcomes from individual courses do not always add up at the end of 4 years of undergraduate education to an educated person. What many wonder is whether curricula as a whole are providing exciting, interesting, useful, and testable experiences (see Caudill, Ashdown, & Caudill, 1990). Those in higher education are being asked to be accountable for what and how they teach. Ervin (1988), for example, identified six major recommendations from the National Governors Association that will have an impact on assessment. Many of the recommendations call for a re-emphasis on undergraduate education. These recommendations state that Governors, state legislatures, state coordinating boards, and institutional governing boards should:

1. Clearly define the role and mission of each institution of public higher education in their state. Governors should also encourage the governing board of each independent college to clearly define its mission.
2. Reemphasize the fundamental importance of undergraduate instruction — especially in universities that give high priorities to research and graduate instruction.
3. Adjust funding formulas for public colleges and universities to provide incentives for improving the learning of undergraduate students, based on the results of comprehensive assessment programs. Independent colleges and universities should be encouraged to do likewise.
4. Reaffirm their strong commitment to access to public higher education for students from all socioeconomic backgrounds.
5. Implement systematic programs that use multiple measures to assess the

learning of undergraduates. The information gained from such assessments should be used to evaluate the quality of the institution and of this program. Information about institutional and program quality should also be made available to the public.
6. Require colleges and universities to collect and use information about student outcomes among undergraduates. Demonstrating levels of student learning and performance should be considered for institutional accreditation. (pp. 19–23; different order)

In a recent study of 180 Association of Schools of Journalism and Mass Communication (ASJMC) schools in which 91 participated, 25 schools, or 27.5%, said that they either had operative outcomes assessment programs or were "in the process of exploring and/or establishing formal systems of assessment for their academic units" (Eshelman, 1991, p. 3). Eshelman identified ten assessment strategies, gave examples of schools that used the different strategies, and critiqued each strategy (for other discussions of assessment see Denham, 1988; Guterman, 1991a; Harwood, 1985; Hutchings & Reuben, 1988; Linn, 1989; Terenzini, 1989; Westling, 1988). Part of that paper is summarized in the following discussion.

Assessment Strategies

Formal Course Evaluation. Evaluations of teachers and courses is standard fare in higher education. As controversial as they are prolific, formal course evaluation is one way of determining if students think they are learning (cf. Thayer, 1990). An advantage of this approach is that it takes place after each course and can give a sense of overall improvement of the teaching in a unit. A disadvantage is taking the evaluations as "gospel" to be used as the only tool faculty evaluation. (For a discussion about variables that might affect course excellence in newspaper writing courses see Stone, 1990).

Exit Test. Another way of assessing outcomes is through an exit exam during the senior year. As with all assessment strategies, the major problem is determining what to assess. The field is so broad and there are so many ways of approaching mass communication, that "tests" are difficult to develop. Eshelman (1991, p. 18) argued that comprehensive senior exams "would be considered a 'barrier' assessment instrument (if you pass you don't graduate) as contrasted to a 'facilitative' assessment strategy (improvement plans based on data derived)." Some schools use the Graduate Record Examination (GRE) as an exit test. The problem with the GRE, according to Eshelman, is that it is not "discipline specific." An advantage of GRE tests or their equivalent is that the results can be compared nationally.

The Exit Interview. A variation on the exit test is the exit interview. Here students submit portfolios or make presentations to the faculty and can be asked questions about their work. The advantage of this approach is that it allows for a very thorough evaluation. A disadvantage is that it is very time consuming for students and faculty alike.

The Capstone Course. It is very appealing to have classes or experiences that pull together 4 years of what a student has learned. The University of Kansas School of Journalism and Mass Communication

> requires exit interviews with a representative sample of graduating seniors; assessment of interns by employers; and capstone courses with a product (Advanced Reporting and Advanced Editing on University Daily Kansan, Magazine Layout Production on Jayhawk Journalist, Advertising Campaigns, and Special Projects in Broadcasting which involves a product and an internship). Also, student success in national competitions in all sequences is used as an assessment indicator. . . . (Eshelman, 1991, p. 6)

The capstone experience may be difficult for broadbased programs due to the problem of integrating diverse experiences.

The Professional Portfolio. The professional portfolio does not have to be a function of one course but rather is developed throughout a student's 4 years. The advantage of this strategy is that it prepares the students for their job interviews. The disadvantage is that it tends to stress only one part of mass communication: the production part.

The Professional Advisory Council. For those who have capstone courses, or require professional portfolios, an advisory board can be a useful, outside forum for critiquing a student's work. (Units that have developed practica—see chapter 6—might find a practitioner's critique of projects informative.) Besides being used to critique student projects, some units use the advisory council for a variety of outcomes assessment concerns. Although we are opposed to practitioners telling the academy how to teach our mass communication students, Eshelman (1991) identified several possible advantages: "Some of the functions of the advisory council can be to review the curriculum; provide resources to the faculty for guest speakers and/or field trips; review course syllabi to determine the adequacy of the objectives, methods and assignments; evaluate the adequacy of the facilities of the unit; and assist the unit in making recommendations to the central administration for improvement of the program" (pp. 13-14). A disadvantage of the professional advisory council is coordinating very busy practitioners. And, as in any attempt to move away from the unit to "outside" people, it is not always easy to communicate mission, philosophy, ethos, and expectations to others who come to the experience with their own assumptions.

The Internship. For applied areas, the internship has been used by some schools to assess success. As with the professional advisory council, practitioners are often given the task of evaluation. An advantage of this approach is that it verifies whether or not a student has learned "practitioner values." A disadvantage is that it abdicates the faculty's responsibilities for evaluation unless the internship experience is separated from the student's careful critique of the experience (see chapter 6).

Regional/National Competitions. A natural extension of the internship or portfolio outcome assessment strategies is to have students actively participate in regional or national competitions. Eshelman (1991) identified several disadvantages with this approach, the most severe being established through the asking of a question: "Are courses being utilized to facilitate entry in competitions, and in this way are competitions replacing the curricular intentions of the courses?" (p. 24). Orienting a course around competitive student products/projects may not serve the students.

The Alumni/Employer Survey. Asking alumni what they think about the program gives former students the time to reflect on their 4 years. Eshelman suggested that "this technique is one of the most common forms of outcomes assessment utilized by departments and universities. The testimony of alumni and/or employers regarding the adequacy of the educational experience can be useful in outcomes assessment" (p. 12). A problem with this kind of strategy is that what students see as successful after 3 months to 30 years after college varies depending on "numerous intervening variables" (p. 12).

Accreditation Standards. As will be clear from our discussion later in this chapter, we think the accreditation standards need to be modified. This does not mean that all of accreditation needs to be thrown out with our critique. It can be beneficial to units to seek accreditation (see Oukrop & Parsons, 1991). As Eshelman (1991) pointed out: "The twelve standards for accreditation have a myriad of outcomes assessment implications. Those, if identified and met, can accomplish two goals: first, the establishment of an extensive and identified outcomes assessment strategy for the discipline, and second, the attaining of the stature and validation of the program which discipline specific accreditation carries" (p. 24).

Outcomes assessment, or some variation of it, seems to be or will soon be a reality for many mass communication units. In order to build bridges between the academy and a public that is looking for the academy to be accountable, units need to be able to show a variety of "clients" that what they do has value. What is needed is a coherent, logical, defensible strategy that takes into account a variety of outcomes assessment measures. And, as we wrote in chapter 5, a good place to start with outcomes assessment is to try and articulate a unit's mission and all that implies.

ACCREDITATION

The accreditation of programs in communication and media education is under the exclusive jurisdiction of the Accrediting Council on Education in Journalism and Mass Communications (ACEJMC). This jurisdiction is both protected and periodically reviewed and evaluated by the Council on Post-secondary Accreditation (COPA) (cf. Keel, 1988; Mullins, 1988). Accreditation, because its purpose is to certify whether professional programs meet prescribed standards and follow certain guidelines, tends to support the status quo. Its evaluation criteria do not call for change. ACEJMC's standards, against which programs are evaluated, include such matters as governance, budget, student records, instruction, faculty, equipment, public service, minorities and female representation (see Ford, 1987; Gutierrez, 1987; Hall & Ruggles, 1987), alumni, and curriculum (see Hoskins, 1988).

Being accredited does not guarantee that a program will be spared intensive scrutiny on its own campus, including calls for its elimination. Iowa State University's journalism program, which has been a model of an accredited department, has been under attack from within its own institution. Another journalism program at Oregon State University, which was repeatedly re-accredited for years, was simply eliminated as not essential to the mission of that university. As cited earlier, accreditation guidelines are too inflexible. Contrary to the claims of ACEJMC, we think accreditation works against the intended result of providing students with a broad-based education. The bottom line for communication and media education is that being accredited is not necessarily a positive assessment in the reformed university or the New Professionalism (see Wartella, 1992).

Challenging Accreditation

In 1980, the ACEJMC began to redesign its accreditation standards. Before drafting, debating, and finally agreeing on 12 new standards, the Council approved a statement of philosophy of accreditation ("Accredited journalism," 1991). The general principles were designed "to recognize, protect and ensure the integrity of the academic institutions that participate in the accrediting process" (p. 4), and to protect institutional diversity and the "spirit of liberal education" (p. 6).

The new standards and the manner in which they are interpreted and enforced are, in fact, contrary to principles of diversity and integrity of institutions, to the development of both the spirit and integregation of liberal arts in communication and media education units, and to the development of curricular innovation.

As Vernon Keel (1991), a long-time member of the ACEJMC wrote:

> Before we began our discussion of proposed changes in our standards and procedures, members of the council approved a statement of our philosophy of accreditation. This was important to us then and it should be important now because it is an expression of our underlying beliefs in what accreditation should foster and accomplish. It is published each year in the accrediting booklet. This statement of philosophy proposes, among other things, that accreditation in our field should foster innovation, respect institutional diversity and not be an undue burden for our schools. As I participated in the debate and later watched the council grapple with issues, it seems to me that this basic philosophy is not being respected. In fact, I think accreditation tends more to discourage innovation and ignore institutional diversity in the application of its standards to the schools. And despite efforts to streamline the process, accreditation is still a heavy burden for schools to bear in terms of time, effort and expense. (p. 4)

One of the most restricting standards of the ACEJMC is the "liberal arts standard," which limits the number of courses communications students can enroll for in the major. The "spirit of liberal education" is expressed through an illiberal formula that requires that "students take a minimum of 90 semester hours in courses *outside* the major area of journalism and mass communication, with no fewer than 65 semester hours *in the liberal arts and sciences*" ("Accredited journalism," 1991, p. 6, italics added).

This standard has created a 25-hour grey area, consisting of courses that have to be outside the communication unit but which do not have to be liberal arts. So, for example, students could take courses in another professional area, such as business or nursing—as long as it is outside the communication major and as long as they take 65 hours in the "traditional liberal arts." This grey area, in effect allows the student to take *any subject other than communication.*

This standard stated, in effect, that all courses in the communication unit are nonliberal arts and that "traditional liberal arts" are the only source of liberal education. As we found in chapter 1, there is nothing inherently "liberal arts" in the "traditional" humanities, and social and natural sciences. The standard's premise is that the liberal arts and communication and media education programs should be kept separate. As we pointed out in chapter 3, this position is out of step with contemporary thinking among authorities in undergraduate reform. The Carnegie Foundation, (Boyer, 1987), Syracuse University (Marsh, 1988), University of Michigan ("Strengthening the ties," 1988), and American Association of Colleges (AAC, 1985) studies have concluded that distinctions between professional and liberal studies not only are artificial but that their continued separation and antagonisms will destroy undergraduate education. They call for the "mixing," "blending," or "integration" of the two realms. They also found that liberal and professional outcomes overlap considerably.

The ACEJMC's position ignored the fact that, in our time, new media elevated the study of communication and media to a high level of importance in human society. A key component in any liberal undergraduate education for the information society—the liberal arts of the 21st century—will have to include study of media technology, professions, institutional systems and other aspects of media and social problems that result from the impacts of new communication technologies.

As we discussed in chapter 3, the liberal arts standard ignores that a new discipline of communication is emerging on major campuses where its PhD programs and research are recognized and respected by the other academic disciplines. But, at least partially because of accrediting standards, this level of achievement has not been matched at the undergraduate level, where instruction has been greatly restricted to teaching occupational perspectives and skills. As we have argued earlier, undergraduate programs must expand their teaching of these broader concepts and issues if they are to achieve a position of intellectual leadership on campus. Equally important is the need to offer students a broad-based conceptual map of the field that systematically considers theoretical underpinnings, connections with the sciences and liberal arts ("Planning for curricular change," 1987).

Liberal Outcomes Enrichment Electives

The restrictive aspects of the liberal arts standard would be greatly reduced if units applying for ACEJMC accreditation were allowed to designate Liberal Outcomes Enrichment Electives (LOEE) that could be counted by communication and media education majors as part of the 90 hours "outside the unit" (in the 25-hour grey area allowed for non-"traditional liberal arts and science" coursework).

This allowance would be contingent on the unit demonstrating in its self-study that the LOEE substantially contribute to liberal outcomes and enrich the major. The self-study must also clearly demonstrate and document how the LOEE are consistent with the curricular missions, policies, and practices of the unit and its college or university, and consistent with authoritative, national criteria and standards on liberal outcomes and enrichment of the major.

This flexibility would not dilute the "spirit of the liberal arts" because it would not alter the requirement that 65 hours be taken in the "traditional" liberal arts and sciences. In fact, it would potentially expand liberal education, because units would have to demonstrate, for instance, that up to, 12 hours in the 25-hour nonliberal arts grey area meet liberal education criteria. Under the present application, none of the 25 hours is required to have any redeeming liberal education value whatsoever.

The proposal would require any exception to the 90-hour rule to be made only for reasons that, in the council's judgment made after due process, would result in more, not less, liberal education. It would be a more even-handed way of making exceptions to the liberal arts standard. At some meetings attended by the first author, the ACEJMC reaccredited some programs that technically violated the 90-hour rule. But, in at least one case, it granted accreditation because of the visitation committee's subjective judgment that the unit's students "were getting a good liberal arts education." We believe an openly stated and even-handed allowance for exceptions would be fairer, more orderly, and structured. It would require units to justify any additional hours by linking them not only with generally accepted standards of liberal outcomes and enrichment, but also with the mission of their university or college, which reflects different geographic mandates and other factors that make them distinctive. This proposal would allow for, or at least not inhibit, the innovation and pluralism our general principles say ACEJMC should be fostering. It rests on the belief, supported in chapter 1, that "liberal arts" is ultimately defined by outcomes.

Identifying Liberal Enrichment Outcomes

A great deal of literature on what constituted liberal arts has been generated, dating back to the classical tradition. The resulting generic criteria have been fairly uniform both over time and across the philosophical/political spectrum. Authoritative liberal-outcome criteria are readily available and could be used by the ACEJMC in its deliberations.

We suggested earlier that communication and media education has a variety of ways in which it could generate liberal outcomes. These are not limited to one curriculum component, for experiential learning has important liberal elements. The conceptual enrichment component of communication and media education, however, is the "flagship" for liberal outcomes and for the discipline's involvement in campus-wide liberal education.

As a first step toward the development of liberal outcomes in this curriculum component, we compared the Oregon Report's recommendations with liberal outcomes synthesized in the Carnegie (Boyer, 1987) and

Michigan Professional Preparation Network ("Strengthening the ties," 1988) reports, summarized in chapter 1. The Oregon Report includes eight conceptual enrichment areas in any model curriculum ("Planning for curricular change," 1987, pp. 48-55):

1. mass communication and society—a conceptual map of the literature and documented experience that explains the relationship of media to society and to individuals in society;
2. historical aspects—an overview both in conceptual and chronological terms of the history and traditions of mass communication, its institutions, people and enterprises, with a strong linkage to intellectual, cultural and economic history;
3. economic aspects—an examination of the economic basis of media activity in the U.S. and worldwide, and structural analysis of media institutions tied to economic history and microeconomics political economy;
4. philosophical and ethical aspects—a cultural review of the values on which modern mass communication is based; theories of ethics and standards of professional practice, tying in university courses in philosophy and ethics;
5. legal and regulatory aspects—the system of freedom of expression under which media operate, communication law, regulatory patterns;
6. technological aspects—the relationship of mass communication to developments in communication technology; communication concerns; a contemporary portrait of new technology and its meaning for society and individualism; understanding about the consequences of the new technology; how its various manifestations are related to patterns of thinking and analysis;
7. communication theory—an advanced examination of the various theories of mass communication and the differing scholarly traditions from which they evolve. Scholarly methods and connections to other fields that study media and communication should be emphasized; and
8. international communication systems—comparison of the U.S. media system with other national systems and the emerging global system.

Most of these conceptual enrichment areas have obvious linkages with traditional disciplines. To the extent that the content of traditional academic disciplines are assumed to be liberal arts, certainly most of these conceptual enrichment areas are, too. But we agree with the authorities we cite in chapter 1 that outcomes and even method of presentation of content, more than the curriculum content itself, determine what is liberal education.

Although preliminary and speculative because of the potential diversity among individual reformed curricula, we find that outcomes are implied in these conceptual enrichment content areas when matched with Carnegie and Michigan outcomes. For example, outcomes such as acquaintance with the major institutions that "make up our world," understanding "the universal experiences of producing and consuming," and placing "work in larger context" (Boyer, 1987, pp. 92–99) could be linked to such areas as mass media and society, philosophical and ethical, economic and technological aspects, and comparative media systems, because they address one of the major institutional systems and important professional fields in our society.

Even at this exploratory stage, not much imagination is needed to match at least one communication conceptual enrichment outcome with some of the liberal outcome categories synthesized by the Michigan report:

Contextual competence, "an understanding of the societal context or environment in which one is living and working" . . . comprehending "complex interdependence between the profession and society." Potentially contributing areas: economic, technological, legal, philosophical and ethical aspects, and mass media and society;

Professional identity, "concern for improving the knowledge, skills, and values of the profession," which "parallels and supplements the liberal education goal of developing a sense of personal identity." Areas: communication theory, historical, philosophical and ethical aspects;

Professional ethics, "liberally educated individuals are expected to have developed value systems and ethical standards." Area: philosophical and ethical aspects;

Adaptive competence, "a liberally educated person has an enhanced capacity to adapt to and anticipate changes." Areas: technological, legal and historical aspects, communication theory;

Scholarly concern for improvement, "recognizing the need to increase knowledge and advance the profession through both theoretical and applied research." Area: communication theory; and

Motivation for continued learning, exploring and expanding personal, civic and professional knowledge and skills throughout a lifetime. "All knowledge . . . is liberal (i.e., it enlarges and liberates the mind) when it is committed to continuing inquiry" (Bell, 1968, p. 8). Area: communication theory.

Dressel's (1960) Carnegie Corporation-funded study of liberal and professional education established that there was "liberal arts content" in the conceptual communication and media education courses. It outlined four areas in which "elements in liberal education have been injected into professional journalism courses" (pp. 53–55). These include:

1. The interrelationship between media and society in a way "not unlike those social science courses which concentrate on a particular social

institution or issue and develop an examination in depth of factors involved and of possible ways of dealing with problems which arise." A course on the press or the media and society was noted as an example.

2. Problems and issues about which "a journalist may be expected to write," such as a course on "Interpretation of Contemporary Affairs," in which students conduct in-depth research on an issue "in order to organize and synthesize all of the different points of view." The "constant emphasis on writing and expression . . . is in itself in accord with the best tradition of the liberal arts."

3. The "increasing tendency to interpret" the field "broadly as a behavioral science or as mass communication . . . utilizing concepts, principles, and research findings" reflecting the field as a discipline in its own right. Courses cited as examples were "Communication Media Analysis, Theory of Mass Communications, Communication Research Design," which bring together a body of materials from statistics, psychology, economics, sociology and "organizing [them] in reference to the need for understanding and research in the field of communications."

4. Offerings that closely parallel, if not in fact duplicate, courses offered in traditional departments, such as "Journalistic Writing," corresponding to a course in short story writing in English (pp. 53–55; see also Cowdin, 1985 and Rowland, 1992)

Becoming More Intellectually Competitive

We believe the intellectual vitality of media education programs would benefit from the LOEE proposal. It would generate enrollments that would justify the offering of more conceptual courses. As a result, faculty would be assigned time to develop and teach such courses. This would attract and retain faculty with interests and capabilities for conceptual courses.

These practical considerations would lead to the emergence of a liberal ethos that goes beyond narrow occupational perspectives to broader intellectual views more consistent with the university tradition and more in concert with the academic community. With a stronger conceptual component—a "critical mass"—in the curriculum and the faculty, the media education units would be more intellectually active and competitive. That means more "brain power" to generate offerings for the general or core curriculum, more interdisciplinary collaboration with other disciplines and programs, and more elective courses to serve the interests of students campus-wide. In short, media education programs could join the intellectual mainstream of the university.

Students majoring in the unit seeking accreditation would benefit from the LOEE allowance. They would be encouraged to explore enriching theoretical, conceptual, and liberal aspects of media studies beyond their professional/craft instruction. This allowance would not require students to take additional hours in the major. It would *allow* them to take additional hours as enrichment electives that would serve as links to the liberal arts. Currently, ACEJMC denies students in accredited programs the opportunity to take electives in their major other than the one or two that might be available after the unit requirements in occupational craft courses are prescribed. The elective component of a student's degree program should be respected, not restricted, by the accreditation process and should allow up to the one-third of the student's degree program to be taken in the major as recommended by the leading authorities of undergraduate education.

How the LOEE Could be Implemented

The Department of Communication at Typical University, Midwest, USA, limits its majors to 30 hours because of ACEJMCs 90-hour rule. But, because of the intellectual caliber of its faculty and its desire to join the intellectual mainstream and revitalize the liberal arts on the campus, the Department proposes two Communication courses—Mass Media and Society and Mass Communication Ethics—to be included in Typical University's liberal arts "Common Curriculum," which all students are required to take. The university-wide Common Curriculum Faculty Committee is impressed with the intellectual, conceptual, and liberal arts content and approach in the courses, and it approves them. Because both courses are required of Communication majors, the faculty believes that its majors should be allowed to take up to 36 hours in the Department. This would exceed the 90-hour rule.

To justify to the ACEJMC the additional 6 hours that many of the majors would take, the Department does the following:

1. It presents evidence that the courses were reviewed and approved by the university-wide Common Curriculum Faculty Committee as meeting the university's liberal arts criteria. Because of this and because the courses meet that university's liberal arts mission and goals, the Department requests that the ACEJMC respect and recognize this certification; that it allow Communication majors to enroll in those courses without being penalized by not being able to take other courses in the Department, and that its major general principles of flexibility and pluralism be applied.

2. It presents appropriate liberal outcome categories identified by the Carnegie Foundation and the Association of American Colleges (AAC, 1985, pp. 15–24; Boyer, 1987, pp. 92–99). The liberal outcomes selected are Communication Competence (ability to read, write, speak, and listen to and use these processes effectively to acquire, develop, and convey ideas and information), Critical Thinking (ability to examine issues rationally, logi-

cally, and coherently), Contextual Competence (an understanding of the societal context or environment in which one is living and working; to comprehend the complex interdependence between one's profession and society and the ability to make judgments in light of historical, social, economic, scientific, and political realities), Personal and Professional Ethics (the development of value systems and ethical standards), Adaptive Competence (anticipating, adapting to, and promoting change).

3. It presents appropriate liberal outcome categories synthesized with liberal components in professional programs by the Professional Preparation Network Report ("Strengthening the ties," 1988, pp. 23–25), some of which parallel or overlap with the Carnegie and AAC outcomes. Other outcomes selected are Professional Identity (concern for improving the knowledge, skills, and values of one's profession, which both parallels and supplements the liberal education goal of developing a sense of personal identity), Leadership Capacity (exhibiting the capacity to contribute as a productive member of one's profession and assuming appropriate leadership roles, requiring intelligent, humane application of knowledge and skills), Scholarly Concern for Improvement (recognizing the need to increase knowledge and to advance the profession through both theoretical and applied research, fostering the spirit of inquiry, critical analysis, and logical thinking), and Motivation for Continued Learning (exploring and expanding personal, civic, and professional knowledge and skills through a lifetime, because all knowledge that enlarges and liberates the mind is liberal when it is committed to continuing inquiry).

4. The Department demonstrates how the two sets of nationally recognized liberal outcomes are reflected in the appropriate content, methods, and objectives of Mass Media and Society and Mass Media Ethics.

5. The Department demonstrates how these courses enrich the major, using the Carnegie Foundation's criteria (Boyer, 1987, p. 110): "What is the history and tradition of the field to be examined? What are the social and economic implications to be understood? What are the ethical and moral issues to be confronted."

The accrediting visitation team reviews the documentation supporting the justification for the 6 additional hours that the majors could take above the limit and makes its recommendation to the ACEJMC.

Finally, there have been several questions raised regarding this proposal that need to be addressed:

Wouldn't This Proposal Result in Fewer Skills Courses?

Not necessarily. The additional enrollments might justify new faculty positions. Or, more likely, the faculty would integrate the skills component of the curriculum along the lines recommended by the Oregon Report. Curriculum reform away from the industrial-based sequence system to a more generic skills curriculum component appropriate to the information age is long overdue in most media education programs.

How Does This Benefit the Media Professions and Industries?

As Chuck Sherman of the National Association of Broadcasters said at the ACEJMC meeting May 7, 1989, the media/communication professions and industries need all the help they can get. They should encourage the development of broad-based, innovative, intellectually competitive communication and media education programs to explore new avenues and provide new ideas, as well as media-knowledgeable graduates, for the information and media industries. If communication and media education departments don't grow into new conceptual and intellectual realms they probably will not survive. And the industry might suffer, also. With media education programs limited to training students in contemporary, but usually short-span or obsolete techniques, what departments would you assign the role of conducting research in and teaching about media?

Wouldn't Implementing This Proposal Require a Lot of Work?

It would require more thought and analysis. But it would require less bean counting. This shift in activity would be a more appropriate role for the type of people who serve as ACEJMC visitation and accrediting committees and council members. The proposal would require units seeking the 12-hour flexibility to clearly think through and articulate how certain courses would result in liberal outcomes and how they enrich, rather than narrow, the student's undergraduate experience. This would shift the documentation focus and efforts—and visitation and accrediting committee efforts and council discourse—from the counting of hours and enforcement of artificial liberal versus professional education distinctions, to substantial, intellectually compelling decision-making on a case-by-case basis.

EPILOGUE: ON WISCONSIN AND WICHITA STATE

The inflexibility of accreditation standards once again became apparent in December 1991 when the faculty of the School of Journalism and Mass

Communication at the University of Wisconsin, Madison voted not to seek reaccreditation of its program.

"Ideally we would like to remain an accredited program," said Robert Drechsel, Director of the school, "but the . . . curriculum standards . . . would force us to sacrifice the integrity of our program and limit flexibility for students . . ." ("Journalism school won't," p. 1).

The reaction of the University of Wisconsin administration to the journalism faculty's decision reflected a national reaction against specialized accrediting agencies (Leatherman, 1991), like ACEJMC. UW Chancellor Donna E. Shalala, for example, said she was "proud of my journalism school" for its faculty's decision not to seek reaccreditation.

"Some of these accrediting organizations are stepping over the line," she said. "It takes a first-rate program in a first-class university to stand up to these groups. . . . This won't be the last time," indicating other departments at Madison may take similar actions (Shively, 1991, p. 6A).

"Many administrators charge that the [specialized accrediting] groups operate like guilds," reported the *Chronicle of Higher Education*. "They promote the special interests of their professions, with little concern for the health of the whole institution, the critics argue" (Leatherman, 1991, p. 22).

We believe that, in the decade of the 1990s, specialized accreditation of undergraduate programs—as we know it—will decline in importance and power as undergraduate reforms we described in chapter 1 take hold in colleges and universities throughout the nation. We have argued that occupational specialism has inhibited the development of more integrative curricula.

In reaction to the decision by Wisconsin's faculty not to seek reaccreditation, the Association for Schools of Journalism Mass Communication (ASJMC), the national organization of administrators in the field, initiated a study of Standard 3 which we believe will lead to some changes in the direction of more flexibility. Although the result may be satisfactory to many programs, some, like Wisconsin, will be seeking alternatives to accreditation.

Wisconsin's journalism faculty considered alternatives before deciding to withdraw from accreditation. The decision followed an extensive review of the accreditation process, begun a year earlier by the JMC faculty. An ad-hoc committee studying accreditation concluded that an external review process was an extremely valuable tool for maintaining quality. As a result, the faculty began considering a set of general standards for the program, including a proposal to create an outside team of four members who would conduct an extensive review every 7 years. This external panel would include at least one person who represented the mass communication industry, one from an academic mass communication department and one from another scholarly field such as English, law, history political science, sociology, or psychology ("Journalism school won't," p. 3).

We believe that alternatives would not be necessary if the ACEJMC had adhered to its own general principles. One major principle, for example, was recognition of and respect for institutional diversity, that "each institution has its own unique situation, particular mission, and special resources, and that this uniqueness is an asset to be safeguarded" ("Accredited journalism," 1991, p. 4). Yet, the ACEJMC had not recognized the fact that some universities require more BA credits than others. Wisconsin students were required to take only 120 hours for the BA, so were limited by the 90–65 rule in the number of hours they could take in the major. Students at other universities that required more hours in the BA, could take more JMC courses. The only option Wisconsin had was to require its students to take additional credits, forcing many to take longer to graduate.

The ACEJMC general rule on uniqueness also was violated by Standard 3 because it did not allow for special aspects of the University of Wisconsin curriculum. For example, the College of Letters and Science recognized, through a rigorous process, 11 school of journalism and mass communication courses as part of the general education requirements. These included such courses as international communication, mass communication in developing nations, mass media and youth, mass media and political behavior, mass media and minorities, communication and public opinion, effects of mass communication, mass media and the consumer, mass communications history, and law of mass communication.

"It seems to us that since these courses can be taken for social science credit by all other students in the College of Letters and Science," then-Director James L. Hoyt wrote to members of the ACEJMC in 1990, "our own students should be able to take at least some of them without having them count 'against' them under the 90–65 rule. They are genuinely 'liberal arts' courses—in most cases taught by faculty members with PhD's in other disciplines . . . psychology, sociology, history, etc.—and, importantly, the final determination is made by the College, not by our faculty" (Hoyt, personal communication, January 5, 1990).

Hoyt's letter, by the way, was a plea to "a group of ACEJMC veterans and journalism unit administrators" for advice and suggestions "as we decide whether to seek reaccreditation in the future." He said Wisconsin JMC faculty views "have been shaped both from our own experiences undergoing accreditation visits here . . . and from my chairing various accrediting teams at other universities."

> . . . [O]ur dilemma is obvious. Given the unwillingness of the (ACEJMC) to recognize that any liberal arts education can occur within the unit, we are faced with *either* meeting the standards of our own College of Letters and

Science *or* meeting ACEJMCs 90/65 rule. . . . Because we have a broad-based faculty interested in teaching many of these liberal arts courses, we believe our curriculum is considerably enriched by such offerings. (Hoyt, 1990)

A related ACEJMC principle was that "accreditation seeks to promote educational innovation, not stifle it, and, [it] puts emphasis on the *outcome of the educational process* [italics added]. Innovations in programs and procedures, courses, and curricula are not judged by abstract and universal rules, but in light of evidence presented as to the actual educational success realized" ("Accredited journalism," 1991, p. 4). Standard 3 ignored liberal arts outcomes by relying entirely on the apparent content categories of courses by the departmental location of courses. It consistently ignored Wisconsin's evidence, and pleas, that an important component of its curriculum was making a significant contribution to the general education liberal arts core of the university.

Another related ACEJMC principle was: "true to the spirit of liberal education, the Council asks that [JMC] programs *not isolate themselves from the larger intellectual life of the institution*. Those programs should be integrated as fully as possible into the facilities, courses, programs, and scholarly activities of the institution as a whole" (p. 4, italics added). Standard 3, by designating all JMC courses as non-liberal arts and all courses in the "traditional" disciplines as liberal arts, drove a wedge and built a wall between JMC programs and the intellectual mainstream of their campuses. As we argued earlier, this contradicts the liberal arts principle.

Wisconsin's decision to withdraw from ACEJMC has historic significance. In 1905, Wisconsin's Willard G. Bleyer established what had become "the Wisconsin model" of undergraduate journalism and mass communication education: "He built a model of an undergraduate curriculum that still is echoed in today's national undergraduate accrediting standard—one quarter journalism, three quarters primarily liberal arts" (Boylan & Sims, 1988, p. 53). And Wisconsin pioneered the practice of adding history and other liberal arts content to courses in the JMC curriculum. This was in contrast to the model pioneered by the Missouri School of Journalism with its strong vocational emphasis. In 1992 the University of Wisconsin joined other respected mass communication programs at Stanford, Michigan, the Annenberg schools at Pennsylvania and the University of Southern California and others in not applying for accreditation. But, rather than abandoning its pioneering tradition, we believe Wisconsin, in fact, reaffirmed its liberal arts spirit and leadership for the New Professionalism in the 21st century. Short of substantial reform in the JMC accrediting process, we believe other schools will follow Wisconsin's lead and withdraw from the ACEJMC.

Media educators who would not consider Wisconsin, Stanford, Michigan, and Pennsylvania appropriate models for their schools, might consider Wichita State's communication program, under the leadership of Vernon Keel, former president of the Association for Schools of Journalism and Mass Communication (ASJMC). The faculty of the Elliott School of Communication and Director Keel developed an integrative, cross-media curriculum, knowing that it probably could not meet ACEJMC's rigid 90–65 hour standard.

"We designed our curriculum to develop well-rounded communicators who not only would possess professional skills in communication, but who would develop their abilities to plan, organize, evaluate and think strategically," Keel said. "We wouldn't have been able to do this if we had concerned ourselves with meeting rigid accreditation standards" (Keel, personal communication, March 30, 1992). The new comprehensive communication degree consolidated former programs in journalism, speech communication and radio-television-film and, according to Keel, had three distinguishing characteristics:

1. It was interdisciplinary, "reflecting the contemporary belief that all media of communication are engaged in essentially the same functions (gathering information and creating and disseminating messages)." It combined disciplinary strengths in an "interdisciplinary matrix" (Keel, 1992).

2. It was consistent with the mission of Wichita State to offer programs that were responsive to the needs of the urban community that the university served.

3. Because the Kansas communication industry had its focus in Wichita, the major media center of the state, the program was designed to exploit its location to integrate teaching and research and theory and practice.

The curriculum required students to complete at least 84 credits outside of communication which falls short, by 6 hours, of the rigid 90-hour ACEJMC rule.

"We require 84 credits because at least 6 hours of our own courses have been accepted as general education courses in the university," Keel said. "In fact, six of our courses or 18 credits in our program are accepted in the university general education component. We in communication have a lot to offer to liberal education for the 21st century. Why should we exclude our own majors from it?"

The 84 hours included three required courses in art and business—visual communication, introduction to business, and marketing. In the communication program, students were required to complete an 18-credit communication core that included communication and society, writing for the mass audience, speaking in business and the professions, and communication analysis and criticism, and two of the following three courses: communication law and responsibility, historical and theoretical issues in communication, and communication research and inquiry. A minimum of 15 credits was required in an open emphasis in communication that was "developed in a manner consistent with their educational and professional goals" (Keel, 1992).

In 1992, The Wichita Symposium, "Beyond Agendas: New Directions in Communication Research" was scheduled for September. We believe its call to action, when applied to undergraduate education, could help herald in the New Professionalism.

> We need to go beyond agendas, beyond turf battles, beyond the conflicts of mass communication versus speech communication, professional versus liberal arts, old liberal arts versus new liberal arts, positivistic versus naturalistic. Above all, we need to remember that communication is an essentially human process even if it is mediated by the technologies of the 21st century. It remains a process that affects the lives of all. (Keel, 1992)

References

Accredited journalism and mass communications education 1990-91. (1991). Accrediting Council on Education in Journalism and Mass Communications. Lawrence, KS: University of Kansas.

Ackoff, R. L. (1986). *Management in small doses.* New York: Wiley.

Adams, H. (1976). *The academic tribes.* New York: Liveright.

Adams, P. (1987). Personal computer, VDT use increases in journalism classes. *Journalism Educator, 42*(1), 24, 57.

Ahlgren, A., & Boyer, C. M. (1981). Visceral priorities: Roots of confusion in liberal education. *Journal of Higher Education 52*(2), 173-180.

Anderson, D. (n.d.). Director's statement. *Excellence.* Tempe, AZ: Arizona State University's Walter Cronkite School of Journalism and Telecommunication.

Arcenas, E. M. (1991, May). *Constructing a "communication" lexicon—a study of how "communication" entered the linguistic mainstream of journalism education.* Paper presented at the International Communication Association convention, Chicago, IL.

Armstrong, R. (1988). *The next hurrah: The communications revolution in American politics.* New York: William Murrow.

Association of American Colleges (AAC). (1985, February). *Integrity in the college curriculum: A report to the academic community.* Washington, DC: Author.

Association of American Colleges (AAC). (n.d.). *A search for quality and coherence in baccalaureate education* (Project on redefining the meaning and purpose of baccalaureate degrees). Washington, DC: Author.

Badgett, M. (1989, September). They're imitating *USA Today* around the world. *Gannetteer,* pp. 12-13.

Ball-Rokeach, S. (1985, October). Convention speaker questions communication theory, structure (keynote speech, convention of the Association for Education in Journalism and Mass Communication). *AEJMC News,* pp. 1, 4-5.

Beard, F. K. (1991). Implementing PC technology with organizational change. *Journalism Educator, 46*(1), 70-73.

Behnke, R. R., & King, P. E. (1986). Computer eases teacher workload in writing course. *Journalism Educator, 40*(4), 26-23.

Bell, D. (1968). *The reforming of general education: The Columbia College experience in its national setting.* New York: Columbia University Press.

Bell, D. (1973). *The coming of the post-industrial society.* New York: Basic Books.

Benson, T. W. (Ed.). (1985). *Speech communication in the 20th century.* Carbondale, IL: Southern Illinois University Press.

Berger, C. R., & Chaffee, S. H. (Eds.). (1987). *Handbook of communication sciences.* Newbury Park, CA: Sage.

Berger, C. R., & Chaffee, S. H. (1988). On bridging the communication gap. *Human Communication Research, 15*(2), 311-318.

Birkhead, D. (1986). News media ethics and the management of professionals. *Journal of*

Mass Media Ethics, 1(2), 37-46.
Birkhead, D. (1988). On the margins: Journalism and journalism education. *ACA Bulletin,* (No. 64), pp. 23-27.
Blanchard, R. O. (1986). Why a department of communication? Hanging together or hanging separately. *ACA Bulletin,* (No. 58), pp. 32-34.
Blanchard, R. O. (1987a, July/August). Is interior decoration more of a "liberal art" than journalism? *Bulletin of the American Society of Newspaper Editors,* (697), pp. 16-18.
Blanchard, R. O. (1987b, September). *"University tradition" is keystone.* Report of the Journalism Education Committee of the Associated Press Managing Editors Journalism Education Committee, Des Moines, IA.
Blanchard, R. O. (1987c). Re-inventing the corporation and rediscovering the university. *ACA Bulletin,* (No. 62), 25-28.
Blanchard, R. O. (1987d). The third revolution: Integration in research and curricula. *Feedback, 28*(2), 7-10.
Blanchard, R. O. (1988a). Academic values are losing out to the narrow values of industry representatives in the accreditation process. *ACA Bulletin,* (No. 64), 50-53.
Blanchard, R. O. (1988b). Put the Roper report on the shelf: We have our own agenda. *Feedback, 29*(3), 3-6.
Blanchard, R. O. (1988c). Our emerging role in liberal and media studies: How do we break the news to the media professionals? *Journalism Educator, 43*(3), 28-31.
Blanchard, R. O. (1988d, March). The changing curriculum in journalism and mass communication. *Insights* (p. 2). Columbia, SC: ASJMC.
Blanchard, R. O. (1988e, May). A first convergence: ACA, ASJMC, and BEA leaders meet in Las Vegas "summit." *Journalism and Mass Communication Administrator* (Newsletter of the Association for Schools of Journalism and Mass Communication), p. 3.
Blanchard, R. O. (1989, October). There are no liberal arts any more. . . . In *The Education of Journalists* (Report of the Associated Press Managing Editors Journalism Education Committee, Des Moines, IA), p. 16.
Blanchard, R. O., & Christ, W. G. (1985). In search of the unit core: Commonalties in curricula. *Journalism Educator, 40*(3), 28-33.
Blanchard, R. O., & Christ, W. G. (1988a). Beyond the generic curriculum. *Insights* (pp. 1-3). Columbia, SC: ASJMC.
Blanchard, R. O., & Christ, W. G. (1988b). Introduction: It's time to hang together. *ACA Bulletin,* (No. 64), 1-2.
Blanchard, R. O., & Christ, W. G. (1988c). Professional and liberal education: An agenda for journalism and mass communication education. *ACA Bulletin,* (No. 64), pp. 3-9.
Blanchard, R. O., & Christ, W. G. (1990). Broadcast curriculum: Essential outcomes. *Feedback, 31*(3), 6-7.
Bloom, A. (1987). *The closing of the American mind.* New York: Simon & Schuster.
Bogart, L. (1991, March). *The American media system and its commercial culture* (Occasional paper No. 8, Columbia University). New York: Gannett Foundation Media Center.
Bohn, T. W. (1988). Professional and liberal education. *ACA Bulletin,* (No. 64), pp. 16-32.
Bolduc, W. J., & Medoff, N. J. (1990). Preparation for entry level jobs in video production. *Feedback, 31*(4), 20-21.
Books in print index. (1991). New York: R. R. Bowker.
Botstein, L. (1979a, July 9). Liberal arts and the core curriculum: A debate in the dark. *Chronicle of Higher Education,* p. 17.
Botstein, L. (1979b, September). A proper education: The trade-off between method and motive. *Harpers,* pp. 33-37.
Bowen, H. R., & Schuster, J. H. (1986). *American professors: A national resource imperiled.* New York: Oxford University.
Boyer, E. L. (1987). *College: The undergraduate experience in America.* The Carnegie

REFERENCES

Foundation for the Advancement of Teaching. New York: Harper & Row.
Boyer, E. L. (1990). *Scholarship reconsidered: Priorities of the professoriate*. New York, NY: The Carnegie Foundation for the Advancement of Teaching, Princeton University Press.
Boyer, E. L., & Levine, A. (1981). *A quest for common learning*. Washington, DC: The Carnegie Foundation for the Advancement of Teaching.
Boylan, J., & Sims, N. H. (1988, Spring). Stand and deliver. Six teachers who made a difference. *Gannett Center Journal, 2*(2), pp. 49–60.
Branscomb, L. (1979). Future computer: The shock will be extraordinary—and one hopes, benevolent. *Across the Board, 16*(3), 61–68.
Brimelow, P. (1990, May 14). American perestroika? *Forbes*, pp. 82–86.
Broadcast Education Association Constitution. (1990). Washington, DC: Author.
Brody, E. W. (1990). *Communication tomorrow: New audiences, new technologies, new media*. New York: Praeger.
Burkhart, F. N. (1988). Using computers to teach statistics in reporting labs. *Journalism Educator, 42*(4), 4–6.
Butler, J. F. (1986). Spreadsheet tasks are worthwhile as teaching tools. *Journalism Educator, 40*(4), 28–31.
Carey, J. W. (1969). The communications revolution and the professional communicator. *The Sociological Review Monograph, 13*, 23–38.
Carey, J. W. (1978). A plea for the university tradition. *Journalism Quarterly, 55*(4), 846–855.
Carnegie Foundation. (1977). *The missions of the college curriculum* (A Commentary of the Carnegie Foundation for the Advancement of Teaching.) San Francisco: Jossey-Bass.
Carroll, R. (1987). No "middle ground": Professional broadcast education is liberal education. *Feedback, 28*(2), 7–10.
Carroll, R. L. (1985). Context of the study of mass communication. *Feedback, 27*(3), 3–8.
Caudill, E., Ashdown, P., & Caudill, S. (1990). Assessing learning in news, public relations curricula. *Journalism Educator, 45*(2), 13–19.
Cherrington, R. (1991). *China's students (the struggle for democracy)*. London, New York: Routledge.
Christ, W. G. (1975). *The role of television production in a liberal arts education*. Unpublished master's thesis, University of Wisconsin-Madison, Madison, WI.
Christ, W. G. (1986). Who is teaching our students? A preliminary inquiry. *Feedback, 27*(6), 32–33, 44.
Christ, W. G. (1990, August). *How shall I teach thee? Let me count the ways*. Paper presented at the 73rd annual meeting of the Association for Education in Journalism and Mass Communication, Minneapolis, MN.
Christ, W. G., & Blanchard, R. O. (1985, Winter). Teaching broadcast sales or "something like that." *Feedback, 27*(3), 32–35.
Christ, W. G., & Blanchard, R. O. (1987). Implementing a "generic" curriculum. In R. O. Blanchard (Ed.), *Partial Proceedings from the Second ASJMC Administrators Workshop* (pp. 7–9), Columbia, SC: ASJMC.
Christ, W. G., & Blanchard, R. O. (1988). Professional education: Who needs it? *Journalism Educator, 43*(2), 62–64.
Christians, C. G. (1989). *History of journalism ethics instruction*. Unpublished manuscript.
Cleveland, H. (1985, July/August). Educating for the information society. *Change*, pp. 13–21.
Cloud, B., & Sweeney, J. (1988). Effective guest speakers require thought and care. *Journalism Educator, 42*(4), 30–31.
Cole, R. R. (1989, June). *Creating excellence in mass communication* (1988–89 annual report). Chapel Hill, NC: School of Journalism University of North Carolina-Chapel Hill.
Communication studies (literature). (1988). Iowa, City, Iowa: The University of Iowa's

Department of Communication Studies.
Consoli, J. (1989, June). Erasable laser disk storage devices. *Editor & Publisher,* pp. 13, 42.
Cost of the ANPA/NAB. (1991, February 23). *Editor & Publisher,* p. 6.
Courson, P. (1989, March). Cellular telephones for radio electronic news gathering. *RTNDA Communicator,* pp. 15–17.
Cover story. (1988, December). *ASNE Bulletin,* pp. 3–7.
Cowdin, H. P. (1985, July/August). The liberal art of journalism. *The Quill,* pp. 16–23.
Curriculum guide for students/advisors 1990–1991. (1990). University Park: PA: Pennsylvania State University's School of Communications.
Dagnoli, J. (1990). Consumer union hits kids advertising. *Advertising Age, 61*(30), p. 4.
Dates, J. L. (1990). The study of theory should guide curriculum. *Feedback, 31*(3), 10–11.
Dates, J. L. (1991). Announcing? Not as a requirement. *Feedback, 32*(2), 22.
Davlin, J. A. (1965). A newcomer looks at the broadcast curriculum. *Journal of Broadcasting, 6*(4), 333–337.
de Sola Pool, I. (1983). *Technologies of freedom.* Cambridge, MA: The Belknap Press.
Delia, J. G. (1987). Communication research: A history. In C. R. Berger & S. H. Chaffee (Eds.), *Handbook of communication science* (pp. 20–98). Newbury Park, CA: Sage.
DeLoughry, T. J. (1989, January 18). Study of transcripts finds little structure in the liberal arts. *Chronicle of Higher Education,* pp. 1, 32.
Denham, C. (1988). Student outcomes assessment in higher education. *Teacher Education Quarterly, 15*(2), 82–89.
Dennis, E. E. (1986a, June). *Commentaries on journalism education.* (Leadership Institute for Journalism and Mass Communication Education.) New York: Gannett Center for Media Studies.
Dennis, E. E. (1986b, July). *A coming of age: Sea changes for the mass media.* (Speech delivered to the Council for Advancement and Support of Education.) New York: Gannett Center for Media Studies.
Dennis, E. E. (1986c, November 15). Quality control for the media. (Speech delivered to the Miami International Press Club, September 30, 1986.) *Vital Speeches of the Day, 53*(3), pp. 93–96.
Dennis, E. E. (1986d). Media researcher as sense-maker. (A reprint from the November/December 1986 issue of *Content for Canadian Journalists*). NY: Gannett Center for Media Studies.
Dennis, E. E. (1987, April). News, advertising, and the public. *Communique,* a publication of the Gannett Center for Media Studies, p. 1. New York, N.Y.
Dennis, E. E. (1988a, Spring). The making of journalists: A roundtable discussion. *Gannett Center Journal,* pp. 85–100.
Dennis, E. E. (1988b, Spring). Whatever happened to Marse Robert's dream? The dilemma of American journalism education. *Gannett Center Journal,* pp. 2–22.
Dennis, E. E. (1989). *Technological convergence and communication education.* New York: Gannett Center for Media Studies.
Dennis, E. E. (1990a). Communication education and its critics. *Syracuse Scholar, 10*(1), 7–13.
Dennis, E. E. (1990b). Educating the university about communications: An agenda for students, society and "the usual suspects." (Speech delivered at a colloquim of the department of communication at the University of Michigan, October 4, 1990). New York: Gannett Center for Media Studies.
Dennis, E. E., & DeFleur, M. L. (1991). A linchpin concept: Media studies and the rest of the curriculum. *Journalism Educator, 46*(2), 78–80.
Department of journalism (literature). (n.d.). Corvallis, OR: Oregon State University's Department of Journalism.
Deppa, J. (1986). Creating and using on-screen tutorials for word processing. *Journalism Educator, 41*(3), 43–49.
Deppa, J. (1989). *The computer connection* (a report on using the computer to teach mass

communications). Syracuse, NY: Syracuse University, The S.I. Newhouse School of Public Communications.

Dervin, B., & Voigt, M. J. (Eds.). (1984). *Progress in the communication sciences.* Norwood, NJ: Ablex.

Diebold, J. (1973). *The world of the computer.* New York: Random House.

Dizard, W. P., Jr. (1989). *The coming information age* (3rd ed.). New York: Longman.

Dominick, J. R. (1987). *The dynamics of mass communication.* New York: Random House.

Donner, F. J. (1981). *The age of surveillance: The aims and methods of America's political intelligence system.* New York: Vintage.

Dressel, P. L. (1960). *Liberal education and journalism.* New York: Columbia University Teachers College.

Eastman, S. T. (1985). Directions for telecommunications. *Feedback, 27*(3), 23-27.

Eastman, S. T. (1987). A model for telecommunications education. *Feedback, 28*(2), 21-25.

Eastman, S. T., & Adams, B. (1986). A radio-tv profile. *Feedback, 27*(5), 10-12.

Ehrmann, S. C. (1990). Reaching students, reaching resources: Using technologies to open the college. *Academic Computing, 4*(7), 8-14, 32.

Ehrmann, S. C. (1991, July). Computer correspondence.

Elmore, G. C. (Ed.). (1990). *The communication disciplines in higher education: A guide to academic programs in the United States and Canada.* Indianapolis, IN: Association for Communication Education and the Association of Schools of Journalism and Mass Communication.

Ervin, R. F. (1988). Outcomes assessment: The rationale and the implementation. In R. L. Hoskins (Ed.), *Insights* (pp. 19-23). Columbia, SC: ASJMC.

Eshelman, D. (1991, April). *Outcomes assessment strategies: Implications for broadcast education curricula.* Paper presented at the 36th annual Broadcast Education Association Convention, Las Vegas, NV.

Evans, C. (1979). *The micro millennium.* New York: Washington Square Press.

Fedler, F., Counts, T., & Stoner, K. R. (1989). Adjunct profs grade higher than faculty at three schools. *Journalism Educator, 44*(2), 32-37.

Fedler, F., & Smith, R. (1985). Administrators feel traditional research has highest value. *Journalism Educator, 40*(3), 51-52.

Filling the upcoming channel cornucopia. (1991, May 27). *Broadcasting,* pp. 44-47.

Finney, R. G. (1990). Wanted: Reading and writing skills. *Feedback, 31*(3), 10.

Fiske, E. B. (1987, April 12). Changes sweeping universities' curriculum. *The New York Times,* pp. 1, 36.

Fitzgerald, M. (1992). Wake-up call (newspaper audiotex ringing up dollars in bad economic times). *Editor & Publisher, 125*(7), pp. 16-17.

Fletcher, J. E. (1988, April). Graduate education in mass communication: Meaningful goals. *ACA Bulletin,* (No. 64), pp. 23-27.

Fletcher, J. E. (1990). Toober ain't couch potatoes. *Feedback, 31*(3), 9.

Footlick, J. K., Wingert, P., & Leonard, E. A. (1990, December 10). Decade of the student. *Newsweek,* pp. 70, 72.

Ford, C. A. (1987). Black student retention. In R. O. Blanchard (Ed.), *Partial proceedings from the second ASJMC administrators workshop* (pp. 24-27). Columbia, SC: ASJMC.

Fox, D. (1983). Personal theories of teaching. *Studies in Higher Education,* (Oxford, England), *8*(2), 151-163.

Funkhouser, E., & Savage, A. L., Jr. (1987). College students' expectations for entry-level broadcast positions. *Communication Education, 36*(1), 23-27.

Gabor, D. (1973). Social control through communications. In G. Gerbner, L. Gross, & W. H. Melody (Eds.), *Communications technology and social policy: Understanding the new "cultural revolution"* (pp. 83-93). New York: Wiley.

Garland, E. G. (1983). The status of broadcast education in institutions of higher learning.

Communication Education, 32(1), 69–77.
Garrison, B. (1981). Post-internship seminar can solve academic credit, grading problems of internship programs. *Journalism Educator, 36*(1), 14–17, 48.
Gendion, G., & Brown, P. B. (1989). A gathering place. *Inc., 11*(11), 32–54.
Gerbner, G. (1984). Defining the field of communication. *ACA Bulletin,* (No. 48), pp. 10–11.
Gomery, D. (1986). Media economics. *Feedback, 27*(5), 3–6.
Gray, R. G. (1983, July/August). If I were an editor. *ASNE Bulletin,* (661), p. 13.
Grow, G. (1990, August). *Enhancing self direction in journalism education.* A paper presented at the Association for Education in Journalism and Mass Communication, Minneapolis, MN.
Grow, G. (1991). Higher-order skills for professional practice and self-direction. *Journalism Educator, 45*(4), 56–65.
Gumpertz, G., & Cathart, E. (Eds.). (1982). *Inter/media: Interpersonal communication in a media world.* New York: Oxford University Press.
Guterman, J. C. (1991a, April). *Assessment in broadcast education: Does it apply to us?* Paper presented at the annual convention of the Broadcast Education Association, Las Vegas, NV.
Guterman, J. C. (1991b). Theory is important. *Feedback, 32*(2), 25–26.
Gutierrez, F. (1987). Racial inclusiveness: A second chance for journalism education. In R. O. Blanchard (Ed.), *Partial proceedings from the second ASJMC administrators workshop* (pp. 14–21). Columbia, SC: ASJMC.
Hall, D., & Ruggles, R. (1987). Gameplan for recruiting and retaining minorities. In R. O. Blanchard (Ed.), *Partial proceedings from the second ASJMC administrators workshop* (pp. 22–24). Columbia, SC: ASJMC.
Hanson, B. (1988, Summer). Profile: The electronic darkroom team. *AP World,* pp. 10–11.
Hanson, L. (1990). Computer-aided remediation for grammar, punctuation. *Journalism Educator, 44*(4), 43–49.
Harwood, K. (1985). Accreditation and the Broadcast Education Association. *Feedback, 27*(3), 15–18.
Hawkins, R. P., Wiemann, J. M., & Pingree, S. (Eds.). (1988). *Advancing communication science: Merging mass and interpersonal processes.* Newbury Park, CA: Sage.
Head, S. W. (1985). The telecommunication curriculum: A personal view. *Feedback, 27*(3), 9–12.
Head, S. W., & Martin, L. A. (1956–1957). Broadcasting higher education: A new era. *Journal of Broadcasting, 1*(1), 39–46.
Highton, J. (1989, Summer). Green eyeshade profs still live uncomfortably with "Chi-squares." *Journalism Educator, 44*(2), 59–61.
Hilt, M. L. (1991). Viewpoint: Improving broadcast internships. *Feedback, 32*(1), 6–7.
Hirschorn, M. W. (1987, October 14). Programs in advertising and public relations fuel growth of journalism school enrollment. *The Chronicle of Higher Education,* p. A36.
Honig, B. (1990, Summer). Should schools turn off Channel One? *Business and Society Review,* (No. 74), pp. 11–14.
Hoskins, R. (1988). A new accreditation problem: Defining the liberal arts and sciences. In R. L. Hoskins (Ed.), *Insights* (pp. 3–8). Columbia, SC: ASJMC.
Hudson, S. (1988). Communication's oratorical and natural rights heritage and the liberal arts. *ACA Bulletin,* (No. 64), pp. 10–15.
Hume, S. (1991, February 18). 900 numbers: The struggle for respect, *Advertising Age,* p. S-1.
Hutchings, P., & Reuben, E. (1988, July-August). Faculty voices on assessment. *Change,* pp. 48–55.
Ismach, A. (1987). The Oregon report: Curriculum reform. In R. O. Blanchard (Ed.), *Partial proceedings from the second ASJMC administrators workshop* (pp. 5–7). Columbia, SC: ASJMC.

REFERENCES

Ismach, A. (1990, Summer). Dean's Column. *Slugline* (University of Oregon School of Journalism newsletter), *3*(5), pp. 2-3.
Jacobson, R. L. (1986, January 22). Academic leaders showing new optimism about reform of undergraduate education. *Chronicle of Higher Education,* pp. 1, 24.
Jankowski, G. F. (1986). Television and teachers: Educating each other. *Feedback, 27*(5), 13-15.
Jansen, S. C. (1988). *Censorship: The knot that binds power and knowledge.* New York: Oxford University Press.
Janis, P. (1991, July/August). Workplace of the future. *Ganetteer,* pp. 18-19.
Jaschik, S. (1985, August 7). Governors weigh role of the states in reform efforts. *The Chronicle of Higher Education,* pp. 1, 14.
Johnson, O. (Executive Ed.). 1991. *1992 Information please almanac atlas & yearbook.* Boston: Houghton Mifflin.
Johnson, S., & Christ, W. G. (1985). Print, broadcasting examined together in vis-comm class. *Journalism Educator, 39*(4), 22-24.
Journalism at Eastern Illinois University (brochure). (n.d.). Charleston, IL: Eastern Illinois University's Department of Journalism.
Journalism at the Ohio State University (literature). (n.d.). Columbus, OH: The Ohio State University's School of Journalism.
Journalism goals and objectives (literature). (n.d.). Carbondale, IL: Southern Illinois University's School of Journalism.
Journalism school won't seek reaccreditation. (1991, December 3). Press release from News and Information Service, Madison, WI.
Junod, J. (1989, September). A time for technology talk. *Gannetteer,* pp. 3-5.
Kamalipour, Y. R. (1990, November). *Broadcast education: Fighting the trade school image.* Paper presented at the annual meeting of the Speech Communication Association, Chicago, IL.
Kanigel, R. (1986, March/April). Technology as a liberal art: Scenes from the classroom. *Change, 18*(2), pp. 20-27, 30.
Keel, V. A. (1988). The academy and the professions: Inherent tensions in professional accreditation. *ACA Bulletin,* (No. 64), pp. 46-49.
Keel, V. A. (1991). A note from the president. *Journalism and Mass Communication Administrator* (pp. 3-5). Columbia, SC: ASJMC.
Kimball, B. A., (1986). *Orators and philosophers.* New York: Teachers College Press.
Kipper, P. (1989). Television's future is interactive. *Feedback, 30*(4), 43-48.
Kittross, J. M. (1989). Six decades of education for broadcasting . . . and counting. *Feedback, 30*(4), 30-42.
Kliebard, H. M. (1972). Metaphorical roots of curriculum design. *Teachers College Record, 73*(3), 403-404.
Kliebard, H. M. (1982). Curriculum theory as metaphor. *Theory In Practice, 21*(1), 11-17.
Koerner, J. D. (1984). *The new liberal arts program—a status report.* New York: Alfred P. Sloan.
Krukowski, J. (1985). What do students want? Status. *Change, 17*(3), pp. 21-28.
Kubey, R., & Csikszentmihalyi, M. (1990). *Television and the quality of life: How viewing shapes every day experiences.* Hillsdale, NJ: Lawrence Erlbaum Associates.
Laakaniemi, R. (1986). Coaches need tact, patience, especially with publishers. *Journalism Educator, 41*(2), 19-20.
Lambeth, E. B. (1986). *Committed journalism: An ethic for the profession.* Bloomington, IN: Indiana University Press.
Lasswell, H. (1948). The structure and function of communication in society. In L. Bryson (Ed.), *The communication of ideas* (pp. 37-51). New York: Harper & Row.

REFERENCES 169

Lavine, J. M., & Wackman, D. B. (1988). *Managing media organizations: Effective leadership of the media.* New York: Longman.

Lawson, R. G. (1983). Liberal arts and television production training: The University of Wisconsin Program. *Feedback, 25*(1), 6–10.

Leaming, D. R. (1986). Marshall's campus, J-majors work to attract new students. *Journalism Educator, 41*(2), 19–20.

Leatherman, C. (1991, September 18). Too much power? Specialized accrediting agencies challenged by campus officials. *Chronicle of Higher Education,* pp. 1, 22.

Leiss, W. (1989). The myth of the information society. In I. Angus & S. Jhally (Eds.), *Cultural politics in contemporary America* (pp. 282–298). New York: Routledge.

Lessersohn, J. (1989, May/June). Readers are dialing their daily newspapers to hear the news that is most important to them, *ASNE Bulletin,* (714), pp. 12–14.

Lester, P. (1989). Computer aids instruction in photojournalism ethics. *Journalism Educator, 44*(2), 13–17, 49.

Levine, J. (1990). The last gasp of mass media? *Forbes, 146*(6), pp. 176–182.

Lieb, T. (1990). Computer conferencing offers new way to think about writing. *Journalism Educator, 45*(2), 32–37.

Linn, M. P. (1989). Influence on institutional values: Accreditation and planning in the assessment movement. *Education Record, 70*(2), 48–49.

Lisensky, R. P., Pfnister, A. O., & Sweet, S. D. (1985). *The new liberal learning: Technology and the liberal arts.* Washington, DC: Council of Independent Colleges.

Lowenstein, R. L., & Merrill, J. (1990). *Macromedia.* New York: Longman.

Lull, J. (1988). The family and television in world cultures. In J. Lull (Ed.), *World families watch television* (pp. 9–21). London: Routledge.

Lull, J. (1991). *China turned on (television, reform, and resistance).* London: Routledge.

Major in communications. (1990). Philadelphia, PA: The Annenberg School of Communication-East.

Mann, R. C. (1986). Expectations must be clear to coaches. *Journalism Educator, 41*(2), 13, 15–18.

Marsh, P. T. (1988). *Contesting the boundaries of liberal and professional education: The Syracuse experiment.* Syracuse, NY: Syracuse University Press.

May, W. F. (1986). Professional ethics, the university, and the journalist. *Journal of Mass Media Ethics, 1*(2), 20–31.

McCall, J. M. (1987). Liberal arts focus provides training for media centers. *Journalism Educator, 42*(2), 17–21.

McCall, J. M. (1988). Sharing the responsibility of media literacy—reaching out to other disciplines. *ACA Bulletin,* (No. 64), pp. 34–39.

McCall, J. M. (1990). Beyond the Roper report. *Feedback, 31*(3), 9–10.

McCall, J. (1991, April). *Mass communication education belongs to the university.* Paper presented at the annual conference of the Broadcast Education Association, Las Vegas, NV.

McCombs, M. E. (1988, Spring). Testing the myths: A statistical review, 1967–86. *Gannett Center Journal,* pp. 101–108.

Meeske, M. (1988). Update: Broadcast intern programs and practices. *Journalism Educator, 43*(2), 75–77.

Meyer, P. (1987). *Ethical journalism: A guide for students, practitioners, and consumers.* New York: Longman.

Michigan State University Department of Telecommunications' packet. n.d. East Lansing, MI: Michigan State University's Department of Telecommunications.

Mission and goals of Eastern Illinois University. (n.d.). Charleston, IL: Eastern Illinois University's Department of Journalism.

Moore, R. (1990, April). *Pro: Core courses.* Paper presented at the Broadcast Education Association Convention, Atlanta, GA.

Morgan, H. (1988). Editing, makeup revamped by desktop computer. *Journalism Educator, 43*(2), 83–84.

Morison, E. E. (1986). The new liberal arts: Creating novel combinations out of diverse learning. *Change, 18*(2), 7–8.

Mullins, E. (1988). The basics of accreditation by ACEJMC: Overview. *ACA Bulletin,* (No. 64), pp. 54–57.

National Institute of Education (NIE). (1984, October 24). Involvement in learning: Realizing the potential of American higher education. *Chronicle of Higher Education,* pp. 35–49.

New forum . . . how advertising and education are working together for a better future. (n.d.). New York: The Advertising Educational Foundation.

New telephone technology will change the way you sell, promote and market your radio station. (1989). *Radiotrends, 5*(4), 1–2.

New York, New York. It's a digital town. (1990, October 22). *Broadcasting,* pp. 69–72, 88.

Niven, H. (1961). The development of broadcasting education in institutions of higher education. *Journal of Broadcasting, 5*(1), 241–250.

Oates, W. R. (1986). Faculty help make computer planning comprehensive. *Journalism Educator, 41*(3), 52–53.

Oates, W. R. (1987a). Class computer use need not be limited to electronic typing. *Journalism Educator, 42*(1), 54–55.

Oates, W. R. (1987b). Software exchange available online in AEJMC forum. *Journalism Educator, 42*(2), 47–48.

Oettinger, A. G. (1980). Information resources: Knowledge and power in the 21st century. *Science, 209*(4452), 191–198.

O'Keefe, H. (1986). Internship contest pairs students with advertising pros. *Journalism Educator, 41*(2), 45–46.

Oukrop, C., & Parsons, P. (1991). Benefits of accreditation scrutiny and university support. *Journalism Educator, 46*(1), 66–69.

Palmer, S. E. (1986, May 7). Concern about quality prompts states to undertake reviews of their colleges, *Chronicle of Higher Education,* pp. 13, 18.

Parcells, F. E. (1985). What broadcast managers want educators to teach. *Communication Education, 34*(3), 235–241.

Parker, D. B. (1983). *Fighting computer crime.* New York: Scribner's Sons.

PCs—The new publishing computers. (1989, September). *Editor & Publisher,* pp. 1PC-40PC.

Peirce, K., & Bennett, R. (1990). Interviewing potential faculty: Finding the right person. *Journalism Educator, 45*(3), 60–66.

Pelton, J. (1983). Life in the information society. In J. L. Salvaggio (Ed.), *Telecommunications: Issues and choices for society* (pp. 51–68). New York: Longman/Annenberg.

Pennybacker, J. H. (1965a). Working with universities. *Journal of Broadcasting, 9*(1), 183–187.

Pennybacker, J. H. (1965b). Comment on Woodliff. *Journal of Broadcasting, 9*(4), 332.

Pennybacker, J. H. (1965c). Comment on Davlin. *Journal of Broadcasting, 9*(4), 337.

Pennybacker, J. H. (1965–1966). Leadership and the educator: The middle way. *Journal of Broadcasting, 10*(1), 67–70.

Pennsylvania State University School of Communications (literature). (n.d.). University Park, PA: School of Communications.

Pioneering partnerships: Faculty development opportunities that link journalism and communication education with media industries. (1991). New York: Freedom Forum Media Studies Center.

Planning for curricular change in journalism education (2nd ed.). (1987). (Project on the Future of Journalism and Mass Communication Education) The Oregon Report. Eugene, OR: School of Journalism, University of Oregon.

Plumley, J. P. Jr., (1990). Key factors for evaluating "non-traditional" faculty. *Journalism Educator, 45*(3), 46–53.

Porat, M. U. (1977). *The information economy* (9 vols.), Washington, DC: U.S. Department of Commerce.
Porter, M. J., & Szkolka, P. (1991). Broadcast students' perspectives on the liberal arts. *Feedback, 32*(2), 18–21.
Potter, W. J. (1991). Yes to research. *Feedback, 32*(2), 24–25.
Potter, W. J., & Clark, G. (1991). Styles in mass communication teaching. *Feedback, 32*(1), 8–11.
Quenzel, G. (1990, April). *Against: Core courses.* Paper presented at Broadcast Education Association Convention, Atlanta, GA.
Rafaeli, S. (1984). *If the computer is the medium, what is the message? Interactivity and its correlates.* Unpublished manuscript, Institute for Communication Research, Stanford, CA.
Ralston, J. (1989). Whittling away at the mass media. *Venture, 11*(7), pp. 30–34.
Rambo, C. D. (1989, January). Direct mail's challenge: Competition is hot as the newspapers battle mailers over delivery of ad preprints. *Presstime,* pp. 18–25.
Reardon, K. K., & Rogers, E. M. (1988). Interpersonal versus mass media communication: A false dichotomy. *Human Communication Research, 15*(2), 284–303.
Reed, B. S., & Grusin, E. K. (1989). Adjuncts teach skills courses but lack role in department. *Journalism Educator, 44*(2), 29–31, 37.
Reilly, P. (1988). Media baron for the 1990s. *Advertising Age, 59*(21), 1, 9.
Renz, B. (1988). Broadcast industry perceptions of the relative value of college majors for entry-level employment. *Feedback, 29*(2), 8–10.
Renz, B. B. (1991). Yes to announcing. *Feedback, 32*(2), 22–23.
Rice, R. E. (1985). *The new media: Communication, research, and technology.* Beverly Hills, CA: Sage.
Rice, R. E., Borgman, C. L., & Reeves, B. (1988). Citation networks of communication journals, 1977–1985: Cliques and positions, citations made and citations received. *Human Communication Research, 15*(2), 256–283.
Riesman, D. (1980). *On higher education: The academic enterprise in an era of rising student consumerism.* San Francisco, CA: Jossey-Bass.
Roberts, C. L. (1984). Speech, mass communication faculty strengthen journalism unit. *Journalism Educator, 39*(2), 5–6, 42.
Rogers, E. M. (1986). *Communication technology: The new media in society.* New York: The Free Press.
Rogers, E. M., & Chaffee, S. H. (1983). Communication as an academic discipline: A dialogue. *Journal of Communication, 33*(3), 23–25.
Rogers, J. L. (1982). Defining the outcomes of journalism education: The perceptions of daily newspaper editors in Texas. *Studies in Journalism and Mass Communications,* 13–19.
Rosenbaum, J. (1991, April). *Preparing graduates for careers, not just entry level jobs: Implications for Broadcasting Education Curricula.* Paper presented at the annual convention of the Broadcast Education Association, Las Vegas, NV.
Rossow, M. D. (1986). Make the start of the next term "user friendly." *Journalism Educator, 41*(3), 34–36.
Rothblatt, S. (1976). *Tradition and change in English liberal education.* London: Farber & Farber.
Rowland, W. D., Jr. (1992). The role of journalism and communication studies: A place of honor. In *Insights* (pp. 1–9). Columbia, SC: ASJMC.
Rubin, A. M., & Rubin, R. B. (1985). Interface of personal and mediated communication: A research agenda. *Critical Studies in Mass Communication, 2,* 36–53.
Rudolph, F. (1979). *Curriculum: A history of the American undergraduate course of study since 1636.* San Francisco: Jossey-Bass.
Rudolph, F. (1984, May/June). "The Power of professors," *Change, 16*(3), 13–17, 41.

Salvaggio, J. L. (1983a). *Privacy, freedom and new communications technology.* Paper presented at the Freedom Foundation, Valley Forge, PA.

Salvaggio, J. L. (1983b). Social problems in information societies: the US and Japanese experiences. *Telecommunications Policy, 7*(3), 228–242.

Salvaggio, J. L. (Ed.). (1983c). *Telecommunications: Issues and choices for society.* New York: Longman/Annenberg.

Salvaggio, J. L. (1987). Projecting a positive image of the information society. In J. D. Slack & F. Fejes (Eds.), *The ideology of the information age* (pp. 146–157). Norwood, NJ: Ablex.

Sandage, C. H., Fryburger, V., & Rotzoll, K. (1988). *Advertising theory and practice.* New York: Longman.

Schell, O., Nixon, R. M., & Gardels, N. (1989). The great wall vs. the fax. *New Perspectives Quarterly, 6*(2), 56–59.

Shen, T. (1990). *Almost a revolution.* Boston: Houghton Mifflin.

Schierhorn, A. (1991). The role of the writing coach in the magazine curriculum. *Journalism Educator, 46*(2), 46–53.

Schiller, H. I. (1981). *Who knows: Information in the age of the Fortune 500.* Norwood, NJ: Ablex.

Schudson, M. (1978). *Discovering the news: A social history of American newspapers.* New York: Basic Books.

Schweitzer, J. C. (1989). Faculty research expectation varies among universities. *Journalism Educator, 44*(2), 45–49.

Scully, M. G. (1983, October 19). Condemns "Careerism" in Colleges. *Chronicle of Higher Education,* pp. 1, 21.

Shively, N. H. (1991, December 4). UW Journalism School balks at accreditation. *Milwaukee Sentenel,* p. 6A.

Silberman, A. (1977). Communications systems and future behavior patterns. *International Social Science Journal, 29*(2), 337–341.

Sitton, C. F. (1986). *Liberal arts education as preparation for a journalism career.* Robert W. Woodruff Lecture, Emory University, Atlanta, March 26, 1986. (Available from American Newspaper Publishers Association Public Affairs Department at the Newspaper Center, Box 17407, Dulles Airport, Washington, DC, 20041.)

Slack, J. D., & Fejes, F. (Eds.). (1987). *The ideology of the information age.* Norwood, NJ: Ablex.

Slater, M. D., Rouner, D., & Tharp, M. (1991). Impact of VDTs on structural and mechanical editing. *Journalism Educator, 45*(4), 45–48.

Smith, B. (1986). Interactive tape helps to teach videotape editing. *Journalism Educator, 40*(4), 34–35.

Smith, W. E. (1991). Multimedia computing: Teaching and research with TV and PCs. *Journalism Educator, 46*(2), 74–77.

So, C. Y. K. (1988). Citation patterns of core communication journals: An assessment of the developmental status of communication. *Human Communication Research, 15*(2), 236–255.

SRDS's business publication rates and data. (1991, October 24). C. E. Burr (President and Publisher). *73*(10). Wilmette, IL: Standard Rate & Data Service.

SRDS's consumer magazine and agri-media rates and data. (1991, September 27). C. E. Burr (President and Publisher). *73*(9). Wilmette, IL: Standard Rate & Data Service.

SRDS's spot radio rates and data. (1991, October 1). C. E. Burr (President and Publisher). *73*(10), Wilmette, IL: Standard Rate & Data Service.

Stacks, D. W., Rosenfeld, L. B., & Hickson, M. III. (1989). Perceptions of regional communication associations. *Communication Education, 38*(2), 144–150.

Stallworth, C. (1987). Computing, editing on big TV makes good teaching tool. *Journalism Educator, 42*(1), 46–48.

REFERENCES 173

Starr, D. (1989). Management tips, *Communicator, 43*(3), 37.
Stein, M. L. (1991, July 13). Whittle away at Whittle. *Editor and Publisher, 124*(28), p. 7.
Sterling, C. H. (1985). The meaning of the name. *Feedback, 27*(3), 13-14.
Stone, G. (1990). Measurement of excellence in newspaper writing courses. *Journalism Educator, 44*(4), 4-19.
Stone, G., & Norton, W., Jr. (1980, July). How administrators define the term "faculty research." *Journalism Educator, 35*(2), 40-42.
Strengthening the ties that bind: Integrating undergraduate liberal and professional study (Report of the Professional Preparation Network). (1988). Ann Arbor, MI: The Regents of the University of Michigan.
Sykes, C. (1988). *ProfScam: Professors and the demise of higher education.* WA: Regmery Gateway; WI: Reardon & Walsh.
Tan, A. S. (1991, Spring). Journalism and mass communication programs in the university. *Insights,* pp. 1-17.
Technology redefines the press. (1988, February 15). *Broadcasting,* p. 133.
Teeple-Hewes, J. (Managing Ed.). (1983-1984). *Colleges enter the information age.* American Association for Higher Education, (1). Washington, DC: AAHE.
Telecommunications master's program. (n.d.). Evanston, IL: Northwestern University, Telecommunications Department.
Terenzini, P. T. (1989). Assessment with open eyes: Pitfalls in studying student outcomes. *Journal of Higher Education, 60*(6), 644-664.
Terrell, P. M. (1989, February). Art (Newspapers' historical gray pages have come alive with an explosion of color and graphics, many of them computer-assisted). *Presstime,* pp. 20-27.
Text of Secretary Bennett's address. (1986, October, 15). *Chronicle of Higher Education,* pp. 27-30.
Thayer, F. D. Jr., (1990). Using semantic differential to evaluate courses. *Journalism Educator, 45*(2), 20-24.
Thompson, P. A., & Craig, R. L. (1991). Promises and realities of desktop publishing. *Journalism Educator, 46*(1), 22-28.
Truitt, R. C. (1988, October). Electronic photography. *Presstime,* pp. 30-37.
Truxal, J. G. (1986, March/April). Learning to think like an engineer: Why, what, and how? *Change, 18*(2), pp. 10-19.
Tucker, D. (1991). Delete comm theory. *Feedback, 32*(2), 25.
Ulrich's international periodical directory 1991-92. (1991). New Providence, NJ: R. R. Bowker.
Walcovy, D. E. (1991). Abolishing research for undergraduates. *Feedback, 32*(2), 23-24.
Waldman, S. (1986, May). If we must have J-schools. . . . *The Washington Monthly,* p. 54.
Ward, J. (1987). Developing journalism curriculum in the information age. In R. O. Blanchard (Ed.), *Partial proceedings from the second ASJMC administrators workshop* (pp. 3-5), Columbia, SC: ASJMC.
Warner, C., & Liu, Y. (1990). Broadcast curriculum profile (a freeze-frame look at what BEA members offer students). *Feedback, 31*(3), 6-7.
Wartella, E. (1992). The integration of journalism and speech in communication: Transcending the professional/non-professional divide. In *Insights* (pp. 15-18). Columbia, SC: ASJMC.
Weaver, D., & Wilhoit, G. C. (1988). A profile of JMC administrators: Traits, attitudes and values. *Journalism Educator, 43*(2), 4-41.
Webster, J. (1989, Summer). Media study in a time of technological change. *Feedback, 30*(3), 20-24.
Welke, J. W. (1985). The generic curriculum menace. *Feedback, 27*(3), 21-22.
Wesson, D. (1986). Shareware can save J-schools money, worry. *Journalism Educator,* (2), 40-42.

REFERENCES

Westling, J. (1988, October 19). The assessment movement is based on a misdiagnosis of the malaise afflicting American higher education. *Chronicle of Higher Education,* pp. B1, B2.

White, S. (1981). Comments. In J. D. Koerner (Ed.), *The new liberal arts: An exchange of views* (An occasional paper from the Alfred P. Sloan Foundation.). New York: Alfred P. Sloan Foundation.

Whitfield, J. D. (1982). Journalism school deans show similar attitudes toward curriculum, school organization. *Studies in Journalism and Mass Communications,* 48–52.

Wicklein, J. (1981). *The electronic nightmare: The new communications and freedom.* New York: Viking.

Wiemann, J. M., Hawkins, R. P., & Pingree, S. (1988). Fragmentation in the field—and the movement toward integration in communication science. *Human Communication Research, 15*(2), 304–310.

Wiener, N. (1950). *The human use of human beings: Cybernetics and society.* New York: Houghton Mifflin.

Williams, S. (1992, February). *Innovative techniques for moving toward conceptually based television production courses.* Paper presented at the spring meeting of the Texas Association of Broadcast Educators, Dallas, TX.

Winston, B. (1987). Response. In R. O. Blanchard (Ed.), *Partial proceedings from the second ASJMC administrators workshop* (pp. 11–12). Columbia, SC: ASJMC.

Woditsch, G. A., Schlesinger, M. A., & Giardina, R. C. (1987, November/December). The skillful baccalaureate: Doing what liberal education does best. *Change, 19*(6), pp. 48–57.

Wood, D. (1992, April). *Combining communication theory and critical thinking: A proposal for a foundation course.* Paper presented at the Broadcast Education Association Convention, Las Vegas, NV.

Woodliff, C. M. (1965). Catch me if you can. *Journal of Broadcasting, 9*(4), 329–332.

Woodliff, C. M. (1965–1966). The gingerbreadman revisited, or have I been caught? *Journal of Broadcasting, 10*(1), 71–72.

Wycliff, D. (1990, September 4). Concern grows on campuses at teaching's loss of status. *New York Times,* pp. A1, A9.

Zettl, H. (1990). *Sight sound motion: Applied media aesthetics* (2nd ed.). Belmont, CA: Wadsworth.

Author Index

A

Ackoff, R. L., 82, 83, 84
Adams, B., 122
Adams, H., 5, 111
Adams, P., 27, 125
Adams, R. C., 140
Addison, J., 76
Ahlgren, A., 3, 13
Albers, J., 104, 105, 143
American Council of Education, 5
Anderson, D., 84, 104, 138
Armstrong, R., 28
Arcenas, E. M., xi
Ashdown, P., 143
Association of American Colleges (AAC), 4, 5, 6, 8, 9, 10, 14, 15, 18, 19, 20, 34, 46, 55, 56, 59, 71, 74, 75, 101, 149, 154, 155

B

Badgett, M., 30
Ball-Rokeach, S., 35
Beard, F. K., 126
Becker, S., 89, 90, 93, 103, 108, 112, 113, 115, 122, 136, 137, 139
Behnke, R. R., 27, 126
Bell, D., 16, 17, 22, 34, 68, 70, 152
Bell, T. H., 4, 9, 10, 12
Bennett, R., 137
Bennett, W., 4, 5, 8
Benson, T. W., 35
Berger, C. R., 35
Birkhead, D., 62, 63, 66, 75
Blanchard, R. O., 37, 47, 74, 86, 91, 92, 96
Bleyer, W. G., 159
Bloom, A., 5, 6, 8
Bogart, L., 76, 77
Bohn, T. W., 112
Bolduc, W. J., 114
Borgman, C. L., 37
Botstein, L., 3, 7
Bowen, H. R., 123
Boyer, E. L., 3, 7, 9, 10, 11, 12, 13, 14, 15, 17, 18, 19, 20, 41, 42, 43, 46, 47, 49, 52, 54, 55, 62, 104, 123, 124, 125, 149, 150, 152, 154, 155
Boyer, C. M., 3, 13
Boylan, J., 159
Branscomb, L., 33
Brimelow, P., 123
Brod, D., 90, 97, 108, 119, 141
Brody, E. W., 22
Brown, P. B., 110
Bunge, W., 86, 94, 96, 104
Burkhart, F. N., 126
Butler, J. F., 126

C

Carey, J. W., 42, 43, 63, 66, 67, 72, 73, 74, 75, 76, 77, 78
Carnegie Foundation, 8, 9, 10, 11, 14, 15, 18, 20, 21, 46, 49, 52, 55, 56, 101, 149, 150, 152, 154, 155
Carroll, R. L., 32, 88
Cathart, E., 35
Caudill, E., 143
Caudill, S., 143
Chaffee, S. H., 35
Cherrington, R., 23
Chomsky, N., 106
Christ, W. G., 37, 47, 86, 89, 91, 92, 96, 107, 122, 127
Christians, C. G., 76, 77, 78
Clark, D., 105, 120, 142
Clark, G., 127
Cleveland, H., 107
Cloud, B., 119
Cole, R. R., 90
Consoli, J., 25
Cornell, E., 17
Counts, T., 119
Courson, P., 26
Cowdin, H. P., 153
Craig, R. L., 126
Cronkite, W., 138
Csikszentmihalyi, M., 24

D

Dagnoli, J., 110
Dates, J. L., 92
Davlin, J. A., 88
de Sola Pool, I., 25
DeFleur, M. L., 106
Delia, J. G., 35
DeLoughry, T. J., 6
Denham, C., 144
Dennis, E. E., 22, 38, 39, 44, 45, 60, 61, 63, 65, 66, 67, 69, 70, 103, 106, 121, 125
Deppa, J., 126
Dervin, B., 35
Dewey, J., 76
Diebold, J., 33
Dizard, W. P., Jr., 22
Dominick, J. R., 23, 37
Donner, F. J., 33
Drechsel, R., 157
Dressel, P. L., 10, 38, 48, 152

E

Eastman, S. T., 32, 122
Ehrmann, S. C., 126
Eliot, C. W., 17
Elliott, W. R., 136
Elmore, G. C., xii
Ervin, R. F., 33, 143
Eshelman, D., 143, 144, 145, 146
Evans, C., 33

F

Fedler, F., 119, 123
Fejes, F., 33
Finney, R. G., 92, 115, 135, 139
Fiske, E. B., 5
Fitzgerald, M., 25
Fletcher, J. E., 34, 59, 92
Footlick, J. K., 123
Ford, C. A., 147
Fox, D., 127
Franklin, J., 94
Fresh Prince, 26
Fryburger, V., 106
Funkhouser, E., 114

G

Gabor, D., 33
Gardels, N., 23
Garland, E. G., 114
Garrison, B., 116, 118
Gendion, G., 110
Gerbner, G., 35, 52, 54, 62, 63, 110
Giardina, R. C., 17, 18, 58
Gomery, D., 13, 39, 40, 42, 43
Gray, R. G., 72
Grow, G., 64, 86, 131, 135
Grusin, E. K., 118
Gumpertz, G., 35
Guterman, J. C., 92, 144
Gutierrez, F., 147

H

Hale, F. D., 138, 139
Hall, D., 147
Hanson, B., 25
Hanson, L., 126
Harwood, K., 144

Hawkins, R. P., 35
Head, S. W., 32, 85
Hickson, M., III., 37
Highton, J., 114
Hilt, M. L., 115
Hirschorn, M. W., 40
Hobbes, T., 76
Honig, B., 110
Hoskins, R., 147
Hoyt, J. L., 158
Hudson, G., 6, 12, 36, 75, 76, 89
Hume, S., 26
Hutchings, P., 144

I

Innis, H., 42
Ismach, A., 43, 67, 68, 96, 142
Isocrates, 76

J

Jacobson, R. L., 7, 9
Janis, P., 31
Jankowski, G. F., 67
Jansen, S. C., 63
Jaschik, S., 5
Jazzy Jeff, 26
Jefferson, T., 76
Johnson, O., 29
Johnson, Sammye, 107
Johnson, Samuel, 76
Junod, J., 25

K

Kamalipour, Y. R., 85
Kanigel, R., 9, 19, 58
Keel, V. A., 142, 147, 148, 160, 161
Kennedy, D., 123
Kenny, S. S., 7
Kimball, B. A., 13, 76
King, P. E., 27, 126
Kipper, P., 23
Kittross, J. M., 32
Kliebard, H. M., 127, 130, 131, 132, 133
Koerner, J. D., 9, 19
Krukowski, J., 42
Kubey, R., 24

L

Laakaniemi, R., 127
Lambeth, E. B., 53, 62, 71, 75, 78
Lasswell, H., 105
Lavine, J. M., 64, 75
Lawson, R. G., 89
Leaming, D. R., 127
Leatherman, C., 157
Leiss, W., 33
Leonard, E. A., 123
Lessersohn, J., 26
Lester, P., 126
Levine, A., 18, 55, 104
Levine, J., 110
Lieb, T., 126
Limburg, V., 89
Linn, M. P., 144
Lisensky, R. P., 9, 19
Litman, B., 122
Liu, Y., 82, 85, 92
Locke, J., 76
Lowenstein, R. L., 35
Lull, J., 23, 24

M

Madison, J., 76
Macaulay, T. B., 17
Mann, R. C., 127
Marsh, P. T., 8, 9, 10, 46, 49, 53, 67, 149
Martin, L. A., 85
May, W. F., 12, 42, 62, 77
McCall, J. M., 59, 91, 92, 109, 112, 115
McCombs, M. E., 40
Medoff, N. J., 114
Messke, M., 115
Mellon Foundation, 8
Merrill, J. C., 35
Meyer, P., 77, 78
Michigan Professional Preparation
 Network Report ("Strengthening the
 ties"), 8, 9, 10, 15, 19, 20, 46, 149,
 151, 152, 155
Miller, J., 85
Moore, R., 89, 91, 97, 107, 113
Morgan, H., 27, 126
Morison, E. E., 9, 19
Mullins, E., 147
Murphy, S., 61
Murrow, E. R., 90

N

National Institute of Education (NIE), 4, 8, 9, 10, 14, 18, 46, 51
Niven, H., 85
Nixon, R. M., 23
Norton, W., Jr., 123

O

Oates, W. R., 126
Oettinger, A. G., 33
Office of Technological Assessment (OTA), 25
O'Keefe, H., 115
Oregon Report ("Planning for curricular change"), 35, 37, 38, 41, 44, 46, 47, 48, 50, 52, 54, 57, 62, 63, 67, 68, 85, 96, 149, 150, 151, 156
Oukrop, C., 146
Ottaway, J., Jr., 60, 61, 68, 71, 72

P

Palmer, S. E., 5
Parcells, F. E., 114
Parker, D. B., 33
Parsons, P., 146
Peirce, K., 137
Pelton, J., 33
Pennybacker, J. H., 88
Pfnister, A. O., 9, 19
Pingree, S., 35
"Planning for curricular change" (see Oregon Report)
Plumley, J. P., Jr., 119
Potter, W. J., 92, 127
Porat, M. U., 22
Porter, M. J., 99
Pulitzer, J., 76

Q

Quenzel, G., 92

R

Rafaeli, S., 23
Ralston, J., 110
Rambo, C. D., 26
Reardon, K. K., 36, 37, 38
Reed, B. S., 118
Reilly, P., 110
Renz, B. B., 92, 114
Rhodes, F. H. T., 20
Rice, R. E., 22, 37
Reeves, B., 37
Reuben, E., 144
Riesman, D., 127
Roberts, C. L., 112
Rogers, E. M., 22, 23, 24, 35, 36, 37, 38
Rogers, J. L., 114
Rosen, J., 59
Rosenbaum, J., 85
Rosenfeld, L. B., 37
Rossow, M. D., 126
Rothblatt, S., 12, 13
Rotzoll, K., 106
Rouner, D., 126
Rowland, W. D., Jr., 153
Rubin, A. M., 24
Rubin, R. B., 24
Rudolph, F., 12, 18, 63, 64, 73
Ruggles, R., 147

S

Salvaggio, J. L., 33
Sandage, C. H., 106
Sass, G. D., 60, 66
Savage, A. L., Jr., 114
Schell, O., 23
Schierhorn, A., 127
Schiller, H. I., 33
Schlesinger, M. A., 17, 18, 58
Schudson, M., 75
Schuster, J. H., 123
Schweitzer, J. C., 123
Scully, M. G., 4
Shalala, D. E., 157
Shannon, C., 36
Shen, T., 23
Shively, N. H., 157
Sidorsky, D., 59
Silberman, A., 33
Sims, N. H., 159
Sitton, C. F., 67
Slack, J. D., 33
Slater, M. D., 126
Sloan Foundation, 8, 9, 57
Smith, B., 125
Smith, H., III, 81, 87, 89, 107
Smith, R., 123
Smith, W. E., 126

AUTHOR INDEX

So, C. Y. K., 37
Stacks, D. W., 37
Stallworth, C., 126
Starr, D., 116
Steele, R., 76
Stein, M. L., 110
Sterling, C. H., 32
Stone, G., 123, 144
Stoner, K. R., 119
"Strengthening the ties" (See Michigan Profesional Preparation Network Report)
Sweeney, J., 119
Sweet, S. D., 9, 19
Sykes, C., 123
Syracuse Experiment (also see Marsh, P. T.), 8, 9, 10, 46, 49, 53, 67, 149
Szkolka, P., 99

T

Tan, A. S., 100
Teeple-Hewes, J., 33
Terenzini, P. T., 144
Terrell, P. M., 30
Tharp, M., 126
Thayer, F. D., Jr., 144
Thompson, P. A., 126
Truitt, R. C., 25
Truxal, J. G., 9, 19
Tucker, D., 92

U

Ulrich's, 29

V

Voigt, M. J., 35

W

Wackman, D. B., 64, 75
Walcovy, D. E., 92
Waldman, S., 119
Walters, L., 99
Ward, J., 46, 96
Warner, C., 82, 85, 92
Wartella, E., 147
Weaver, D., 100
Weaver, W., 36
Webster, J., 32, 83, 111
Welke, J. W., 32
Wessen, D., 126
Westling, J., 144
White, S., 9, 19
Whitfield, J. D., 100
Whittle, C., 110
Wicklein, J., 33
Wiemann, J. M., 35
Wiener, N., 38
Wilhout, G. C., 100
Williams, S., 89
Wingert, P., 123
Winston, B., 96, 112, 140
Woditsch, G. A., 17, 18, 58, 88
Wood, D., 92
Woodliff, C. M., 88
Wycliff, D., 123

Z

Zemsky, R. M., 6
Zettl, H., 33

Subject Index

A

Accountability, 142–147, *see also* Accreditation, Outcomes Assessment academic programs, 14
Accreditation, 142, 147–161, *see also* Accountability
  challenges to, 147–149
  intellectual competition, 153–154
  liberal enrichment outcomes, 150–155
  liberal outcomes enrichment electives, 149–150, 153–154
  media industries, 156
  reform of, 149–160
  skills courses, 155–156
  Wisconsin/Wichita State, 156–161
Accrediting Council on Education in Journalism and Mass Communication
  and accreditation, 144, 147–151
  and liberal arts standard, 148–150, 154–160
Adaptive competence, 16, 152
Adjunct professors/guest lecturers, 118–119
Advertising Educational Foundation goals, 120–121
Advertorial, 30
Aesthetic sensibility, 16
American Advertising Federation, 66
American Council on Education, 5
American Newspaper Publishers Association, 66
American Society of Newspaper Editors, 66
  ethics survey, 77–78
Annenberg/Corporation for Public Broadcasting Project
  conversational styles, 126
Assessment strategies, 144–147
  accreditation standards, 146–147
  alumni/employer survey, 146
  capstone course, 145
  course evaluation, 144
  exit interview, 145
  exit test, 144
  internship, 146
  Professional Advisory Council, 145–146
  professional portfolio, 145
  regional/national competitions, 146
Association for Education in Journalism and Mass Communication, 36–37, 42
Association of American Colleges
  and integrated core, 55
  and liberal-professional distinctions, 149
  and New Professionalism, 46
  and professional programs, 10
  and university electives, 56–59
  liberal outcomes, 154–155
  recommendations, 5–8, 14–15, 18–19, 34
  social accountability, 74
  survey questionnaire, 101

182 SUBJECT INDEX

television, 55
Association of Schools of Journalism and Mass Communication
  journalism mass communication educators' leadership default, 43–45
  outcomes assessment, 144
  study of accrediting Standard, 3, 157

B

Baccalaureate degree, 18–21, *see also* electives, enriched major, integrated core, study in depth
  balance of community and individual perspectives in, 18, 42
  media education, 42
Broadcast education, *see* media education
Broadcast Education Association, 36
  Courses and Curricula Committee, 85, 92
  educational goals, 88
  faculty internships, 120
  mission statement, 82

C

Capstone, *see also* experiential learning, internships, media laboratory, media workshop
  course, 145
  experiences, 98–99
Carnegie Foundation
  and balance of individual and community values, 18, 42
  and liberal outcomes, 150–151, 154–155
  and New Professionalism, 46, 149
  and scholarship, 123–125
  and teachers, 123–125
  enriched major, 49
  integrated core, 54–55
  public service, 18
  study recommendations, 8–11, 14–15, 19, 20, 52, 152–153
  survey questionnaire, 101
"Central States Speech Journal," 37
Classroom cultures, 125–135
Communication, *see* interpersonal communication, mass communication, media delivery systems, technology
Communication competence, 15
"Communication Education," 37
Communication and media education, *see* media education

Communication education, *see* media education
Communication models
  Shannon-Weaver, 36, 38
  Lasswell, 105
"Communication Monographs," 37
"Communication Research," 37
Conceptual core in the New Professionalism, 47–48, *see also* integrated core
Conceptual enrichment in the New Professionalism, 48–49
  outcomes, 149, 150–153
Consumption metaphor, 127, 130, 141
Contextual competence, 15, 152, 155
Core, 18–19, 47–48, 91–96, *see also* conceptual core, general education, integrated core
Corn-hog cycle, 38–43
  and the university tradition, 41–43
Council for the Understanding of Technology in Human Affairs, 9
Council on Post-secondary Accreditation, 147
Critical thinking, 15, 154
Culture
  classroom, 126–135
  faculty hiring, 137
  unit, 99–100
  university, 99–100

D

Docudrama, 30

E

Electives
  and the Baccalaureate, 20–21, 45
  and media studies, 56–59
  and New Professionalism, 56–59
  and reform, 45–46, 56–59
Enriched major, *see also* philosophical orientations, study in depth
  and liberal education, 45–46
  and mission statements, 81–84
  and New Professionalism, 46, 72
  capstone experiences, 98–99
  core, 91–96
  conceptualized, 48–49
  defined, 20
  framework, 81–102
  sequences, 96–98

unit culture, 99–100
Experiential learning, *see also* capstone, internships, media laboratory, media workshop
 and New Professionalism, 50–53

F

Faculty forum, 114
Film and Video Association, 37
Freedom Forum Media Studies Center, 121

G

General education, 104–107, *see also* Baccalaureate degree, core, integrated core
 and journalism and mass communication, 104–107
 and media studies, 53–59, 104–107
 and New Professionalism, 53–59
Grammar slammer, 60, *see also* occupationalism
 addressing the issue of, 71–72
 and media educators, 61
Great Lakes Colleges Association, 155
Growth metaphor, 131–132
Graduate Record Examination, 144
Guest lectures, 118

H

Hiring practices, 137–140
 academic hire, 139
 hybrid hire, 139
 hybrid program, 140
 industry giant, 138
 MA/ABD, 138–139
 superperson, 138
"Human Communication Research," 37

I

Integrated communication, 34
Integrated core, 18–19, 45–46
 and New Professionalism, 70
 Carnegie findings, 54–56
 conceptualized, 47–48
 contribution of New Professionalism and media studies to, 53, 54–56
 defined, 18–19
 development of, 91–96
 general education, 54–56
 practitioner vs studies, 94–95
 public service, 18
 universal vs sequence, 92–94
International Communication Association, 36
Internships, 115–118, *see also* capstone, experiential learning, media laboratory, media workshop
 assessment, 146
 apprenticeship, 108
 credit, 116
 distinction between practica/apprenticeships and, 108
 evaluation of, 116
 faculty, 120
 practica, 108
 payment, 117
Interpersonal communication, *see also* mass communication
 and interactive media, 24
 and mass communication, 31, 36–38
 machine-assisted, 37–38
Interpersonal communication education, 35, *see also* media education
 and separation from journalism and mass communication education, 35–38
 and speech communication, 35

J

"Journal of Broadcasting and Electronic Media," 37
"Journal of Communication," 37
Journalism and mass communication education, 35, *see also* media education
 and separation from interpersonal and speech communication, 35–38
"Journalism Quarterly," 37

L

Leadership
 and reform, 43–45
 capacity, 16, 155
Liberal arts, *see also* accreditation, electives, enriched major, integrated core, liberal education, New Liberal Arts
 and professional studies, 8–11, 15–16, 54, 84–91
 and reform, 8–21
 and media studies, 53–59

and New Professionalism, 53-59
career preparation, 11-12
criticisms, 4
defined, 13-14, 53-54
myths, 9, 13
outcomes, compared to professional outcomes, 152
purpose of, 11-12
resistance to, 11-12
subject matter, 16-18
Liberal arts standard in accreditation, 149-150
Liberal education, *see also* liberal arts
and Baccalaureate, 18-21
and enriched major, 45-53
and professional education, 62-64
and subject matter, 16-18
defined, 13-14, 53-54
liberally educated professional, 62-64
outcomes, 14-16, 154-158
Liberal enrichment outcomes, 149-154
Liberal ethos
and media education, 63-64
and New Professionalism, 76-78
and professional education, 63

M

Major, *see* study in depth, enriched major
Mass communication, 22-24, *see also* interpersonal communication, media delivery systems, technology
and interpersonal communication, 31, 36-38, 44-45
and media education, 35
machine-assisted, 38
Mass communication education, *see* media education
Media delivery systems, *see also* interpersonal communication, mass communication, technology
and ACEJMC, 149
and teachers, 125-126
audiotex, 25-26
books, 30
cable, 29
characteristics of, 23
computers, 27
digital, 31
direct mail, 25
economic aspects, 27

fax, 23
magazines, 29-30
media programs, 39
new forms, 30
newspapers, 25
radio, 26, 29
technological impacts, 25
VCR, 27-28
Media education, *see also* media studies, mission statements, philosophical orientations
and liberal arts, 53-59
and mission statements, 81-91
and new media, 50, 107
and professionalism, 74-75
and technology, 22-23
balance of community and individual perspectives in, 62
curricula, 34-35, 38, 42, 125
economic perspective, 12-13, 40, 43
enrollment, 40-43
extra-curricular approaches, 113-114
fragmentation and specialization in interpersonal, journalism, mass communication, speech communication, 35-38, 39-41, 112
implementation of, 122-141
interdisciplinary bridges, 111-112
intradisciplinary bridges, 112-113
media workshop and laboratory, 108-110
minors and electives, 107
occupational vs professional, 63
practica/apprenticeships, 108
reform with practitioners, 114-121
reform within academy, 103-114
skills courses, 104-105
traditionalists vs reformers, 46, 148-150
university tradition, 42
Media educators, *see also* teachers
and becoming more intellectually competitive on their campuses, 153-154
and grammar slammer, 60-61
and occupationalism, 72-74
and professionalism, 74-75
and workshops, 52-53
challenges, 22, 28, 35
curricula development, 30-33, 115
curricula reform, 62-64, 103-121
unit culture, 99-100
Media industry, *see also* media management
accreditation proposal, 156

accountability, 74-75
adjunct professors, 118
and reform, 62-78
and technology, 25-28
cheap labor for, 65-66
internships, 115-118
practitioner associations, 119-121
public service, 75-76
Media laboratory, 57, *see also* capstone, internships, experiential learning, media workshop
conceptualization necessary to distinguish with rootless vocationalism, 50-53
defined and described, 50, 108-110
experiential learning, 98-99
Media management, *see also* media industry and academy, 114-121
and need for cheap labor, 65-66
and curriculum reform, 62-72
and New Professionalism, 60-78
arrogant recruiting practices, 65-66
resistance to reform, 66-72
Media studies, *see also* media education
in general education, 53-59, 104-107
in liberal arts, 53-59
in minors and electives, 107-111
Media workshop, 57, 71
conceptualized, 50-53
defined and described, 50, 108-109
experiential learning, 98-99
Michigan Professional Preparation Project, 8, *see also* professional education, occupationalism, New Professionalism
and liberal, 150-152
and New Professionalism, 46, 149
and reform, 20
conclusions, 15, 19
intellectual competitiveness, 153-154
network report, 9, 155
potential professional outcomes, 15-16, 152
Minors and electives, 107
Mission statements, 81-102, *see also* media education, philosophical orientations
cores and sequences, 91-99
culture, 99-100
hybrid program, 89-91
ivory tower program, 87-89
philosophical orientations, 84-91
professional program, 86-87

student outcomes, 135-137
trade school program, 86
Motivation of continued learning, 16, 152, 155

N

National Association of Broadcasters, 65
accreditation proposal, 120
faculty internships, 120
National Governors Association
assessment recommendations, 143-144
National Institute of Education, 4, 8-9, 18
and New Professionalism, 46
study recommendations, 10, 14, 51-52
New Liberal Arts, 3-21, 35, *see also* liberal arts, liberal education, liberal arts standard in accreditation, liberal ethos
and media education in, 53-59
and New Professionalism, 46, 53-59
and professional programs, 21
defined, 9, 14
Sloan Foundation, 57-58
New Professionalism, 3, 13, 16, 31, 33-34, 41, 45-46, 49, 62-64, 70, *see also* Michigan Professional Preparation Project, professional education, professional outcomes, occupationalism
accountability, 142
and AAC, 46
and Carnegie Foundation, 46, 149
and conceptual core, 47-48
and conceptual enrichment, 48-49
and core, 91-96
and electives, 70
and enriched major, 72
and ethical commitment, 62
and experiential learning, 50-53
and general education, 53-59
and integrated core, 53-54, 70
and liberal ethos, 64-65, 76-78
and media practitioners, 60-78, 110, 114-121
and Michigan Professional Preparation Project, 46, 149
and National Institute of Education, 46
and New Liberal Arts, 46, 53-59
and occupational ethos, 75-78
and Syracuse Experiment, 46
and teaching, 141

186 SUBJECT INDEX

balance of community/public service and individual perspectives in, 46, 62
components of, 46
curricular metaphors in, 127-135
outcomes of, 62, 34, 135-137
public service emphasis in, 62-63
sequence-occupation programs contrast with, 71
Wichita Symposium 1992 heralds in the, 161

O

Occupationalism, *see also* grammar slammer, liberal ethos, New Professionalism
and media educators, 72-74
and New Professionalism, 75-78
defined and distinguished from professionalism, 67-71
ethos of, 64
practitioner perspective, 66, 68, 70
programs in, 62-63
Office of Technological Assessment, 25
Oregon Report, 41, 44, 46, 57
and experiential learning, 50
and liberal outcomes, 150-151
and occupational practitioners, 67-68
and sequences, 96
Outcomes, *see also* outcomes assessment
and New Professionalism, 34, 135-137
conceptual enrichment, 150-153
liberal enrichment, 150-155
liberal outcomes enrichment electives, 149-150, 153-154
liberal, 14-16, 154-155
liberal and professional overlap of, 15-16
potential liberal, 14-16, 152
student, 135-137
Outcomes Assessment, 142-147
defined, 143
NGA recommendations, 143-144
Assessment strategies, 144-147

P

Philosophical Orientations, 84-91, *see also* enriched major, media education, mission statements
hybrid dual tracks program, 89
hybrid integrated program, 90
ivory tower program, 87
trade school program, 86
we-educate-them-you-train-them program, 87
we-train-them-you-educate-them program, 86
Practica/Apprenticeships, 108, *see also* capstone, experiential learning, internships, media laboratory, media workshop
Practitioner, 66, 68, 70, *see also* media industry, media management, occupationalism
associations, 119-121
in the classroom, 113-114, 118-119
Practitioner/occupationalist
perspectives, 66, 68, 70
Production Metaphor, 130-131, 141
Professional, *see* Michigan Professional Preparation Project, New Professionalism, occupationalism
ethics, 16, 152, 154-155
identity, 16, 152, 155
liberally educated media, 62-64
occupationalism distinguished from, 67-71
outcomes, 15-16, 150-154
and liberal outcomes, 15-16
Professional Advisory Council, 145-14
Professional Education, 3, 62, *see also* Michigan Professional Preparation Project, New Professionalism
and AAC, 10
and liberal arts, 15-16, 84-91
and liberal ethos, 63
and liberally educated media professional, 62-64
and university tradition, 42
challenges, 21
criticisms, 7
myths, 10
role of, 7
"Public Opinion Quarterly," 37
Public Relations Society of America, 66
Public Relations Student Society, 69
Public Service
and New Professionalism, 62-63
integrated core, 18
historic roots, 75-75
"Quarterly Journal of Speech," 37

R

Radio-Television News Directors Association, 66
Reform
  academic, 34-78, 103-114
  and New Liberal Arts, 4-13
  and media management, 62-78
  in electives, 56
  leadership, 43-45
  management resistance to, 66-69
  Michigan Professional Preparation Project, 20
  mission, 64
  movement, 34
  occupational program, 62
  principles of, 13-18
  traditionalist opposition to, 12, 45-46

S

Scholarly concern for improvement, 16, 152, 155
Scholarship
  defined, 123-125
  of appreciation, 124, 125
  of discovery, 124
  of integration, 124
  of teaching, 125
Self directed learning model, 135
Sequences, 91, *see also* New Professionalism
  alternatives to, 45-53
  and fragmentation of the fiend, 35-38
  and the corn-hog cycle, 38-41
  and the enriched major, 45-53
  development of, 96-98
  occupational and vocationalism of, 22, 69-71
Sloan Foundation, 8-9, 57
  New Liberal Arts Project, 57-58

Social accountability
  AAC findings, 74
Society of Professional Journalists, 69
Speech Communication Education, 35, *see also* media education
  and journalism and mass communication education, 35
Study in Depth, 10, 19-20, *see also* enriched major
Speech Communication Association, 36
Syracuse Experiment, 8-9, 149
  and conceptual enrichment, 49
  and New Professionalism, 46
  and occupationalism, 67
  findings, 10-11

T

Teaching, 122-141
  advising, 141
  and technology, 125-126
  classroom cultures, 126-135
  hiring practices, 137-140
  self directed learning model, 135
  student outcomes, 135-137
  vs research vs service, 122-125
Teaching metaphors, 134-135
  consumption, 127, 128
  growth, 129, 131-132
  production, 128, 130-131
  route, 129
  travel, 133-134
Technology, *see also* media delivery systems
  and curricular change, 31-33
  and media channels and content, 28-31
  and new media industries, 25-28
  and teaching, 125-126
Travel Metaphor, 133-134, 141

W

Whittle Communications
  and media laboratory, 110

P 91 .3 .B55 1992

DATE DUE			